Education and
the Voice of
Michael Oakeshott

Kevin Williams

imprint-academic.com

Published in the UK by Imprint Academic
PO Box 200, Exeter EX5 5YX, UK

Published in the USA by Imprint Academic
Philosophy Documentation Center
PO Box 7147, Charlottesville, VA 22906-7147, USA

ISBN 978-1-84540-055-2

A CIP catalogue record for this book is available from the
British Library and US Library of Congress

imprint-academic.com/idealists

Printed by Biddles Ltd, King's Lynn, Norfolk

190067799

Contents

Foreword

If raising a child takes a whole village, the same can be said of writing a book. For this reason I take the opportunity to make some acknowledgments.

I am grateful to Anthony Freeman of Imprint Academic for his confidence in the project and to the Research Committee of Mater Dei Institute, Dublin City University for its support.

Many friends and colleagues in the Institute and in the University and from other universities in Ireland and overseas offered scholarly, practical and moral support. I can name but a few but for their support in various ways and especially for reading drafts of different chapters, I am grateful to Caroline Renehan, Gabriel Flynn, John Murray, Clare Maloney, Eoin Cassidy, Ethna Regan, Sandra Cullen, Fiachra Long, Eoin Cassidy, Pádraig Hogan, Paul Standish, Harvey Siegel, Colm Lennon, Michael Hynes, Seán Byrne and Paddy Gillan. I would also like to acknowledge the assistance of the staff in the Institute's library. I wish particularly to thank Noel O'Sullivan for his generous, wise, learned and sensitive editorial advice.

Responsibility for any deficiencies in style or argument is entirely my own.

Most of all for their forbearance, interest and love, I thank my wife Fiona, and children Caitríona, Patrick and Áine.

Kevin Williams

Acknowledgements

Some of the chapters consist of substantially revised, adapted and developed versions of articles that appeared previously in following journals.

Taylor and Francis:

The limits of aesthetic separatism: literary education and Michael Oakeshott's philosophy of art, *Westminster Studies in Education*, 25 (2002), pp. 163–73. Re-printed in *The RoutledgeFalmer Reader in Philosophy of Education* (London and New York, Routledge, 2005), pp. 174–84. Chapter seven.

The discipline of inclination: Michael Oakeshott's treatment of the issue of compulsion in the teacher-pupil relationship', *Westminster Studies in Education*, 19 (1996), pp. 15–23. Chapter eight.

The Dilemma of Michael Oakeshott: Oakeshott's treatment of equality of opportunity in education and his political philosophy, *The Journal of Philosophy of Education*, 23 (1989), pp. 223–40. Chapter eleven.

Blackwells:

The gift of an interval: Michael Oakeshott's idea of a university education, *British Journal of Educational Studies*, 37 (1989), pp. 384–93. Chapter five.

Prospero:

Some puzzling elements in the pedagogy of Michael Oakeshott, *Prospero: A Journal of New Thinking in Philosophy for Education*, Special Issue on Michael Oakeshott, 11, (2005), pp. 15–25. Chapter nine.

Curriculum/Studies in Education Ltd:

The classical idiom in curriculum design: a critical review of Michael Oakeshott's philosophy of the curriculum, *Curriculum*, 11 (1990), pp. 132–9. Chapter four.

Introduction

The foundation in 2000 of the Michael Oakeshott Association reflects the lasting influence of Oakeshott's work. As is evident from the extensive bibliography to be found on the association's website, books and articles continue to appear on aspects of his *oeuvre*. These include consideration of his epistemology and philosophy of mind, his political philosophy, philosophy of law, philosophy of history, moral philosophy and his philosophy of art. As will be clear from this volume, Oakeshott's contribution to the philosophy of education retains a significant profile in contemporary discourse in the discipline. Not only did he write extensively and in detail directly on education but his philosophical work itself is also directly relevant to education. Interestingly, one of Oakeshott's most celebrated essays 'Rationalism in Politics' is more about the folly of rationalism in education than in politics, a point noted by Ephraim Podoksik (2003a). Education also features as a theme in several of the other essays in his volume *Rationalism in Politics and Other Essays* (1981), in the magisterial *On Human Conduct* (1975) and in the posthumously published 'Work and Play' (1995).

A reflection of Oakeshott's status in the field is the inclusion of an essay on his work in the RoutledgeFalmer volume *Fifty Modern Thinkers on Education* (Palmer, 2001) The significance is even more striking because the work of only a handful of philosophers, including Wittgenstein and Heidegger, is considered in the book. The choice of an essay on Oakeshott from the countless articles in the area to feature in *RoutledgeFalmer Reader in Philosophy of Education* (Williams, 2005), a volume with a relatively limited number of articles, indicates the salience of his thinking. *Prospero*, a journal in philosophy of education, in 2005 devoted a special issue to Oakeshott that includes several significant contributions from the philosophical community.

More generally, as Podoksik explains so well (2003a), Oakeshott is also being read in ways that show that his work cannot be dismissed as an expression of a rather dated liberal conservatism. New perspectives on Oakeshott's achievement have emerged from the books by Paul Franco (1990) and Robert Grant (1990) in the early 1990s to the major works that have appeared in this decade, for example, the volumes by Wendell John Coats (2000), Steven Gerencser (2000), Terry Nardin (2001), Kenneth McIntyre (2004), the impressive collection edited by Corey Abel and Timothy Fuller (2005) and Elizabeth Corey (2006). The work of these and other scholars has greatly contributed to debunking the characterisation of Oakeshott as a reactionary thinker.

After all, Oakeshott affirms a world that offers 'neither harbour for shelter nor floor for anchorage, neither starting-place nor appointed destination' (Fuller, 1989, p. 150). This openness to experience and to dialogue has resonated with Richard Rorty and the connection has been noted by several commentators (Lawn, 1996; Arcilla, 1995; Gallagher, 2002) but, as will be shown in Chapter 10, it is a connection that has not always been viewed favourably (see McCarney, 1985, pp. 398–405). Yet Arcilla, a radical in educational thinking, shows a commendable willingness to learn from Oakeshott as well as from Rorty and others (Arcilla, 1995, pp. 3–6, 151). What Rorty and Arcilla find congenial in Oakeshott's work is the anti-foundationalism that leads to his denial of all claims to absolute knowledge, his openness to the world and its varieties of experience without being 'disconcerted by the differences or dismayed by the inconclusiveness of it all' (Fuller, 1989, p. 39). At the same time, we must learn 'to be at home in this commonplace world' (Oakeshott, 1981, p. 196) simply because it is the only one that we know. The enduring legacy of Michael Oakeshott's writing suggests that a substantial study devoted to his educational thought would be worth writing.

Turning to the volume itself, the first chapter deals with Oakeshott's conception of education and its location within the tradition of liberal education. This is followed by his account of the presuppositions of human agency which is an important feature in his development of the tradition of liberal education. In the second chapter following an account of his distinction between work and play, the contrast between closed and open forms of learning and education is explored and Chapter 3 concerns itself with the institutional context in which education is given expression.

Chapters 4 and 5 trace the connection between Oakeshott's conception of education as a practice and the actual content of the curriculum at primary, secondary and third levels. Though it is shown to be possible to adapt the liberal learning advocated by Oakeshott to the conditions of the twenty-first century, these chapters also reveal important difficulties with Oakeshott's epistemology. The difficulties in question arise from his tendency to work with too rigid and restricted a conceptual repertoire and from what I call his dichomotomising impulse, that is, the allocation of experience in an oppositional or either/or way to one of two categories. This generates an epistemological separatism that is unsustainable in the form in which he presents it. In Chapter 4 the distinction between academic and practical pursuits is called into question and in Chapter 5 the distinction between vocational and university education is found to be too rigid.

The two chapters that follow focus specifically on some consequences of Oakeshott's epistemological separatism. In Chapter 6, his resistance to the encroachment of vocational aims into education is defended, but Oakeshott's separatism is found to lead him to espouse an impoverished conception of work. In Chapter 7, the difficulties in giving an account of the relationship between the aesthetic world and the ordinary universe of everyday living are also seen to derive from this separatism. But, as will noted in this and other contexts, Oakeshott's thinking is often more subtle than it first appears in the sharp contrasts that he draws.

The next three chapters deal with the themes of teaching and learning. These themes are related because, explains Oakeshott, his epistemology derives from his reflections on teaching and learning. The treatment of Oakeshott's philosophy of learning deals with the notion of motivation (Chapter 8) where once again Oakeshott's epistemological separatism is seen to give rise to problems. Chapter 9 offers a general account of the teacher-learner relationship and attention is drawn to the nuance in his thinking that does not feature in the over-simplified distinction between instruction and imparting. In Chapter 10 the relationship between conformity and dissent in moral and civic education is explored and Oakeshott's affirmation of individual morality in opposition to a community-oriented morality is shown to reflect once more Oakeshott's tendency to work with over-simplified categories conceived in an either/or way.

This leads to an important issue in his educational and political thought, namely, the issue of access to the emancipatory education that Oakeshott proposes. In Chapter 11, I defend him from the charge of elitism while at the same time disclosing tensions in his theory of civil association regarding any significant re-distributive project. As part of a general review of his educational legacy, the final chapter once more affirms the possibility of making accessible Oakeshott's conception of liberal learning in conditions of mass participation in education. His political philosophy is shown to hospitable to accommodating the re-distributive interventions necessary to maximise access to the intrinsic and positional goods of education. Before concluding the chapter, Oakeshott's prescience in identifying the malign effects of the culture of control in education today is noted and some of the consequences of this culture are explored.

The book aims to offer both a wide canvas as well as fine-grained attention to Oakeshott's work that cannot reasonably be expected in publications referring to his philosophy of education or even in single articles on the subject. Where relevant, I try to give a sense of the texture of the arguments by drawing on literary texts, interpreted broadly to include biography. The difference between philosophy and literature as conduits of human understanding is captured in Goethe's distinction between theory and life itself, mentioned by Robert Grant in his fine mongraph on Oakeshott. '*Grau, theurer Freund, ist alle Theorie,/ Und grün des Lebens goldener Baum* (Grey, dear friend, is theory all/ And green the golden tree of life)' (Grant, 1990, p. 118).[1] Of necessity there is a greyness in some philosophical work but literature does offer something of the 'green' of life's 'golden tree'. Noel O'Sullivan (2005, p. 13) perceptively notes the potential contribution of imaginative literature in understanding Oakeshott's account of human practices. The volume aims to endorse what is positive and life-enhancing about Oakeshott's philosophy of education and his respect for the integrity or sovereignty of liberal educa-

---

[1]   I have slightly changed Grant's translation.

tion. Rather than being merely an exposition of his arguments, the book attempts to offer a critical account of Oakeshott's views that brings out their continuing relevance in a 'post-modern' world. This study of his philosophy of education is inspired by Oakeshott's vision, insight and wonderful prose and also by the generous, optimistic and, in a non-ideological sense, pro-life spirit of his work, qualities well captured in Noel O'Sullivan's excellent short essay 'Why read Oakeshott?' (*ibid.*). Re-reading Oakeshott's work in order to write this book often revealed to me new insights in his writing as well as prompting new *frissons* of pleasure at the majesty of his prose. My ambition in writing this volume is to capture the spirit and relevance of Oakeshott's thinking for the twenty-first century in a form that readers with an interest either in his work or in educational policy will find engaging. I hope too that this book will serve to promote two of the essential educational aims identified by Oakeshott— 'to enable ... [us] to make ... [our] own thought clear and to attend to what passes before ... [us]' (Fuller, 1989, p. 133).

A Note on Oakeshott's Writings on Education

Most of the essays on education are to be found in the collection edited by Timothy Fuller first published in 1989. Omitted from the collection is 'The Definition of a University', as it repeats many ideas in other essays. Yet this essay does contain insights of its own. Oakeshott did not wish 'The Study of "Politics" in a University' to be included in Fuller's collection and I think that this is a pity as there is much of relevance in the essay. The essays on education were published over a span of many years from the early articles on the university in the late 1940s/1950s to the later ones of the 1960s/1970s. Full details can be found in the bibliography.

Chapter One

The Ordeal of Learning

The central ideas that inform Oakeshott's philosophy of education are located in the tradition of liberal education articulated in the nineteenth century by such writers as Hegel, John Henry Newman and Matthew Arnold. What defines liberal education in this tradition is the conduct of teaching and learning in a context that is set from the world of ordinary human affairs. The content of the curriculum is totally divorced from any instrumental purposes and is pursued for the sake of the enrichment that it engenders rather than for any instrumental benefit. The learning in question also releases or liberates learners into an exhilarating world of ideas and images.

Oakeshott's Educational Thought in Context

Matthew Arnold's theory of culture and of liberal education is of particular relevance in reading Oakeshott (see Novak 2003, p. 377) but it is also worth noting the resonances with the thought of the Hegel and Newman. Hegel is one of the very few thinkers to merit favourable reference in Oakeshott's writing on education. In an address at a prize giving at the *Gymnasium* of Nuremburg where he was principal from 1808–1816, Hegel describes the school in a way that is taken up by Oakeshott in his account of the school's detachment from '*hic et nunc*, the here and now, of current living' (Fuller, 1989, p. 24). Hegel envisages the school as an arena where 'private interests and selfish passions' (2005, p. 9) are not heard and where preparation for public life is conducted in an atmosphere of calm reflection (*ibid.*). This conception of the school is captured in metaphor 'monastic' that appears in Oakeshott's writing (Fuller, 1989, p. 69). The monastic perception of the nature of the school is consistent with the view of the school as a 'sanctuary' apart from the rest of society developed in France in the nineteenth century (see Renaut and Finkielkraut, 2005,

p. 38). The conception of the school as an oasis of humanity set apart from the demands of adult life is also a feature of the tradition in the English-speaking world.

More generally, Oakeshott's theory of liberal education inherits aspects of the spirit of Cardinal Newman's thought. The resonance with Newman is suggested in the titles of two of Oakeshott's essays, 'The Idea of a University' (Fuller, 1989) and 'The Definition of a University' (Oakeshott, 1967). Oakeshott's portrayal of the experience of a university education clearly reflects that of Newman (Newman, 1901, pp. 145–8). Readers of Oakeshott who are already familiar with Newman's work will note shared motifs. Among these is the conviction that at university a person does not become educated simply through study alone. A university offers a curriculum of studies and extracurricular activities, and it also gives students the opportunity to absorb its *genius loci* as part of a human community. Both value specialisation in university studies and are suspicious of general courses of study that provide only a 'smattering' (*ibid.*, p. 144) of knowledge. The self-possession of the gentleman in Newman's celebrated portrait (*ibid.*, pp. 208–11) has resemblances with Oakeshott's conception of autonomous individual, who is the personification of Montaigne's ideal of the man who 'knows how to belong to himself' (Oakeshott, 1981, p. 290 and see Oakeshott, 1975a, p. 240). Newman's disparagement of people who engage in strident, ill-mannered polemics resonates with Oakeshott's preference for conversation over abrasive argument. Though sympathetic to Christianity, Oakeshott does not, however, share Newman insistence on the place of religion in life.

This more modest perception of the role of religion also marks a difference between the views of Oakeshott and Matthew Arnold. A review of Arnold's thought illustrates very aptly that the tradition of liberal education is not composed of a homogeneous set of attitudes. Arnold has a confidence in the competence of the state in promoting culture and education, whereas Oakeshott is hostile to state intervention in such areas. Arnold's belief that culture has 'its origin in the love of perfection' and as being '*a study of perfection*' (Arnold, 1966, pp. 44–5) would not at all consort with Oakeshott's less inflated conception of culture. Oakeshott's valuation of specialisation would make him hostile to Arnold's aspiration to providing students with a synoptic view of culture. Ephraim

Podoksik argues that Oakeshott's scorn of integrating courses of lectures that would aim to unify the pursuit of knowledge 'with a sticky mess called "culture"' (Fuller, 1989, p. 98) is 'almost certainly' a reference to Arnold (Podoksik, 2003a, p. 218). Oakeshott does, however, share Arnold's hostility towards 'the mechanical and material civilisation' that enjoys such 'esteem with us' (Arnold, 1966, p. 49).

The wide compass of Arnold's conception of culture as including not only intellectual endeavour but our moral impulses and aspirations is also compatible with Oakeshott's view. In other words both accept that the cultural dimension of education embraces moral learning. There is another interesting connection between Arnold's characterisation of culture in terms of multifaceted 'voices of human experience' made up of 'art, science, poetry, philosophy, history, as well as of religion' (Arnold, 1966, p. 47) and Oakeshott's description of the modes of experience as voices in the conversation of mankind (Oakeshott, 1981, pp. 197–247). Oakeshott develops his conception of culture or civilisation or of what he refers to in the words of Dilthey as humankind's *geistige Welt* (Fuller, 1989, p. 45) by elaborating on the nature of these modes and through the notion of human practices that he advances in *On Human Conduct* (Oakeshott, 1975a). What is notable is the tension between Oakeshott's broad conception of culture and the narrow selection of activities that he envisages as being eligible for inclusion in the school curriculum.

His writing echoes Arnold's concern regarding the kind of lives young people should be enabled to live in industrial societies of the nineteenth century. He would sympathise with Arnold's rejection of the attempt to provide the general population with a differentiated form of culture, with what Arnold refers to as 'an intellectual food prepared and adapted in the way … (considered) proper for the actual conditions of the masses' (Arnold, 1966, p. 69) such as, for example 'ordinary popular literature' (*ibid.*, p. 70). Arnold believes that it is necessary 'to make the best that has been thought and known in the world current everywhere' (*ibid.*). This, he argues, 'is the *social ideal*; and the men of culture are the true apostles of equality' (*ibid.*). He puts the point memorably in his address to the Royal Society on the theme of equality when referring to the well-being that he associates with being educated and cultured. 'Many are to be made partakers of well-being, true but the ideal of well-being is not to be, on that account, lowered and coarsened' (Gribble, ed., 1967, pp. 160–61). Neither for Arnold nor Oakeshott is culture the special preserve of any social class. In this respect, their views reflect those of the great French socialist, Jean Jaurès in the nineteenth century. Jaurès argues that the children who will be future workers of the soil or labourers in factories should not be disinherited of the joys of art and of the beauty of great works of literature (Jaurès, 2006, pp. 26–7). Oakeshott's philosophy of culture and of the school curriculum contains none of the social divisiveness of the epistemology of the conservative theorist, G.H. Bantock, who argues that different social groups can be distinguished on the basis of their capacity for consciousness and that the school curriculum should be designed to take this into account.[1]

Both Oakeshott's and Arnold's conceptions of education have a connection with the German notion of *Bildung* The term communicates a shared non-instrumental emphasis in educational aims to be found in the German tradition and in the English tradition of liberal education. Novak (2003, p. 278) traces the link between *Bildung* and Arnold's account of culture as an 'idea of perfection' expressed in 'an *inward* condition of mind and spirit' (Arnold, 1966, p. 49). The salience of *Bildung* as an element in Oakeshott's thought has attracted the attention of scholars (see Lovlie and Standish, 2002, pp. 317–340; Arcilla, 2002, p. 257; Podoksik, 2003a, pp. 223–7; Lawn, 1996, p. 267). *Bildung* serves to distinguish between the person who is educated in the wide sense of *gebildet* and the person who is merely cultured and cultivated. Nazi officers who had a great appreciation of music and art could be described as cultured but not as *gebildet* or educated. Their appropriation of high culture failed signally to develop their moral characters.

The notion of *Bildung* also captures the intimate relation between culture, education and personal development in Oakeshott's thought. The conjunction is clear in his characterisation of education as enabling the pupil 'to make the most or the best of himself' (Fuller, 1989, p. 47, see also Oakeshott, 1967, p. 131). Consequently no disjunction exists between the aim of personal development and coming to appropriate

---

[1]   For an illuminating treatment of the relationship between Bantock's epistemology, curriculum proposals and social philosophy see Jonathan (1986).

aspects of a culture. This same point is made memorably and with some metaphorical force by Somerset Maugham.

> Culture is not something you put on like a ready-made suit of clothes, but a nourishment you absorb to build up your personality, just as food builds up the body of a growing boy; it is not an ornament to decorate a phrase, still less to show off your knowledge, but a means, painfully acquired, to enrich the soul. (Maugham, 1971, p. 193)

This means that individuals who are learning to make their own the cultural inheritance become in this way personally enriched. It is through this learning that they develop more finely and more comprehensively their human capacities to think, to feel, and to act, which is what, if anything is meant by 'self-realisation', a term that Oakeshott rightly disparages (see Fuller, 1989, pp. 47–8 and Oakeshott, 1967, pp. 131–2). On account of the connection between them, Oakeshott's philosophy of education admits no distinction between the aims of personal enrichment and of initiation into a culture. This initiation, writes Oakeshott, is the only avenue to 'self-realization' for selves as 'historic, circumstantial personalities' (Oakeshott, 1967, p. 132, see also Fuller, 1989, p. 48).

Turning to the context of the second half of the twentieth century, Oakeshott's work had an important influence on the early publications of Richard Peters and Paul Hirst, two philosophers whose work had an enormous impact on educational thought and practice in the English-speaking world.[2] The currency that Michael Oakeshott's work has continued to enjoy in philosophical discourse about education goes beyond the influence on English-speaking philosophers of education in the 1960s and 1970s. His writings have been drawn upon by scholars such as René Arcilla (2002, 1996), Paul Standish (2000a, 2000b, 2005) and Maxine Greene (2005) who would have little sympathy with the intellectualist orientation of the thought of the early Peters and Hirst. Standish is one of several contemporary philosophers who have turned to Oakeshott's work in criticising the rationalist, instrumental and utilitarian thrust of education policy of our times. Susan Mendus also invokes the work of Oakeshott in her critique of the notion of

---

[2] The intellectualist emphasis of this work is greatly tempered in the later writings of both Peters and Hirst and, indeed, in the case of Hirst this emphasis could be said to be largely abandoned (see discussion and references in Podosik, 2003a, pp. 222-3).

culture as a kind of bolt-on technology to be found in the European Community documentation on higher education, (2000, p. 70). Pádraig Hogan (1998, pp. 372–3), like Standish, emphasises Oakeshott's conception of the 'sovereignty' of educational institutions and activities against the smug reductionism of official European policy on higher education.[3]

Oakeshott's continuing relevance within educational discourse is hardly surprising because he addresses the central issues in philosophy of education. Despite changes in educational debate over the last four decades, most of the same issues remain central and also contested—for example, the nature of knowledge and the moral life and the proper remit of educational institutions. Oakeshott's educational thought is consistent with the tradition of liberal humanist learning to which his thought belongs and for which he is such an eloquent spokesperson. He is the inheritor of a tradition that he develops and expands. There is much in his conception of education that can be preserved subject to the criticisms and qualifications that will be made in the course of this volume.

Yet Oakeshott himself sometimes takes a very pessimistic view of the future of liberal education. Though he is critical of alarmism about education (see Fuller, 1989, p. 109), a marked strain of pessimism can be identified in his later writings. This is very prominent in the essay entitled 'The Tower of Babel' that appeared in 1983 in *On History and Other Essays*.[4] With much literary verve he parodies the notion of a state bent on the pursuit of a futile project and marshalling all its resources to this end. In several of his essays, education is envisaged as an important instrument of manipulative social engineering, supported by the spurious science of behaviourism, designed to realise a common social purpose. In 'The Definition of a University' he describes education conducted in this way as an attempt 'to abolish man' (Oakeshott, 1967, p. 130) and in 'Education: The Engagement and its Frustration' first published in 1972, he presents a gloomy vista of the 'social engineer' intent

---

[3]   Hogan also draws attention to the announcement of the end of ideological debate on the 'objectives of education' and on 'educational principles' in the European Commission's *Teaching and Learning: Towards the Learning Society. White Paper on Education and Training* (Hogan, 1998, p. 373, European Commission, 1996, p. 42; see also Standish, 2000a, p. 225; and also Smith, 2000, p. 196).

[4]   An earlier and completely different essay also entitled 'The Tower of Babel' appeared in *Rationalism and Politics and Other Essays* originally published in 1962.

not merely on 'the abolition of the child but the abolition of man' (Fuller 1989, p. 77). In 1975 in 'A Place of Learning', he criticises the promotion through education of a notion of the human being as a 'role-performer' in a '"social system"', which, he tells us, 'portends the abolition of man' (Fuller, 1989, pp. 31–2). The term 'abolish' that expresses Oakeshott's fears find an ironic echo in the confident imperialism of B.F. Skinner in *Beyond Freedom and Dignity*. 'What is being abolished' through the science of behaviourism, asserts Skinner, 'is the autonomous man — the inner man, the homunculus, the possessing demon, the man defended by the literatures of freedom and dignity' (Skinner, 1973, p. 196). This view and the impulse of current policy to prescribe, control and monitor the work of educators that shall be examined in Chapter 12 leave no room for complacency regarding the future of education. Yet the categories or postulates that form the conceptual infrastructure of Oakeshott's philosophy reveal a conception of the human person that is not susceptible to such reduction. Educational technologists with teaching programmes and devices cannot shape the life of human beings who respond 'in terms of their self-understandings' (Fuller, 1989, p. 28) to what Oakeshott in the words of Henry James refers to as 'the ordeal of consciousness' (Oakeshott, 1975a, p. 326, Fuller, 1989, pp. 23, 28). Nor could any education programme prescribe in advance the achievement of autonomy or of *Bildung* which is the important part of the purpose of education that emerges in Oakeshott's writing.

Learning and Learners

One very important aspect of Oakeshott's contribution to developing the tradition of liberal education lies in positioning this tradition within the context of a comprehensive account of the nature of human agency. In other words, he provides an elaborated philosophical account of what it is to learn and to be a learner. He envisages the capacity to learn or to undergo 'the ordeal of consciousness' as being underpinned by a number of basic categories that he refers to rather loosely as postulates. Crucially this involves the capacity to engage in practices and this capacity assumes that human beings must be possessors of reflective consciousness/understanding and must be able to exercise freedom. So what then is his conception of learning?

Learning

According to Oakeshott all distinctively human conduct must be the outcome of an activity of learning on the part of an individual, and so learning is a necessary condition of such conduct. By learning, Oakeshott means 'an activity possible only to an intelligence capable of choice and self-direction in relation to its own impulses and to the world around him' (Fuller, 1989, p. 43). As a uniquely human activity, learning concerns 'conduct' rather than mere 'behaviour' (Fuller, 1989, p. 44). There is, of course, also a sense in which we speak of learning in respect of behaviour. An example would be an octopus responding and adapting to its environment in order to maintain itself in existence. But the kind of learning involved here, like the achievement of learning marked by the bark of a dog when he sees his mistress produce his lead, is behaviour, not conduct.[5] Learning as behaviour rather than conduct also occurs in the early life of human beings. In this sense of learning, individuals can come to perform a mechanical routine either by making physical gestures or by reciting rote utterances, such as catechism answers, dates, or tables, which they not understand. This, however, is not human learning, properly speaking, because it does not involve understanding. In distinctively human learning, writes Oakeshott, a person 'acquires only what he accepts and makes his own in an understanding' (Oakeshott, 1975a, p. 37). This understanding is required in all human activities and not just in those such as science, history, or philosophy which are themselves activities of understanding. Learning to observe the rules of any practice entails, on the part of human beings, some understanding of what they are doing. For example, it is only through a uniquely human activity of learning that a child can come to participate even in such simple practices as dressing herself or playing hide and seek. Similarly enjoying a relationship with another person means that we have to understand ourselves

---

[5]   Hanna Pitkin claims that Oakeshott in *On Human Conduct* leaves the status of animals curiously ambiguous (Pitkin, 1976, p. 318, footnote 20). In 'A Place of Learning' however, Oakeshott makes it clear that our talk of learning in respect of animals should be understood as 'anthromorphic analogy' (Fuller, 1989, p. 21).

as being related to that person, and such understanding can be acquired only by learning to see ourselves in terms of that relationship (*ibid.*, p. 55). Understanding impresses itself upon the most fundamental of our relationships with others and the mere fact of consanguinity does not prescribe the terms of a genuinely human relationship with another person. Even parents and children must acquire a concept of themselves as standing in a particular relationship to one another. Indeed, it can happen that a parent of a child refuses to enter into relationship with her or his own child. Human beings are not components in a causally determined process and are not predetermined to engage in particular relationships. Human roles and relationships cannot be explained in terms of such so-called processes as psychological tendencies or instincts, or because of resemblances between individuals based on age, disposition, or socio-economic background. Experienced teachers have always been sensitive to the vast difference between young people who may all be the same age and in the same class in school.

Oakeshott also insists that the human potential for learning admits of no teleology, that there is no pre-determined point at which individuals can be said to have exhausted all the possibilities of rational development to them. There are no scripts that govern the unfolding of human lives. Having 'no pre-ordained course to follow' (Fuller, 1989, p. 23) or 'no pre-ordained destination' (*ibid.*) or 'pre-determined end' (*ibid.*, pp. 47–8), an individual can never be said to have finally made 'the most or the best of himself (*ibid.*). The potential for personal development is not fixed in the same manner as the potential for physical development. This means that learning cannot be understood as a process of growth or maturation that the school endeavours to facilitate. The concept of growth applies only to the category of process, it cannot be applied to the procedures involved in education. If learning were merely a matter of maturation, then there would be no need for education.

> The educational engagement is necessary because nobody is born a human being, and because the quality of being human is not a latency which becomes an actuality in a process of "growth".
> (*ibid.*, p. 66)

But, more problematically, Oakeshott would carry his anti-determinism as far as to claim that our character is 'the outcome of a self-education' rather than 'somehow imposed by such circumstances as poverty or wealth' (Oakeshott, 1975a, p. 325, see also pp. 96–7). This dramatic denial of the significant influence of socio-economic circumstances upon the possibilities for personal development open to the individual will be considered in Chapter 11.

Nevertheless the connection between learning and what it is to be human should now be clear. Our achievements in learning are achievements in becoming the kind of persons we are. Our identity as unique individuals is constituted by what we have learned to think, to feel to imagine, and to do. The context through which we express this individuality and 'converse with one another' (*ibid.*, p. 54) is provided by the multiplicity of practices which make up our culture. Our practices constitute, therefore, what might be called a discursive universe. This concept of a practice needs some attention.

The Context of Learning: The Concept of a Practice

Underlying this concept is Oakeshott's distinction between two mutually exclusive categories of phenomena, a practice and a process. A process is causally determined and subject to measurement, whereas a practice, as the context for intelligent, human action, cannot be measured. A practice is both a necessary condition for there being human action and a conceptual category which makes sense only with reference to such action. A practice, in the words of Auspitz, provides the 'ordered context' for all actions (Auspitz, 1976, p. 271) which go beyond the instinctive satisfaction of wants, in the manner in which language provides the context for all utterance beyond brutish grunt and gesture. For Oakeshott the term 'practice' comes to assimilate the earlier term tradition which he now finds 'inadequate' to express what he wanted to express (Oakeshott, 1976, p. 364). Each of our many human practices offers itself as a language or living tradition of activity which gives distinctive form to all our human actions. In Oakeshott's words:

> A practice may be identified as a set of considerations, manners, uses, observances, customs, standards, canons, maxims, principles, rules, and offices specifying useful procedures or denoting obligations or duties which relate to human actions and utterances. It is a prudential or an authoritative adverbial qualification of choices and performances, more or less complicated, in which

conduct is understood in terms of a procedure. (Oakeshott, 1975a, p. 55)

According to what Bhikhu Parekh describes as Oakeshott's 'conversational theory of action' (Parekh, 1979, p. 500), all action of a distinctively human nature must be expressed through the metaphorical language of some specific practice in the same way that all speech must be through the medium of some human language. When reflex and involuntary movements are excluded, every human action represents a performance within some practice. Obviously in the early stages of post-natal life human beings can survive in the sense of keeping themselves alive by eating and drinking and sleeping without recognising and observing the conditions of any practice. To live in society, however, requires participation in practices. Even our most familiar and basic diurnal activities of eating, sleeping and washing take their shape from the conditions of the practices which regulate the performance of these functions. The human agent is, therefore, always a practitioner. And, conversely, as no performance can consist merely in the observance of the conditions of a practice, a practitioner is always an agent, that is, someone who is continually judging, choosing, and acting. Just as using a language necessarily involves making a specific, intelligible utterance in some language such as Spanish or German, subscribing to the conditions of any practice means performing a specific, intelligible, concrete action.

In the conduct of our lives we participate in many different kinds of practices. The language we speak and our moral code, which Oakeshott describes as a 'language of moral converse' (1975a, p. 59), are our two 'most important practices' (*ibid.*) and pervade all aspects of our lives. Particular ethical practices, such as pacifism and the sincere observance of any religion, are so inclusive as to constitute ways of life. Rituals, customs, and manners are also practices but these bear less pervasively on our lives. Where they prescribe offices and roles such as husband/wife, employer/employee, musician/audience, or judge/jury, teacher/pupil we speak of practices as institutions. Each human art or skill, such as carpentry or piano playing, is a practice, the rules of which, like those of any practice, are sometimes formulated in canons, standards, maxims, or principles. Science, history and art are, as Auspitz puts it succinctly, practices that have achieved such 'conceptual integrity that we call them "modes"' (Auspitz, 1976, p. 271). Experience in these modes is contrasted with experience within what Oakeshott calls the world of practice (see Oakeshott, 1978, pp. 247–321 and Oakeshott, 1981, pp. 206–12).

A brief consideration the nature of this epistemological universe is appropriate here. According to Oakeshott experience offers itself in terms of discrete and autonomous modes: the mode of practice or practical living and the modes of scientific, historical, and aesthetic experience—philosophy, as shall be explained in more detail in Chapter 11, has an ambiguous status in his epistemology. The activities, practices, or forms of life that make up these modes are described in a memorable metaphor as voices in the conversation of mankind (Oakeshott, 1981, pp. 197–247) a metaphor, which as already noted, echoes that of Matthew Arnold (1966, p. 47). In what he calls practical experience our concern is with the world in terms of its usefulness in promoting our survival. Human activity in this mode enjoys a certain priority, primacy, or primordiality over that in other modes so that the practical is the dominant mode in which we live out our lives. The world of practical experience is constituted by inclinations which are expressed in the form of 'habits of desire and aversion' (Oakeshott, 1981, p. 206). We conceive everything in it entirely in relation to ourselves and to our occurrent wants and in terms of its worth, usefulness or convenience in the satisfaction of these wants. It is the universe of 'common discourse' (Oakeshott, 1983, p. 11), and the objects of which this universe is constructed are 'the language in which we compose our wants and conduct the transactions designed to satisfy them' (*ibid.*, p. 12). The universe of practical experience is then the world '*sub species voluntatis*' (Oakeshott, 1981, p. 206), the world of 'desiring and obtaining' (*ibid.*, p. 224) or what Wordsworth in the poem, 'The World Is Too Much with Us', describes as the world of 'getting and spending'.

But practical experience is not exclusively functional or instrumental because it also accommodates moral conduct. And the world of practical experience assumes a moral status where we come to recognise other selves as 'equal members of a community of selves' (Oakeshott, 1981, p. 210) and not merely as means to our ends. Determined then by our desires/aversions and by our moral approvals/disapprovals the practical is the mode in which we conduct the greater part of our lives. The notion of the practical as a separate mode of experience serves therefore to distinguish the ordinary world of human affairs from the scholarly and contemplative forms of understanding or experience. In the revised terminology of *On Human Conduct* the modes of scientific, historical and aesthetic experience call upon knowledge or expertise which pertains to participation in a practice. Here Oakeshott makes explicit his intention to use the adjective 'practical' to refer to participation in any practice (Oakeshott, 1975a, p. 57, footnote 1).

Practices may be deliberately designed as, for example, a game such as monopoly has been, but they usually emerge as a by-product of human performances and, of course, they are often constituted by a combination of premeditated and unplanned activity. Education, for example, developed from the practice of initiating young people into the skills of adult life. The development of the school as an institution, and in particular the introduction of compulsory schooling, imposed a deliberate design on this practice of initiation. Consequently, education has largely become the specific practice of initiating young people into particular aspects of their cultural inheritance. Oakeshott's philosophy of education makes much of the distinction between the learning that is acquired by virtue of being a member of a society and the learning that it is the business of the school to promote. For Oakeshott the concern of school education is, pre-eminently but not exclusively, with the modes of experience represented in the forms of knowledge and understanding. The activity of educating has also come to prescribe a unique relationship, that between teacher and learner, which is categorially distinct, that is, it belongs to a separate category, from all others (for example, from such relationships as buyer/seller, doctor/patient, or lawyer/client).

Practice refers therefore to the 'adverbial qualification of choices and performances' (Oakeshott, 1975a, p. 55). The face that we present to the world in pursuing our basic wants and desires becomes qualified by the considerations of practices. Even the activities of eating and washing are shaped from the social rules that regulate the performance of these functions. The curiosity that is prompted by the desire for knowledge and understanding has its rules, namely, the rules that apply to the universe of discourse involved. The practices that qualify desires and wants of a prudential or intellectual character require learning. This learning that enables human beings to become participants in practices assumes a particular philosophy of the human person that next needs some attention.

Learners

Oakeshott's philosophy of education is grounded in a considered philosophy of the person that is sketched in 'A Place of Learning' (Fuller, 1989), first published in 1975a, and elaborated in some detail in *On Human Conduct* published in the same year.

This discussion of his conception of the human learner underlying his educational thought that follows will be more curtailed than I would like because a comprehensive exploration of every nuance of Oakeshott's philosophy of mind and the person would require a separate volume. His philosophy of the human learner assumes the presence of two postulates — reflective/consciousness and freedom — and these need closer examination.

Reflective Consciousness/Understanding

In ascribing reflective consciousness to persons, we mean that human beings understand themselves as creatures with certain desires or wants, together with certain capacities to satisfy, or to fail to satisfy, these wants. It is the 'formal character' of all human action to seek the satisfaction of wants — not in some general sense but in terms of desires to do specific things, 'to idle in Avignon or hear Caruso sing' (Oakeshott, 1975a, p. 53; see also p. 39). People understand the world, or more precisely their situations, as favourable or unfavourable in relation to these desires (*ibid.*, pp. 32, 36–7). This notion of reflective consciousness applies even where the understanding that people have of themselves and of their situation is limited and even where this understanding is incorrect. When they misunderstand, people make judgments, interpretations, diagnoses, or appraisals of themselves or their situation and so a misunderstanding is an expression of distinctively human intelligence. For example, a pupil's mistaken belief that she is being victimised by her teacher is an expression of her understanding of her situation, through perhaps mistaken in this instance.

Oakeshott's claim here has been criticised by Anne Seller, a criticism that is rather surprising because it arises in the context of a careful and helpful review of *On Human Conduct* (Seller, 1976). Seller argues that Oakeshott's claim that our situation is 'what we understand it to be' is exactly what that bank managers have occasion to deny (*ibid.*, p. 56). What Seller wants to point out is that our understanding of our situation may be incorrect but this is precisely what Oakeshott is at pains to stress (Oakeshott, 1975a, pp. 38, 52). The relative truth of our appraisal is not relevant to its status as an expression of human intelligence. According to Oakeshott all that matters is that a person can give reasons for her understanding of her situation.

This emphasis on the individual's own distinctive judgment, appraisal, or interpretation of his situation might seem to attribute an excessively subjective quality to human understanding. Oakeshott is careful to reject any account of understanding as 'merely subjective' (*ibid.*, p. 52). Any act of understanding is necessarily and inherently subjective in the sense of being personal and unique to one individual. Yet this does not mean that such an act is 'merely subjective' in the sense of being an inner, private matter, secure from evaluation in terms of publicly accepted standards of reasonableness and correctness. According to Oakeshott's view, 'I feel warm', for example, is a statement which is subjective in that it applies to me, but it is objective in that it conveys a public meaning which is open to appraisal by myself and others. I may, for example, ask myself or be asked by others whether my feeling of warmth is due to the temperature or whether it is due to fever or embarrassment. Or, to return to our previous example, the pupil's conviction that she is being victimised is subjective in that it is her own, but it also has an objective meaning in virtue of which its reasonableness can be assessed by others. If we established that the teacher and the girl's class-mates unanimously considered that she was persistently idle, disruptive, and provocative, we would doubt the reasonableness of the young person's feeling of victimisation, though we may be unable to dispel her feeling of grievance. In Oakeshott's sense of the term, 'objectivity' in interpreting a situation signifies only that we understand our situation as having a particular meaning which can, in principle, be grasped by someone else. Therefore, the objectivity of our understanding of our situation implies nothing of the relative correctness of our appraisal of it. In any event, if our appraisals were simply subjective in the sense of being merely inner experiences, then we could never learn to describe them. This is because it is through our participation in the public world of language that we become able to understand the world and to share our understanding with others.

Oakeshott affirms very emphatically the inherently subjective nature of human understanding. But he also makes it clear that this emphasis should not be understood to imply that people must understand their situations in terms of narrow self-interest (Oakeshott, 1975a, pp. 52–3). Human beings are capable of understanding situations in terms of the interests of others and of acting accordingly. The capacity for such understanding is the basis of our sympathy and concern for other people. Indeed, in their professional role it is the duty of teachers to understand and to respond to situations in terms of the interests of their pupils, as it is with anyone whose work entails responsibility for the interests of others. The human capacity to participate in practices, to be examined in more detail later, means that we that we are not genetically programmed to act in any particular way nor are we subject to genetic laws that oblige us invariably to act in terms of our narrow self-interest. Consequently, in responding to the wants, interests, or needs of another, we are not simply seeking self-gratification under the guise of altruism. Implied therefore in Oakeshott's work is the belief that if generous or kind actions were merely disguised expressions of human selfishness, it would be hard to see what sense could be made of our ordinary language distinction between such actions and those that are ungenerous and narrowly selfish, or those that show only a hypocritical concern for others. The wants that we seek to satisfy may therefore be non-self-regarding and take the form of a concern for the interests of others. This point leads to the important conceptual category of freedom.[6]

---

[6] For example, readers who wish to explore Oakeshott's theory of human freedom will find it treated very comprehensively in Liddington (1984) and Podoksik (2003b).

Freedom

According to Oakeshott, the understanding that informs distinctively human actions is composed of contingent beliefs, that is, beliefs which could have been other than they are and, as such, they are unlike the components of a causally determined process. And the actions which give expression to these beliefs likewise enjoy 'freedom from a natural necessity' (Oakeshott, 1981, p. 60; see also p. 248) of a biological or environmental kind. Peter Winch puts this point as follows in the context of a discussion of Oakeshott:

> Since understanding something involves understanding its contradictory, someone who, with understanding, performs X must be capable of envisaging the possibility of doing not-X. This is not an empirical statement but a remark about what is involved in the concept of doing something with understanding. ... Now though it is true that this 'alternative' need not be consciously before the agent's mind it must be something which *could* be brought before his mind. (Winch, 1980, p. 91 and p. 65)

For example, a person who invariably votes for the same political party may never have even considered voting for any other party or of abstaining from casting a vote. But she must be able to understand the possibility of acting differently if this possibility is brought to her mind. This is why understanding presupposes freedom because an action performed with understanding is one to which there is, in principle, an alternative. The freedom in question here is a *formal* quality of human conduct and does not imply anything of an individual's power of self-direction, self-determination, or autonomy.

This means that for Oakeshott an action performed under constraint can, in this sense, still be deemed to be free. Seller suggests that many will balk at Oakeshott's view 'that we are always free because we can always choose our response', and she observes sharply that 'some seen to have martyrdom thrust upon them, while others work hard at it' (Seller, 1976, p. 56). This criticism makes perfect sense because Oakeshott does say that 'when alternatives present themselves', individuals 'must be able to choose between them and decide upon a performance' (Oakeshott, 1975a, p. 36). The point that he wishes to make is that for both kinds of martyr their respective reluctance and willingness represent choices of response which could have been different. These choices of response are therefore, in principle, alterable. The reluctant martyr could choose to embrace his fate with less reluctance in order, for example, to demonstrate his faith in God or his contempt for his executioners. The willing martyr could choose to resist her fate in order, for example, to engage in dialogue with her executioners in an attempt to bring them to an awareness of the evil of their actions. In the sense in which the term is used in this context, the inevitability of the outcome and the impossibility of escaping from it do not qualify the martyrs' formal freedom. Oakeshott's point is that in the response of human beings to their situation nothing is determined in advance by causal laws and that, even where the freedom of physical movement has been taken away, the formal freedom inherent in human agency cannot be. The kind of freedom to which Oakeshott is referring is communicated by one of the characters in Irène Némirovsky's novel, *Suite Française* (Némirovsky, 2006), Jeanne Michaud is addressing her husband, Maurice, about his capacity to cope with the deprivations and humiliation of the German occupation. Yet, remarks, Jeanne, '"you're not unhappy, I mean, not really unhappy inside!"' (Némirovsky, 2006, p. 168). His state of mind, Maurice replies, is due to his '"certainty that deep down I'm a free man ... It's a constant, precious possession, and whether I keep it or lose it is up to me and no one else ..."' (*ibid.*).

According to Oakeshott, the freedom that is enjoyed by human beings is not merely the exercise of the individual's will. Willing to perform an action is a feature of action rather than something superimposed upon it. In his terms, all distinctively human action is willed and only such behavior as involuntary reflex can be described as unwilled (Oakeshott, 1975a, pp. 37, 39). Human freedom, as Mary Midgley writes in *Beast and Man*, 'flows from something natural' (Midgley, 1980, p. XVII) to a person 'his special kind of intelligence and the character traits that go with it ... It is not something added by his own will after birth ...' (*ibid.*). Almost aphoristically, Oakeshott observes that 'what is called "the will" is nothing but intelligence in doing; in denying "will" to an ebbing tide we are refusing to recognize it as an exhibition of intelligence' (Oakeshott, 1975a, p. 39). Therefore, in so far as it derives from the free, intelligent engagement of the participant, all human action, from playing marbles to playing the music of Debussy, from teaching a military salute to teaching atomic physics, is *ipso facto* an outcome of the human will.

The exercise of the will is therefore a feature of the reflective/consciousness and freedom required to learn engage in any practice. In this way human beings are enabled to achieve their own versions of autonomy and this achievement is an important part of the purpose of education that emerges in Oakeshott's writing.

Autonomy, *Bildung* and the Purposes of Liberal Learning

There is an interesting relationship to be noted between becoming autonomous and becoming responsible. This is suggested in Oakeshott's metaphor of education as a preparation to participate in a conversation which implies becoming 'responsible' with its etymological connotation of being able to answer for oneself. This relationship is even more clearly marked in German term *mündig*, which means being of age and literally capable of speaking for oneself. Indeed *Mündigkeit is* a common translation of autonomy. In common with many philosophers of education, Oakeshott places great emphasis on this value in the hierarchy of human goods. But the version of autonomy that he envisages and which is canvassed in the philosophical literature tends to be limited to the scholarly, moral and civic spheres. Yet the concept embraces more than the capacity to make informed and unconstrained life choices and becoming adept in scholarly conversation and in the conduct of moral and civic life. The contexts in which human beings can give expression to autonomous capacities are multifarious. As George Eliot puts it in *The Impressions of Theophrastus Such*, 'a man may be a sage in celestial physics and a poor creature in the purchase of seed-corn, or even in theorising about the affections; ... he may be a mere fumbler in physiology and yet show a keen insight into human motives' (Eliot, 1995, p. 63). And in Oakeshott's writing there is also something to suggest a vision of autonomous action that is broad and nuanced. This suggestion is to be found in the connection between his conception of education and the German notion of *Bildung*, mentioned previously.

Bildung implies an expansive sense of human development as well as an activity of identity creation and formation that are consistent with Oakeshott's educational thought. All of this is captured in Oakeshott's characterisation of education as a matter of '(l)earning to make something of ourselves' (Oakeshott, 1981, p. 303) or of a person's learning to 'make the most of or the best of himself' (Fuller, 1989, p. 47, and see also Oakeshott, 1967, p. 131). In this endeavour the teacher's task is to enable the learner 'to recognize himself in the mirror of the human achievements which compose his inheritance' (*ibid.,* p. 48). The term *Bild* also has an etymological connection to image, picture or model and this connection is further reinforced by his reference to learners recognising themselves in the 'mirror' of their 'inheritance' (*ibid.,* pp. 48–9, where the terms mirror and image recur, and also pp. 36, 67). The mirroring is not something passive, it is rather acquiring the character of what he describes in the words of Leibniz as '*un miroir vivant, doué d'action interne*' (*ibid.,* p. 67).

This expansive sense of human development in Oakeshott's work makes for a conception of education that still has purchase in this era of almost universal participation in education until the mid-teens and of almost 50% participation in higher education. His thinking gives expression to a tradition of liberal education that can be adapted in coherent and imaginative ways to meet the challenge of providing education in mass industrial democracies. His articulation of this tradition can therefore be preserved subject to the criticisms, qualifications and elaboration that will be made in the course of this volume. An important strand in criticism of his thinking is the rigidity of his demarcation between the practical and other areas of experience. As noted previously there is a tension between Oakeshott's broad conception of culture and the narrow selection of activities that he envisages as being eligible for inclusion in the school curriculum. The tension emerges clearly in respect of the sharp contrast that he makes between work and play which is the subject of the chapter that follows.

Chapter Two

Work, Play and Learning

In the posthumously published article 'Work and Play' Oakeshott (1995) re-affirms the epistemological categories explained in Chapter 1 but bases them on a distinction between work and play. This distinction needs closer scrutiny since it goes to the heart of much that is both positive and, at the same time, questionable in his philosophy of education.

Distinguishing Between Work and Play

Human beings, unlike animals, have wants as well as mere needs that are related to the business of survival. These wants are in principle 'inexhaustible' (Oakeshott, 1995, p. 30) because they have a propensity endlessly to proliferate. As creatures of wants, human beings, argues Oakeshott, look upon the world as 'something to be used' (*ibid.*, p. 29) and almost as 'an enemy to be conquered, and having been conquered, to be exploited'(*ibid.*). This impulse to seek mastery over the world is recognised to have some limits and these limits are set by what 'we call morality' (*ibid.*, p. 30). Morality he defines as the adoption of a different attitude towards 'other human beings' than towards 'the other components of the natural world' (*ibid.*). This is expressed in a 'refusal' to regard others instrumentally, that is, 'simply as materials to be used' (*ibid.*). The knowledge and skills necessary to equip people to undertake this exploitation of the earth are passed on from generation to generation 'in an appropriate sort of education—an education in "useful knowledge", as we call it' (*ibid.*). According Oakeshott, the activity of satisfying wants came to the regarded as '"the great business and occupation of life"' (*ibid.*)[1] and people came to refer to this as '"work"'. This he defines as 'a continuous and toilsome activity, unavoidable in creatures moved by wants, in which the natural world is made to supply satisfaction for those wants' (*ibid.*). Through work, '*Homo sapiens*' becomes '*Homo laborans*' (*ibid.*).

According to Oakeshott, two beliefs accompanied this attitude and he identifies the genesis of these beliefs in the sixteenth century. This first was that 'work' in the sense of exploiting the natural world became conceived as the proper occupation and morally appropriate activity of humankind to which everything else should be subordinated. This was reinforced by an acceptance among religious believers that work was the curse of Adam and thereby a divine punishment visited upon all human beings. Accompanying this moral belief was huge confidence about the eventual success of the endeavour to subdue nature to the purposes of humankind. This aspiration or dream of ever increasing productivity is part of the legacy of western civilisation to the whole world. Yet along with the endeavour of 'getting and spending'[2] has come a recognition that wants can never be fully satisfied and that human beings who see the satisfaction of wants as the main purpose of existence will end up like Sisyphus encountering repeated frustration in spite of all their efforts.

Understanding 'Play'

There is, argues Oakeshott, another form of human endeavour that is qualitatively different from work and this is 'play,' the activity of '*Homo ludens*'(*ibid.*, p. 32). How then is 'play' to be understood? It is defined as 'activity that, because it is not directed to the satisfaction of wants, entails an attitude to the world that it is not concerned to use it, to get something out of it, or to make something of it, and offers satisfactions that are not at the same time frustrations' (*ibid.*). Games provide a clear example of what play involves. In playing a game the prize is 'incidental' to the 'experience of enjoyment': it has no other 'ulterior purpose' and 'begins and ends in itself' (*ibid.*). A game

[1] Oakeshott takes this phrase from an unnamed 'eighteenth century writer'(*ibid.*).
[2] Oakeshott (*ibid.*, p. 31) uses this expression of Wordsworth's without attribution—something which goes to show how our reading can become so much part of us that we are at times unaware of the provenance of some of our phrases.

will demand energy and effort from the participants but it has none of the 'seriousness, the purposefulness, and the alleged "importance" of "work" and the satisfactions of wants' (*ibid.*). 'Play' belongs to the world of leisure or what Aristotle called '"non-laborious activity"' (*ibid.*). 'Play' is not a mere respite from 'work' and so must be distinguished from rest and relaxation. It occurs only we when are free of the burdens imposed by 'work' and is conducted with a kind of commitment that is of a qualitatively different character from that which is required when engaged in 'work'.

Next he goes on to relate 'play' to the endeavour 'to understand and to explain the world' (*ibid.*). Unlike the aim of 'work,' which is to exploit the world and to exert power over it in the interests of satisfying wants, the aim of understanding and explanation, is, claims Oakeshott, 'to discern the intelligibility of the world' (*ibid.*) and, as he puts it in a phrase reflecting a rather surprising philosophical realism, 'to reveal the world as it is' (*ibid.*). This activity is to be found in the 'great explanatory adventures of mankind' (*ibid.*) conducted by philosophers, scientists and historians. The knowledge generated in 'play' by 'pure' scientists is not to be confused with that produced by applied scientists whose aim is essentially instrumental, that is, to use that knowledge in a transaction with the world of 'work'. The former's activity is governed by notions of truth and error and the latter's by notions of usefulness. The sole purpose of the explanatory languages, modes of thinking or forms of thought is to contribute to our understanding of the human or natural world rather than to produce a result which can be used in the world of practical activity. We can describe these activities as being valuable in themselves, which means that the point of these activities lies within themselves, rather than in what they enable us to fabricate. The distinction between instrumental and explanatory activities remains tenable for all that the exercise of instrumental skills is informed by understanding and that our achievements in understanding are realised through the exercise of intellectual skills. In other words, the exercise of instrumental skills requires understanding and our achievements in understanding contain a skill factor.

Explanatory activities are not co-extensive with activities engaged in for their own sake or on their own account. Engaging in activities for their own sake or on their own account means engaging in them for the sake of the satisfaction provided by participation in such activities, rather than for the sake of a 'profit, a reward, a prize, or a result in addition to the experience itself' (Oakeshott, 1981, p. 175). Typical of such activities within the world of practical experience would be sailing, pony trekking, and enjoying human relations. One distinction between the two classes of activity is that the achievements of explanatory activities, a scientific hypothesis or an historian's account of an event, are public in that they can be shared with others, whereas the experiences in sailing or in friendship are private and exclusive to the individuals enjoying them. A. Phillips Griffiths says of explanatory, theoretical activities that their 'objects are universal, and at the same time concrete ... All such objects are qualitatively and not numerically identified ...' (Phillips Griffiths, 1972, p. 192). By contrast the objects of the other class of intrinsically valuable activities, such as the enjoyment of a friend's company, are non-universal, 'concrete and unique' (*ibid*.).

This distinction between the two kinds of 'playful' activity also helps us to account for the place of the language of artistic experience in Oakeshott's epistemology. A work of art, unlike a friend, is a publicly realised form of experience that can be shared with an indefinite number of people. In being publicly available and universal, a work of art belongs, therefore, to the same category of universal activities as the explanatory languages. Aesthetic experience is, according to Oakeshott, even more obviously distinct from the world of work. In creating and responding to works of art, the world is 'something to be contemplated', it is a 'dream enjoyed for it own sake ... it is an end in itself' (Oakeshott, 1995, pp. 32–3). In this essay it is worth noting Oakeshott's rejection of the Greek distinction between the arts of music, poetry, drama and dancing and arts like sculpture and painting that were perceived as mere crafts because they involved interaction with the material world (*ibid*, p. 33).

Educational Applications

In the final part of the essay, Oakeshott draws together the educational implications of the distinction that he has drawn. Where the system of formal learning attributes 'work' aims to education, this subverts the properly ludic mission of the school. He refers to this in earlier writings as 'socialisation'. From the ancient Greeks, however, we have also inherited another conception of the school as an arena for the pursuit of *schole*, that is, of leisure or of time free from the pressure of the 'working day world' (Shakespeare, 1997a, *As You Like It*, Act 1, Sc. iii, line 10). This understanding of education was also embraced by the Romans in their design of the *liberalia studia*. Indeed Oakeshott's distinction is captured in the contrast between the Greek *schole* and the Latin *otium*, which mean leisure, and *ascholía/negotium* which mean work or business, that is, the opposite of leisure. *Schole/otium*/leisure can result in an end-product (writing a poem, composing a piece of music, for example), or it can include simply reading a poem or listening to music. (*Schole*, of course, provides the root of the word 'school' and equivalent terms in many languages.) According to Oakeshott, if we fail to allow young people enjoy the legacy of *schole* and of *liberalia studia*, we bequeath to them an impoverished and impoverishing education.

The account in 'Work and Play' of the proper purposes of education reflects that in the major essays on the subject. Based on this rigid distinction which he draws between 'work' or practical experience and 'play' or the scientific, historical, aesthetic and philosophical modes of experience, he believes that genuine education, i.e., as conducted in schools and colleges, consists in the initiation of young people into the metaphorical conversation made up of the languages of human understanding (including that of art) which are rigorously set apart from the world of 'work' or practical experience. Coming to acquire a facility in using these explanatory languages of human understanding is for Oakeshott the characteristically educational endeavour. Yet moral and political education, which are both aspects of the world of practical experience, although non-instrumental in nature, come within the legitimate province of the educator's concern. Moreover Oakeshott can also be understood to imply that the school may, on prudential grounds, have to provide some instruction in the practical aspects of living.

For Oakeshott, genuine education is of necessity liberal. It is liberal in that it is conducted in an arena which is a 'place apart' (Fuller, 1989 pp. 69 (twice), 71–2, 76) from the rest of society and which is free from intrusion by the demands of the language of practical activity, the 'language of appetite' (*ibid.,*

p. 41). But education is also liberating or emancipatory in that it liberates us from the grip of this language: it emancipates us from servitude to the world *sub species voluntatis*, 'from the here and now of current engagements' (*ibid.*, p. 37). Through his/her education the young person is offered 'a release from the immediacies, the partialities and the abridgements of the local and contemporary world' (*ibid.*, p. 86). This 'release' constitutes 'an emancipation from the mere "fact of living", from the immediate contingencies of place and time of birth, from the tyranny of the moment and from the servitude of a merely current condition' (*ibid.*, p. 93).

A closer examination of the relationship between the kinds of learning associated respectively with the worlds of work and play is next necessary.

Instrumental/Closed Learning and Non-instrumental/Open Learning

There is a form of education concerned with acquiring instrumental skills and knowledge of the world of work/practical activity. There are two kinds of learning that characterise this education of an instrumental nature. Firstly, there is what it is proposed to call education in the practical aspects of living, the concern of which is to improve the skills and to increase the knowledge necessary to cope with the tasks of everyday survival in society. It would include health education, for example, as well as instruction in such home-crafts as cookery and needlework. (The place of such activities in Oakeshott's curriculum will be considered later.) Secondly, there is the more specialised vocational education which is the endeavour of teaching and learning occupational skills. Now Oakeshott makes it clear that the acquisition of vocational skills does require 'genuine learning' (Fuller, 1989, p. 26). But it is not the learning characteristic of the genuine education that it is the business of schools and universities to provide. The point of vocational education is strictly instrumental. Its aim, rationale, or intention is to equip the learner with a specific and circumscribed skill which is to be used in maintaining a 'current manner of living' (Oakeshott, 1981, p. 307). The case of the individual of independent means who studies, say medicine or engineering, for the sheer satisfaction of mastering the skills in question must, of necessity, be exceptional. By definition vocational education is concerned with the teaching and learning required to practise particular occupational skills.

By contrast, it is freedom from considerations of utility which represents the 'liberality' of non-instrumental/open learning and which constitutes the 'common formal character' (Fuller, 1989, p. 37) of this learning. On this point Oakeshott's metaphor of education as a conversation is most appropriate. Where considerations of utility apply, we are not speaking of genuine conversation but of transactional or instrumental discourse, that is, of discourse where our concern is with the expeditious satisfaction of wants. With genuine conversation 'we do not ask what it is "for"' (Fuller, 1989, p. 98) because the point of conversation lies within the activity of conversing itself, i.e., in the pleasure, stimulation and enlightenment that it provides. This is why we can speak of conversation as valuable in itself or for its own sake, and this is what Oakeshott means when he speaks of the non-instrumental nature of educational pursuits.

Many conversations are also open in the sense that they have no definable end point and they can be suspended and taken up again on future occasions. Likewise the activities with which education is concerned, in particular science and history, have no terminus prescribed or prescriptible in advance. There is no point at which we can say that we have finished learning about science and history, and this is what is meant by saying that these pursuits involve indeterminate learning. Of their nature science and history 'remain always activities of learning' (Fuller, 1989, p. 43); in the practice of science or history 'learning itself is the engagement' (*ibid.*, p. 24). Though in the exercise of vocational skills there is 'probably a component of learning in every notable performance' (*ibid*), learning itself is not the purpose of the activity. With regard to the study of science or history, not only is the learning involved inexhaustible, but it also presents itself as a permanent challenge to the learner. To increase one's capacity to participate in a tradition of learning demands sustained and concentrated effort and to succeed in making a personal contribution to such a tradition is the exemplary intellectual achievement.

But the presence of challenge alone does not confer educational value upon an activity. Chess is a challenging and intellectually demanding game but the conceptual boundaries of the activity, unlike those of science or history, are prescribed and limited. Of chess we might say that it 'does not significantly look outside itself' (Oakeshott, 1967, p. 136 and Oakeshott, 1981, p. 308). The tendency of our times has been to try to convert the open learning that traditionally characterised university studies into a 'closed economy' with everything as tightly prescribed as moves in chess (see Standish, 2005, p. 54).

Learning in Oakeshott's terms is also open in that it is not conducted in the pursuit of some transcendent, absolute truth of which the various modes of experience are a reflection. Nor within the modes of science of history is there a single 'truth' which is the subject of enquiries within these modes. Rejecting all claims to absolute knowledge, Oakeshott envisages the conversation of mankind as a contingent, continuing dialogue between those willing to participate in it. With intellectual pursuits, as in political activity, there is neither a 'safe harbour' nor 'a destination to be reached' (Oakeshott, 1981, p. 133). The voices in Oakeshott's conversation, as Richard Rorty notes, is each a 'cultural genre ... which centres on one topic rather than another at some given time not by dialectical necessity but as a result of various things happening elsewhere in the conversation' (Rorty, 1998, p. 264).

Aims and Learning

As Geoffrey Hinchliffe points out, Oakeshott uses the distinction between open and closed practices in his defence of liberal education (Hinchliffe, 2001, p. 42). But his conception of the liberality and openness of education leads to a general question. What, if any, sense does it make to speak of engaging in learning for its own sake? Sometimes hostility to the Oakeshottian notion of learning for its own sake is based on a difficulty with the logic of claims which characterise activities in terms of their intrinsic value, as being worthwhile for their own sake or on their own account. Much of this hostility stems from a confusion regarding the relationship between means and ends in such claims and next I wish to suggest how these standard objections might be met.

But first two qualifications must be entered (see Fuller, 1989, p. 79). In the first place, the fact that the qualities of educated people have socially useful functions does not mean that education is designed with this end in view. Secondly, it is true that part of what it means to be educated involves being able to relate to other people and that the cultivation of this capacity is rightly viewed as an important feature of education. However, increasing one's capacity to engage in human relationships is part of what is meant by education; education is not a means or an instrument to this end. Interestingly enough, P.A. White (White, 1975, p. 127) cites Oakeshott in her argument that it is a conceptual truth that education unavoidably involves socialisation in this sense. Obviously it would be nonsense to claim that cultivating a capacity to engage in personal relationships occurs exclusively in schools. Oakeshott is making the same point as Newman mentioned in Chapter 1 — since education takes place in a community of teachers and learners, by virtue of this fact alone, it involves learning to relate to others. Certainly education in human relationships need not be made into the discrete, formalised activity that the preoccupation with pastoral care frequently tends to make it.

This leads to first objection to the notion of learning for its own sake that needs to be considered.

The Socio-Political Argument

The first argument is the dramatic claim that all knowledge, including the curriculum of liberal learning, is simply an instrument of the vested interests of the rich and powerful in society. What we count as knowledge is not merely influenced, but is actually determined, by what is in the economic interests of the agencies of social and political control. If, however, all knowledge were simply a reflection of vested interests, then the claim to this effect would be similarly a reflection of these interests. If the proponent of the determinist argument seeks to attribute a special status to her knowledge claim, then she refutes her proposition that all knowledge is a reflection of the vested interests of the rich. If she continues to maintain that all knowledge claims, including her own, are explicable in terms of their connection to socio-economic ends, then it is hard to see how arguments regarding the intrinsic merits, plausibility, or validity of claims to knowledge can be conducted. No enquiry whatsoever is possible unless the participants accept the principle of non-contradiction as being compelling in itself. Questions regarding the validity of claims to knowledge must be carefully distinguished from questions regarding the genesis of the knowledge concerned. Even if a theory could be constructed which explained the genesis of knowledge in terms of its propensity to serve the interests of the agencies of social and political control, this would not affect the validity of argument conducted within the scientific, historical, or philosophical forms of discourse.[3] In any case, commitment to this view is scarcely compatible with normal functioning in the practical world of teaching and learning. When operating in this practical world, where students have to be taught and their work appraised, even the most radical philosophers have to be as epistemologically conservative as they tend also to be where their personal interests regarding publication are involved. After all, authorless texts do not feature on bookshelves and the narratives of the most thorough-going radicals assert fairly unambiguous claims to personal ownership.

A less dramatic version of this argument, and one that Oakeshott ignores completely, is the claim that conventional schooling really serves as a covert mechanism of vocational selection in the interests of the middle classes. The standard school curriculum is portrayed as part of the ideological apparatus used by the 'contented classes' as a means to facilitate the passage of their children into prestigious and well-paid employment. Although hardly anyone could deny the force of the evidence which indicates that conventional schooling works to the advantage of the middle classes (see Wolf, 2002, pp. 168–99), the association of the school curriculum with the middle class is contingent rather than necessary. Attributing the relative lack of success of individuals at conventional school subjects to a conspiracy on the part of a socio-economic elite to contrive criteria and norms which prevent the poor from achieving success at them is seriously misguided. Economic factors play an important role in determining the distribution of many of the benefits of education but these factors do not define the criteria of success or the norms of achievement within school subjects.

---

[3]   The work of Harvey Siegel provides a formidably cogent and detailed elaboration of the argument presented here. See, for example, Siegel (1997), especially pp. 129–39.

The Psychological Argument

The second, psychological, argument concerns the instrumental credential effect of education, i.e., the use of scholastic performance to determine suitability for particular kinds of employment and for further education. Oakeshott is aware of its prevalence (see Oakeshott, 1967, pp. 140-1), yet he would hardly go as far as Karl Popper who claims that the demands of such selection have the almost inevitable result that students will study only for reasons of crude personal ambition rather than out of love for their subjects (Popper, 1999, pp. 135-6). Nor should the almost unavoidable presence of a credential effect lead to the kind of disillusion experienced by D.H. Lawrence's character, Ursula Brangwen in *The Rainbow* (Lawrence, 1977, 434-6). For Ursula 'the life went out of her studies' when she realised that she did not dwell in a world of 'pure learning' and that 'the religious virtue of knowledge was become a flunkey to the god of material success' (*ibid.*, pp. 434-5).

On a measured note, Oakeshott observes that 'although there may be ways of discovering … the relation between … abilities and … ambitions, these devices will not be infallible, even if the criterion itself remains uncorrupted' (Oakeshott, 1967, p. 140). The criterion is, of course, the aptitude for and the 'willingness to submit to the discipline of academic study' (*ibid.*). Specifically with reference to university education, Oakeshott regrets the 'recognition of a university career as the passport to social prestige, to power and to emolument' (Oakeshott, 1967, p. 141) and he criticises 'the vulgarisation of learning which regards it merely as a means to passing an examination or winning a certificate' (Fuller, 1989, p. 99). This attitude to the status of university degrees has had the unfortunate consequence of depressing that of other qualifications and of 'prejudicing the appearance of new ways of acquiring esteem' (Oakeshott, 1967, p. 141). However, in the light of 'human servitude to the scarce resources of the world' (Oakeshott, 1975a, p. 45, note 1), and as position and prestige must necessarily be limited, competition for these resources and for position and prestige are likely to remain features of human life. On this matter perhaps one can say no more than that, when engaged upon any endeavour, including the pursuit of knowledge, human beings tend to act from an inextricable multiplicity of motives. The responsibility of teachers is to try and get their pupils to learn for the right reasons, that is, on account of the intrinsic interest of what they are learning.

There is no doubt that human beings tend to act from multiple motives and that there will be some tension inherent in a system which uses academic success for instrumental purposes thereby conferring upon it a status as a positional good. Yet it does not mean that the educational value of all learning conducted in this context is compromised by the intrusion of external motivation. There is a passage in John Knowles's novel, *A Separate Peace* that captures two extremes on this issue. The narrator has a strictly instrumental approach to learning because he is not 'really interested and excited by learning itself' (Knowles, 1966, ibid., p. 46), whereas his friend and academic rival, Chet Douglass, studies without any concern for examinations.

> But I began to see that Chet was weakened by the very genuineness of his interest in learning. He got carried away by things; for example, he was so fascinated by the tilting planes of solid geometry that he did almost as badly in trigonometry as I did myself. When we read *Candide* it opened up a new way of looking at the world to Chet, and he continued hungrily reading Voltaire, in French, while the class went on to other people. He was vulnerable there, because to me they were all pretty much alike—Voltaine and Molière and the laws of motion and the Magna Carta and the Pathetic Fallacy and *Tess of D'Urbervilles*—and I worked indiscriminately on all of them. (*ibid.*)

But we do not have to choose between these extremes and there is no reason why students studying for examinations should not also derive pleasure and satisfaction from their study. My own experience as learner and teacher suggests to me that many people manage to enjoy at least some of their studies.

Some Conceptual Tensions

The third and most persistent objection to the notion of learning for its own sake is one that I propose to call the means–ends fallacy. This is the fallacy that views the qualities and pleasures that characterise learning as related instrumentally to education. Here is the view articulated very explicitly by a character in Richard Hawley's novel *The Headmaster's Papers.*

I am no foe of "learning for its own sake", although I happen to think that the term is tossed about a good deal as an intrinsic educational good, but rarely examined for meaning. Considered seriously, the notion poses problems. Learning seems to me to be perfectly instrumental, to be invariably for the sake of something else: reward, promotion, amusement, mastery. Different souls learn things for different ends, and some ends are undoubtedly nobler than others, but learning itself is never the end. (Hawley, 1984, p. 121)

It is also the view which underlies the following observations of F.W. Garforth's:

[E]ducation is essentially instrumental; it is not an end in itself ... but a means both to fulfilment in the individual and to stability and progress in society. It is a tool ... to achieve the aims which society sets before itself. (Garforth, 1964, p. 25)

More surprisingly in their philosophically sophisticated article, I.M.M. Gregory and R.G. Woods make a similar point. In discussing the status of claims that ascribe intrinsic value to certain educational pursuits, they suggest that this may be a way of talking about the effects of such activities in developing certain desirable personal characteristics. Thus, for example,

talking about the study of English literature being valuable in itself is a way of saying that this study may be instrumental in the creating of persons who are sensitive, imaginative, affectively well balanced and so on. (Gregory and Woods, 1971, p. 59)

But, as with other human activities that have certain purposes, ends or outcomes written into them, educational activities should not be conceived in terms of means-ends logic. A means-ends model can no more be applied to the benefits that attend liberal learning than the activity of sailing would be proposed as a means to the pleasurable end of enjoyment. The exhilaration, the sense of mastery, well being, and closeness to nature that a person gets from sailing are not ends to which certain physical arrangements are the means. From the enthusiastic and practised participant's point of view such feelings are what sailing is for him; they are not ends which are instrumentally related to participation in the activity itself. Or, to consider a context that will arise again in Chapter 7, feelings of increased sympathy towards others, an understanding of, and a sense of outrage at, the human havoc wrought by market economics are not ends, effects, results, or consequences which may or may not follow a sensitive reading of Dickens's

Hard Times. An understanding of the corrosive power of ambition is not the end to which watching a performance of Macbeth is the means. Responding to novels and plays actually means having these and similar experiences. (This, of course, is not to suggest that all readers will respond in the same way or have the same kinds of experiences.) Accordingly enjoying the benefits of learning entails the development of understanding and sympathy as a feature, rather than as an effect or result, of the pursuit of learning. Education involves engaging in activities, it is not something which comes as a by-product of engaging in them. Outcomes or ends are built into the learning involved rather than being bolted on in the form of almost arbitrary 'learning outcomes' or 'benchmark standards'.[4]

For these reasons, as Oakeshott notes, the achievement of understanding and the satisfying experiences which are a feature of learning for its own sake are not to be conceived as 'marginally different' (Fuller, p. 92, note 10) extrinsic ends to education. To speak of these as extrinsic ends is like speaking of pleasure and stimulation as extrinsic ends of conversation. Personal enrichment is not an end at all: it is part of what being educated means. To describe an educational activity as valuable in itself or as worth pursuing for its own sake is not, therefore, to ascribe to the activity a status independent of what it contributes to enabling us to live fuller and richer lives. To learn for its own sake is to learn in order to have our lives enriched.

This argument also applies the version of the means-ends fallacy used with regard to science. According to this argument the significance of science lies in what it can contribute in enabling us 'to resolve practical problems' (Gregory and Woods, 1971, p. 62) and in the 'implications' that it has 'for the business of living and so on' (*ibid.*, p. 61). But the significance of scientific enquiry need not be defined solely or primarily in terms of its useful consequences. The pursuit of scientific understanding is also significant in other and richer terms. As well as satisfying intellectual curiosity, the pursuit of scientific understanding offers experiences of 'wonder and delight' (Fuller, 1989, p. 40) and provides a context in which rationality

[4]   For examples of 'learning outcomes' and 'benchmark standards' see Wolf (2002, pp. 116, 229). I trust that this clarification answers criticism of my argument about the nature of learning for its own sake by Ian Gregory (1999).

and intellectual connoisseurship can be at once exercised and developed. Though the medical/engineering scientists may also enjoy these satisfactions, their enquiries have a different point from those of pure scientists. Enquiries of the former kind derive their value from what they enable us to do, those of the latter kind from what they enable us to understand. Normally too applied research presupposes and depends upon the existence of pure scientific enquiry.

In practice, of course, enquiries in pure and applied science have much in common—both are complex and inexhaustible and both present taxing intellectual challenge (see Gregory and Wood, 1971, p. 60). The distinction between them may not therefore always be clear-cut. A pure physicist may well become preoccupied with some practical problem in designing a space shuttle, and the designer of a space shuttle may find herself becoming interested in some purely theoretical aspect of her work. There is absolutely no reason why research in engineering or medicine should not provide pure as well as applied knowledge. Yet, in principle, unlike the researcher in applied science, 'pure' scientists work 'undistracted by practical concerns' (Oakeshott 1981, p. 310), that is, without regard for the consequences of their discoveries for the world of practical experience. In Oakeshott's metaphors, the theoretical scientist uses the capital of scientific learning, not to spend it in the production of some technological device, but rather to reinvest it in the effort to learn more (see Oakeshott, 1981, pp. 307–11). And it is precisely its non-instrumental nature which constitutes the defining formal characteristic of pure as opposed to applied science. (This relationship between pure and applied learning will be raised again in Chapter 5.)

In the final section of this chapter, it is necessary to consider the relationship between aims and values in education.

Learning and Values

However people conceive of the aims of education, these aims must be rooted in values. Human beings must in the end find value somewhere. For example, the narrow view of education as preparation for work is predicated on the values of providing employment and producing wealth normally with the aim of supporting a way of life considered good in itself. To argue that education should prepare young people for working life, or that it should serve to undermine the capitalist system, assumes some view of what constitutes the good life for humankind. And here one must point to the danger in not treating education as being itself of intrinsic value. By treating education as something to be endured rather than enjoyed in order eventually to pursue activities in which we find intrinsic value, education becomes, in the words of P.S. Wilson, 'a sort of confidence trick' or 'a mere token activity' (Wilson, 1974, pp. 124 and 126). The experience of being educated becomes, in Oakeshott's words, 'a passage of time hurried through on the way to more profitable engagements' (Fuller, 1989, p. 70). '(G)rowing up', writes Oakeshott, is 'something to be enjoyed, not merely got through' (Grant, 1990, p. 120). Otherwise education becomes an experience merely to be endured until, as Wilson puts it, 'the great day dawns (e.g. on retirement) when at last one will be "free" to do what one can see the *intrinsic* point and value of doing' (Wilson, 1974, p. 124). Though their views on what constitutes appropriate curriculum content diverge dramatically, Oakeshott and Wilson are in agreement on this point.

As with a commitment to a moral position, an individual commits herself to the value of a particular educational pursuit by her preparedness in practice to be bound by her decision to this effect. (Compare the attitude of those who advocate work-related learning for other people's children but who strive to secure a good academic education for their own in Wolf, 2002.) This requires a willingness in practice 'to act on it, to suffer the consequences of it and, in short, to try to live by it' (Wilson, 1974, p. 74). Genuinely to subscribe to a moral principle clearly involves living one's life according to it. For example, a person cannot be said really to believe that birth control is wrong if, in practice, for the sake of expediency he or she uses some form of contraception. In the context of education, teachers demonstrate their commitment to the value of educational pursuits by their willingness to take them seriously in their own life, that is, by the quality of their engagement with them. This means that the activity must matter to them and have some roots in their personal life. However efficiently they might discharge the technical side of their duties in terms of maintaining control over the class or of securing good examination results, to teach any subject sincerely requires that teachers really care about it themselves. We would deny the integrity of the commitment of teachers to their subject if they valued only its credential effect in providing an examination result. Commitment to the educational value of a pursuit also means making a genuine effort to communicate to pupils something of the intrinsic interest of the subject. It is the teacher's professional responsibility, as P. S. Wilson puts it, 'to *teach* them the interest of it' (Wilson, 1974, p. 57).

Commitments to particular educational pursuits, like moral commitments, must ultimately be grounded in values which, although rational and defensible, are irreducible. Like the advocate of a point of view on, for example, the morality of capital punishment, the proponent of a position on what is educationally most worthwhile reaches a point at which she can no longer offer further argument in defence of her point of view. Having explained what it is about educational pursuits that she finds valuable, eventually the individual can only employ what Raziel Abelson calls '*reason terminating* locutions' (italics in original) (Abelson, 1965, p. 550) such as 'these are my reasons and such is my personal commitment' or 'this is what I believe should be done and these are my reasons'. But finding value in the explanatory languages of human understanding and the language of art is not simply a question of personal preference or taste, like a preference for strawberries over raspberries, although commitment to such pursuits is related to liking or even to loving them (see Phillips Griffiths, 1974, pp. 191–2). This is because commitment to curricular principles is a matter about which argument is possible. Argument is possible precisely because the values involved are rational and defensible.

Commitment to the educational value of any activity, like commitment to a particular moral principle, relates to our conception of what constitutes a desirable form of human life. And Oakeshott's curricular prescriptions derive their value from a conception of a form of life in which the supremely rational activities of human beings, namely, science, history, art, and philosophy are given a special place. I believe, however, that the school curriculum should include more than these areas. In particular, Oakeshott is insufficiently alert to the educational value of practical subjects and to the joy and great playfulness of overt interaction between beings and their material environment. Identity creation, making 'the most or best' (Fuller, 1989, p. 47) of oneself or *Bildung* can assume an embodied quality and can also be related in educationally significant ways to work. More generally, I hope to show that the contrast that Oakeshott draws between work and play in this chapter is too stark and needs far greater nuance. What is deemed educationally worthwhile can be conceived more generously while, at the same time, retaining his proper emphasis on the priority of learning for the sake of human enrichment.

Next therefore the shape of Oakeshott's version of liberal learning as he envisages it taking place in schools and in institutions of higher education needs to be examined.

Chapter Three

An Exclusivist School?

This chapter explores the nature of the school as the institutional arena in which initiation into the conversation of mankind takes place. It will firstly examine the nature and status of Oakeshott's characterisation of the school as 'a place of its own' (Fuller, 1989, p. 40 and as 'a place apart' (*ibid.*, pp. 41, 69, 71–2, 76) from the demands of the world of practical experience/work. The chapter will concentrate on his conception of the school, although Oakeshott also refers to universities as 'special places' and 'places apart' (Fuller, pp. 23–4, 27).

School: A Place of its Own

I begin with an image suggested to me by a student that captures very well the relationship between the school and education. For Oakeshott the school is like a church in being a 'place apart' from other human institutions. In a church through religious practice and in a school through education, people are offered a release from their practical concerns. This conception of the school as a 'place apart' from the world of practical experience is consistent with his conception of education as initiation into the languages of human understanding that make up the conversation of mankind. Just as the languages of this conversation are disjoined form the mode of practical experience, Oakeshott envisages the school as an institution upon which, in principle, social and economic interests should have no influence. The school here represents the appropriate arena in which this initiation is undertaken. In the school, therefore, the voice of the 'language of appetite' (*ibid.*, p. 41) is replaced by the voices of the languages of human understanding. What distinguishes the school is its insulation from the activity of satisfying the desires of the world of practical experience. The school, writes Oakeshott, is 'liberated from the distracting business of satisfying contingent wants' (*ibid.*, p. 28).

It is 'a place apart', a 'special place' (*ibid.*, p. 24) in 'its seclusion, its detachment from what Hegel called the *hic et nunc*, the here and now, of current living' (*ibid.*, p. 24) and of 'current happenings and engagements' (*ibid.*, p. 39). '(S)heltered ... from the demands of utility' (*ibid.*, p. 27) and from 'the language of appetite' (*ibid.*, p. 41), the school is '"monastic"' (*ibid.*, p. 69) in respect of this seclusion from 'the current engagements and occupations of the world outside' (*ibid.*, p. 69). Through this detachment from 'the immediate, local world of the learner' (*ibid.*, p. 69) and her or his occurrent inclinations, the school provides to the young person an arena in which she or he may find release from the 'grip' (*ibid.*, p. 78) of 'the immediacies, the partialities and the abridgments of the local and contemporary world' (*ibid.*, p. 86).

As noted in Chapter 2, Oakeshott also refers to institutions devoted to vocational training as 'special places' (Fuller, p. 26), but that this special quality is, however, of only a limited nature. Both school and institutes for vocational training are educational institutions but, because of the distinctive nature of the education promoted there, the school is 'a place of its own' (Fuller, p. 40). Unlike what is learned in an institution for vocational training, what is learned in school has, in Oakeshott's view, no function in equipping the learner with skills related to the satisfaction of desires associated with the everyday business of survival. Only in the school is knowledge pursued solely for the sake of the interest that it offers on its own account.

Oakeshott then resists any attempt to represent the school itself other than as a specific institution with any identity distinct from that of any other. Accordingly, the role of the school cannot be assimilated by putative substitute institutions. Examples of these include community or cultural centres where young people might come and engage in the pursuit of whatever activities interested them. To proponents of such proposals Oakeshott ascribes a mélange of ill-defined, progressive ideas. Such people, Oakeshott claims, affect to believe that the traditional school is a place where children are

> ... condemned to a prison-like existence in cell-like classrooms, compelled by threats to follow a sordid, senseless and rigid routine which destroys all individuality, dragooned into learning what they do not and cannot understand because it is remote from their 'interests'. (*ibid.*, p. 73)

Consequently they wish children to '"burst out of the class-room box"' and to 'win their "education" from the open book of life', free from the '"intrusion of adult interference"' (*ibid.*, p. 76). Oakeshott's tendentious rhetorical presentation of his argument detracts from its essential reasonableness. It is possible to argue for the distinctiveness of the school as an institution without presenting the opposing conception in this exaggerated fashion.

Oakeshott also rejects the view that the community can come to discharge the educative role of school. According to proponents of this view, the boundaries between school and community should be dismantled, and education should occur through participation in the community's activities (*ibid.*, p. 76). According to Oakeshott what is distinctive of school is that there one learns precisely 'what never could be learned' (*ibid.*, p. 89) merely by participation in the everyday life of the community. Participation in this life normally offers initiation only into practical activity and rather than into the pursuits proper to education.

Similarly dismissed is the notion that the school can be replaced by a form of distance education or what is referred to nowadays as e-learning whereby tuition is dispensed by means of television and computer centres linked to a console situated in the learner's home. He disparages arrangements that purport to provide children with access to a learning package which would enable them to choose their own educational goals without having to 'jostle their way into class' (*ibid.*, p. 77). In an Oakeshottian idiom, Paul Standish also draws attention to the poverty of a commonly canvassed and very limited conception of the role of ICT in education as 'canned learning accessed by information skills' (Standish, 2005, p. 67). Oakeshott believes that there is no substitute for the school as a specific institution where, in a personal transaction, a young person is initiated by a teacher into the languages of human understanding.

How Plausible is Oakeshott's Philosophy of the School?

At this point it is appropriate to deal with some issues that have been raised by commentators regarding Oakeshott's understanding of the nature of the school. I shall start with the view that Oakeshott's conception of the school is merely aspirational.

Is It Merely Aspirational?

John Kleinig, for example, suggests that Oakeshott's characterisation of the school is an 'idealised' somewhat idiosyncratic account of 'schools-as-they-ought-to-be' (1982, p. 92). It is true that his conception of the school, like his conception of education itself, is stipulative in that it stipulates the context or parameters of what kind of institution a school is, just as his concept of education stipulates what constitutes education. His understanding of the school and of education can also be said to be normative or evaluative in that both relate to, and derive their value from, a conception of what constitutes a desirable form of human life. Yet Oakeshott's conception of the school is neither idealised nor idiosyncratic, rather it is the institutional expression of 'an historic educational engagement (with all its faults and shortcomings)' (Fuller, 1989, p. 91) to initiate young people into crucial aspects of their cultural inheritance. It is an engagement which has found, and which continues to find, concrete realisation in 'the *Gymnasium*, the *Lycée*, the grammar and collegiate schools and elsewhere' (*ibid.*, p. 87). Though Oakeshott's conception of the school is historically specific, it must not be understood as a description of what all schools are actually like or of what they do. In 'Education: The Engagement and its Frustration', for example, he speaks of the 'idea "School"', and this idea he contrasts with actual schools as individual institutions (*ibid.*, pp. 68, 69, 71, 80, 87). The purpose of this contrast is to distinguish between 'the contingent vices of schools' and the 'virtues embedded in the idea "School"' (*ibid.*, p. 87). Unfortunately, however, Oakeshott fails to spell out what the contingent vices or faults and shortcomings of these schools might be. Such elucidation would at least make clear what kinds of institutional practices he would find undesirable and would provide valuable elaboration of his thinking.

How about Its Monastic Character?

The characterisation of the school as a monastic arena set apart from the rest of society is not all idiosyncratic or peculiar to Oakeshott. In Chapter I its connection to the view held by

Hegel was noted as well as to the aspiration in France that the school can serve as a sanctuary apart from the rest of society. According to this tradition, initiated by Jules Ferry and so dear to the philosopher and inspirational teacher, Alain, the school is meant to be a safe place where childish blunders do not have the consequences they have in the adult world and where encounters with this world occur vicariously through the study of literature.[1] The school has also famously been described by Jean Zay as 'an inviolable refuge into which the quarrels of humankind do not enter' (quoted in Debray, 2004, p. 32 — my translation).[2] This conception of the school as a sanctuary from the rest of society runs deeply in France. For example, in a major address on religion in the public space in December 2003 the President at the time, Jacques Chirac, affirmed the role of the school as a *'sanctuaire républicain'* (Costa-Lascaux and Auduc, 2006, p. 102). This is an expression of the underlying rationale of the French state school and of the passionate commitment to its status as a secular sacred space apart from the family and wider community.[3]

The conception of the school as an oasis of humanity set apart from the demands of adult life in Oakeshott's writing is also reflected in the tradition of the English-speaking world. The school is often perceived as an extension of the home in terms of providing personal support and overall care for young people. This conception of the school is most conspicuous in the case of boarding schools. Novelist, Monk Gibbon,

---

[1] In a recent interview with Nicolas Truong, distinguished French historian, Mona Ozouf, offers an interesting review of this tradition, with telling use of some apposite quotations from Alain (Truong, 2007, pp. 68–73, pp. 70–1).

[2] The French version is *'(U)n asile inviolable où les querelles des hommes ne pénètrent pas'* (quoted in Debray 2004, p. 32). Jean Zay was Minister for Education in the Government of the *Front Populaire* of 1936 and assassinated by collaborationists in 1944.

[3] Oakeshott, though, has some difffficulty with what he seems to perceive as the excessively negative attitude towards religion in education in France (Fuller, 1989, p. 83). This is due to the rigorously neutral and non-confessional (*laïc*) character of the school from which any expression of religious commitment is prohibited including, most controversially, the wearing of Islamic dress. Accordingly even the teaching of history of religions or religious studies may be rejected as a Trojan horse designed to subvert neutrality of the state in matters of belief (see Debray, 2002, p. 22). This is an expression of the Republican ideal in France deriving from the French Revolution and culminating in the Law of Separation between Church and State just over one hundred years ago in 1905. The reason for his reservations about the exclusion of religion from the school is on account of what religion has to intimate of a "'a quality of life beyond "the fact of life"'" and of what the Bible has to offer as a source of 'human understandings' (Fuller, p. 83).

for example, uses the metaphor 'oasis' in his description of the school in England that features in his novel, *The Pupil*. The narrator experiences the school as a 'kind of miniature Plato's Republic', a 'cultured oasis' animated by the conviction of the principal that a '"school should be a large family — a small nation"' (Gibbon, 1981, pp. 21, 75, 14).

Oakeshott's own reminiscences echo the tradition of the school as a sanctuary and an oasis. The happiness that Oakeshott experienced at school was 'a kind of serenity' and, as noted in the previous chapter, a sense that 'growing up was something to be enjoyed, not merely got through' (Grant, 1990, p. 120). The school was 'surrounded by a thick, firm hedge' and offered 'a feeling of safety' (*ibid.*). He also communicates something of the positive character of the school as a human community. As a community it 'was remarkably equipped with heroes, with a past and a relationship to that past' (Grant, 1990, p. 119).

> Religion did not appear as a set of beliefs but as a kind of *pietas*; morals was knowing how to behave; Florentine and Pre-Raphaelite art was on the walls. These things were very little 'intellectualised', and afterwards, when some of them were left behind, I never felt that they were things I had to be released from. (*ibid.*)

The loyalty provoked by the principal was 'very much a loyalty to the community' (*ibid.*). 'There was a great deal of laughter and fun; there was a great deal of seriousness' (*ibid.* p. 120).

Is It Exclusivist?

Oakeshott's reminiscences may give the impression that the school experience he advocates is the preserve of a middle/upper class constituency of learners. In a letter to me Oakeshott urges passionately that the kind of schooling he enjoyed and wished others to enjoy also should not be restricted to the well-to-do. Even where it was the only education enjoyed by the inhabitants of his native village, they remembered the local school 'with immense gratitude'.[4] Commitment to the quality of the experience of school is not confined to teachers in upper middle-class schools. Christopher Winch refers to the 'heroic efforts made by many secondary

---

[4]   See the Michael Oakeshott website. See Oakeshott (1983b) Photocopy of letter from Oakeshott to Kevin Williams, library. 2.lse.ac.uk/archives/handlists/Oakeshott/m. html. Accessed 11 March 2007.

modern teachers to give their children a worthwhile experience at school' (2002, p. 115, note 20). Here is an account of the role of the school that would be shared by committed teachers in many schools in the English-speaking world. Gervase Phinn, a school inspector, arrives in a boys' school in an area of disadvantage catering for children who have failed to get places in the traditional, academic secondary school. By virtue of attending this school, the boys are already 'deemed to be failures' and arrive 'under-confident, with low self-esteem' (Phinn, 2000, p. 152). The task of the school, explains the principal, is:

> first and foremost ... to build up their confidence and self-esteem, continue to have high expectations for them and be sure they know, give them maximum support and encouragement, develop their social skills and qualities of character to enable them to enter the world feeling good about themselves ... so they develop into well-rounded young people with courage, tolerance, strong convictions, lively enquiring minds and a sense of humour ... I do really believe ... that those of us in education can really make a difference, particularly in the lives of less fortunate children, those who are labelled failures. (*ibid.*, pp. 152/3, 171)

He tries, he says, to make the school 'like the good home that I was brought up in, a place where there is work and laughter, honesty and fairness' (*ibid.*, p. 171). The reference here and in Oakeshott's reminiscence to laughter is interesting because the humorous aspect of school life is very little acknowledged in educational literature.

Most schools that I have the privilege of visiting are nurturing and protective environments where good humour and banter are common. The notion of the school serving as a sanctuary is especially striking in areas of social disadvantage. These schools allow young people to be children, secure for a while from the cramped toughness of their world outside the classroom where the demands of a precocious adulthood urge themselves so insistently upon them. This is captured succinctly in the description of the primary school in Roddy Doyle's *A Star Called Henry* where the brother of the eponymous hero cries on being withdrawn from school, missing 'the warmth, the singing, making words, the chalk working across his slate, the woman who'd made him feel wanted' (Doyle, 1999, p. 79). Clearly a positive experience of schooling is not the sole prerogative of the middle-class and those bound for university.

Narrowness of Focus?

Oakeshott does argue that the formal curriculum is the main business on the school but in no sense does he conceive it as the only business. As well as offering 'a feeling of safety', his own school also offered 'an immense variety of outlets' and 'a world of beckoning activities and interests' (Grant, 1990, p. 120). These emanated from the principal or 'were the private enterprise of members of staff ... (or were) made for oneself' (*ibid.*). Notable also in these reflections is the wide compass of activities included within the school. The positive educational experiences to be found even in traditional schools are often much more embracing than those offered by the formal curriculum. An 'immense variety of outlets' in a 'world of beckoning activities and interests' hardly reflects a narrowly academic conception of school experience.

Yet there is some force in John Wilson's point that there is no necessary connection between Oakeshott's conception of school as a place apart from economic and social conditions and initiation therein into predominantly academic pursuits (1977, p. 22). Wilson argues that the school's detachment from instrumental considerations is consistent with its promoting the pursuit of any non-instrumental activities such as woodcarving, metal work, needlework, hobbies or sports. In Wilson's words, Oakeshott fails:

> to disentangle ... the admittedly still vague notion of schools as 'detached', 'apart', specifically separated and shielded from the outside world, perhaps 'monastic', etc., from his quite different ideas about the particular scholarly or 'academic' functions or régimes in them. (*ibid.*)

This criticism will have to be considered in more detail later but for the present Oakeshott's account of how the school can be subverted or undermined needs to be examined.

School and the Assimilationist Project

What Oakeshott calls socialisation is the endeavour to usurp the school's function in the educational engagement (Fuller, 1989, pp. 79–94, Oakeshott, 1975a, pp, 306–7) by deflecting it from its institutionally appropriate role. Socialisation means the suborning of this role by insisting that the school serve economic needs. It involves therefore the imposition on the properly educative task of the school of instrumental purposes foreign to this role. Rather than being perceived as a 'place of its own' or a 'place apart', the school is assimilated into society's 'sovereign common purpose' (Oakeshott, 1975a, p. 315).

Before exploring Oakeshott's account of socialisation, it might help if we distinguish between the various purposes of the school. The first aim is to equip young people with enabling skills, i.e., the skills of literacy and numeracy necessary for future education and to live in, and to contribute, to society. The second aim of schooling is to provide personal enrichment: this might be called its most conspicuously educational dimension. The third aim is to provide young people with a nurturing environment and to cultivate moral character. But schooling has another feature that is an unavoidable consequence of the institution in almost any society. This is its facilitation of positional advantage, i.e., the labour market advantage conferred by the exchange value of education. Many negative manifestations of schooling derive from the consequence of its having this exchange value.

Schooling the Nation

According to Oakeshott, advocates of socialisation assume that contributing to society is the only purpose of the school and that the teaching of enabling skills and the development of character are all part of this purpose. He identifies the genesis of this assimilationist project in the actions of those Catholic and Protestant rulers who, at the time of the Reformation, assumed for themselves the *auctoritas docendi* which had hitherto been exercised by the papacy. For these rulers the authority to rule, to '"command for truth"' (Oakeshott, 1975a, p. 284) and to educate all went together. They used this newly appropriated authority to promote through the schools a uniform cultural and religious identity that would serve to integrate the inhabitants of their kingdoms. Though confessional requirements were imposed on teachers, the general school curriculum was left intact. Consequently these rulers 'did not otherwise seriously modify the educational engagement' (Fuller, 1989, p. 80). Indeed, as 'patrons of learning' rather than as 'managers of a system of education' (Oakeshott, 1975a, p. 306), many Reformation princes helped to spread the new humanism of the Renaissance.

On this feature of the activity of these princes Oakeshott is not very convincing. The role of patron of learning is hardly consistent with that of rulers concerned with the 'moral and religious integration of their subjects' (*ibid.*, p. 301) whose aim was to ensure the cultural and religious homogeneity of the population. It is hard to see how this concern to impart an orthodoxy from which no divergence was permitted and that was to be 'learned by rote in schools and universities' (Oakeshott, 1975a, p. 283) is compatible with being a genuine patron of learning. The historical accuracy of Oakeshott's reading of history need not, however, concern us here. More inimical to the education was what Oakeshott calls the Enlightenment conception of schooling. This conception of the role of the school, claims Oakeshott, was given exemplary expression in the Prussian *Landschulregiment* of 1763 and had as its progenitor the 'audacious imagination of Francis Bacon' (Oakeshott, 1975a, p. 287; see also *ibid.*, p. 307). It made of the school a political instrument in the endeavour to maximise the productivity of the state understood as a corporate 'enterprise association' (*ibid.*, p. 114) or as a 'corporate productive enterprise' (*ibid.*, p. 290).

To appreciate fully Oakeshott's understanding of how the state can come to subvert the properly educative role of the school, it is necessary to explore further this notion of the state as an enterprise association. An enterprise association is an association of individuals joined together 'to procure the satisfaction of a chosen common want or to promote a common interest' (Oakeshott, 1983a, p. 122). In the state conceived as an enterprise association, Oakeshott sees the interests of the inhabitants as being vested in and expressed through the agencies of government. This corporate interest consists in the promotion of the 'well-being' of the inhabitants and this 'well-being' is understood as 'the satisfaction of their endlessly proliferating wants' (Oakeshott, 1975a, p. 290). If within a state the interests of individuals and of organisations diverge from this 'sovereign common purpose' (Oakeshott, 1975a, p. 315), then it is the task of the government to ensure the conciliation and integration of such private interests with the 'general interest' (*ibid.*, p. 152) which represents the 'so-called "common good"' (*ibid.*, p. 315). Oakeshott's state as enterprise association would seem to resemble the state in Orwell's *Animal Farm* with benevolent, rather than self-seeking, pigs as rulers. It is a state in which the rulers have a genuine concern for the welfare of their subjects and in which the ruled can confidently entrust the management of the common good to their rulers. In *On Human Conduct*, in an idiom reminiscent of the work of Michel Foucault, Oakeshott even speaks sharply of an understanding of government, not as management of a productive enterprise, but as a 'therapeutic engagement' (*ibid.*, p. 310) whereby education is conceived accordingly as a 'curative' (*ibid.*) social service designed to provide against the 'universal neurosis' (*ibid.*, p. 309) brought about by the conditions of modern life.

It is Oakeshott's opinion that in most contemporary states government and citizens alike tend to think of the state as an enterprise association. What he calls the 'teleocratic drift' (*ibid.*, p. 311), which mobilisation for two world wars has 'imparted to all European governments' (*ibid.*), has made this concept of the state increasingly pervasive and acceptable. Accordingly, the 'managerial engagements' of early modern European states have become 'the commonplace concerns of modern European governments' (*ibid.*, 300). Consequently, Oakeshott's account of the development of this conception of the state as an enterprise association must not be understood as a 'merely imaginary' (*ibid.*, p. 299) view of the matter. In practice, however, he considers that only Calvin's Geneva, Nazi Germany, and Soviet Russia have come near to the condition of the state as an unqualified enterprise association (*ibid.*, p. 286). But the spirit of the conception of the state as an enterprise association can take less totalitarian forms. In Ireland, Fianna Fáil, the main political party and the dominant party of government since the 1930s, has its two main aims the unification of the country and the revival of the national language. The school has been used as the principal vehicle for a vigorous and unsuccessful attempt to revive the language. The endeavour was perceptively and accurately indicted by Oakeshott as one of the 'progeny of rationalism' (1981, pp. 6/7).[5]

One essential feature of the state's managerial engagement, according to Oakeshott, has been its concern to provide 'com-

---

[5]   Sanity has thankfully prevailed about aim of unification and this has facilitated the progress towards peace throughout the island. But policy towards the Irish language has changed little and study of the language remains compulsory throughout all the years of schooling. Though an Irish-speaker myself I deplore this policy; it has served neither the language nor education (see Williams, 1989). The failure of the policy is a salutary example of the dangers of the politics conducted in pursuit of an ideology.

pulsory generalized education and technological training'
(*ibid.*, p. 301). Clyde Chitty, for example, considers James
Callaghan's famous speech at Ruskin College in 1976 as mark-
ing a significant moment in the articulation of a 'more direct
subordination of education to what were perceived to be the
needs of the economy' (Chitty, 2004, p. 45). And this thrust of
government policy has had adverse consequences for the status of the school as an institutional arena set apart from the
world of practical activity. I shall argue later in this chapter
and elsewhere in the volume that judicious state intervention
can extend the opportunity for participation in education and
so have a positive effect. But this is not to deny that government concern with education tends to be animated by an often
misguided perception of its potential contribution to the pursuit of material prosperity, a theme that will be explored in
Chapter 7. Far from being protected as a 'place apart', the
school is perceived as an arena in which young people are provided with training for their future occupational roles.
Together with this training they are initiated into values
appropriate to an understanding of themselves as 'role performers' (Oakeshott, 1975a, p. 291, 294) in a 'corporate productive enterprise' (*ibid*, p. 290).

Oakeshott claims that vocationally oriented schooling was
originally designed for the poor and peasant classes in order to
provide them with the skills to make them more socially useful
as citizens. With the emergence of industrial society, however,
he maintains that vocationally oriented education has been
gradually extended to include all social classes. Contemporary society emphasises this orientation to such an extent that
it has come to dominate thinking about education, particularly
as all stages of education have fallen increasingly under state
control. In accordance with this conception of education, as
Oakeshott characterises it, human beings are seen primarily, if
not exclusively, as 'human "capital"' and as 'intelligent components' of a state's 'natural resources' (Oakeshott, 1975a,
p. 307 and Fuller, 1989, p. 81). The school has thereby become
an arena in which young people are offered 'a systematic
apprenticeship to domestic, industrial and commercial life in a
"modern" state' (Fuller, 1989, p. 82).

There is no doubt that the language of practical activity, particularly in its vocational idiom, has become increasingly
intrusive in the educational conversation. In Ireland, for exam-

ple, Christopher Whelan and Brendan Whelan, in an ironic echo of Oakeshott's 'capital' metaphor, argue that 'the expansion of the Irish educational system has been consistently justified ... on the grounds of the development of human capital and its contribution to economic growth ...' (Whelan and Whelan, 1984, pp. 186). With erudition and humour, Alison Wolf shows how the vocational purposes of education continue to dominate the thinking of policy-makers, but that this orientation of the school system remains a 'great idea' as long as it is designed only 'for other people's children' (Wolf, 2002, p. 56). Nevertheless, Oakeshott probably exaggerates the extent to which direct economic utility has determined the content of the school curriculum. Little of what is included on school curricula in Britain and Ireland, for example, could be said to be of direct vocational utility, particularly in the areas of the arts and humanities. Moreover, from an historical perspective Richard Johnson has argued that attempts to link educational provision and the Industrial Revolution, 'through some notion of the "need" for labour skills (for literacy or a technical know-how)' are not sustainable in terms of the evidence (Johnson, 1976, p. 47). Referring in particular to the work of Michael Sanderson, Johnson is not convinced by the claim that this phase in the development of capitalism required a close relationship between schooling and the need for labour skills (*ibid.*). Apart from literacy, which was taught in schools, occupational skills tended to be acquired not in the school but rather within the family or by apprenticeship.

In the light of his distinction between education proper and socialisation, it would be mistaken to attribute to Oakeshott the view that schooling and education are synonymous. Surprisingly enough, considering the general philosophical care and rigour characteristic of his book, *Philosophical Concepts and Values in Adult Education*, K.H. Lawson would appear at one point to attribute to Oakeshott the view that the terms are synonymous (Lawson, 1979, p. 57). But precisely what Oakeshott wishes to deny is that schooling and education are synonymous. Indeed, his critique of the subversion of the educational engagement by the demands of socialisation would not make sense unless it were acknowledged that what goes on in schools is not necessarily education. In his denial that all that goes on in schools is genuine education Oakeshott is most emphatic. Consequently in his account of the matter the notions of schooling and education coincide only in principle and not in practice. Perhaps we might say that for Oakeshott school and education are synonymous in the metonymic sense in which sceptre and crown are metonymic for royalty. The term school is used in this sense in his quotation from Ernest Barker: 'Outside the cottage, I had nothing but my school; but having my school I had everything' (Fuller, 1989, p. 40). The expression schooled also has this sense, for example, in Shakespeare's description of Coriolanus as 'ill schooled in bolted language' by which he means that Coriolanus has not been educated in the use of the language of diplomacy (Shakespeare, 1997b, Act III, Sc. i, lines 323–4).

Oakeshott's account of the relationship between education, the economy and employment gives rise to major issues that will be addressed in some detail later in this volume but now the ideological aspect of the assimilationist project needs attention.

The Ideological Remit of the School

Oakeshott is well aware that socialisation also has an ideological form whereby that unique type of human intercourse with which the school is concerned has been suborned in the endeavour to 'propagate beliefs favourable' to particular interests (Oakeshott, 1975a, p. 289). As a result of training in basic literacy and numeracy it was hoped, Oakeshott writes, that the poor would be able to make a larger contribution to the well-being of society and begin to 'recognize themselves more clearly as intelligent components of its natural resources', its "human capital"' (Oakeshott, 1975a, p. 307). And he speaks in a critical tone of the self-appointed:

> right and duty of the government of a modern European state 'to school the nation' in such a manner that each of its component parts might recognize himself as a member of the corporate association and be made fit to contribute to the pursuit of the corporate enterprise according to his abilities and in relation to the current managerial policy. (Oakeshott, 1975a, p. 307)

Oakeshott's point here is consistent with the argument of those historians who suggest that the teaching of literacy was simply a feature of the endeavour to propagate approved social ideology. Indeed, according to Richard Johnson for example, the purpose of the introduction of compulsory schooling, following the Industrial Revolution, was to make the masses into more acquiescent and productive workers. Consequently, argues Johnson, supporting his argument with apposite quotations and illustrations from contemporary records (Johnson, 1976, pp. 47–8), the promotion of literacy and of instruction in new labour skills was less important than the need of employers for workers who were willing to comply with the disciplinary régimes required in factories (Johnson, 1976, p. 48). More important than mere literacy was, therefore, the compliant and orderly disposition created by the authoritarian discipline of the schools. This attitude towards the ideological role of schooling lasted well into twentieth century. Clyde Chitty (2004) quotes from an infamous paper by a DES official in 1984 who argued that educational opportunity must be designed to meet job opportunities otherwise society would have to cope with the demands of an angry, disaffected and *educated* young population.

> There may be social unrest, but we can cope with the Toxteths. But if we have a highly educated and idle population, we may possibly anticipate more serious social conflict. People must be educated to know their place. (Chitty, 2004, p. 8)

People can be over-qualified but the notion of being over-educated is misguided. But perhaps Margaret Donaldson is right in her acid observation that the 'convenience of having educational failures explains why we have tolerated so many of them for so long' (Donaldson, 1987, p. 127).

Academic writing on education has for many years been concerned with the ideological aspect of the school's role and the theme is a common one in much rather repetitive analysis of schooling from the late 1960s to the present. Recent years have witnessed the growth of a whole moralising industry of conspiracy theorists (Margaret Donaldson is not one of these) advocating 'critical pedagogy' (see Williams, 2004). These writers repeat the same arguments made by the historians and sociologists of an earlier generation that the function of schooling is to engender in young people conformity to society's dominant approved beliefs. But these commentators understand the purpose of the ideological aspect of socialisation very differently from Oakeshott. According to Oakeshott young people are socialised into a common social purpose, what he calls 'society's sovereign purpose' (Oakeshott, 1975a, p. 315). By contrast, historians such as Clarence Karier, Richard Johnson, and Elizabeth Vallance, sociologists such as Samuel Bowles, Herbert Gintis, Michael Young, Michael Apple, and Basil Bernstein argue that the socialisation which schooling promotes is socialisation into the prevailing *status quo* in the interests of the rich and powerful in society. For example, in the introduction and in many articles of a standard reader on the subject from the 1970s, the authors allege that the purpose of the 'hidden curriculum' of the school is to impose a form of social control designed to make young people into docile and obedient employees in the future in order to perpetuate the current class structures (Dale et al, 1976). Similarly, in what must be the classic statement of this position,'Unequal education and the reproduction of the social division of labor', Samuel Bowles argues:

> that schools have evolved in the United States to meet the needs of capitalist employers for a disciplined and skilled labor force, and to provide a mechanism for social control in the interests of political stability. (Bowles, 1976, p. 32)

Developing his argument through use of historical sources, he quotes from the conclusion to the annual report of the Lowell, Massachusetts, School Committee that the 'surest safety against internal commotions' was universal education (*ibid.*, p. 39, note 10). Bowles also points to the fact that in England public support for elementary education, although previously widely discussed, received legislative support only after the extension of the franchise by the electoral reform of 1867 (*ibid.* pp. 39/40, note 10). Accordingly, suggests Bowles, the purpose of elementary education was to ensure the compliance of the working class with the prevailing political order. Perhaps no words convey more vividly the establishment view of the purpose of education than the comments of Sir James Graham after the strike movements of 1842 (the Plug Riots). 'The police and soldiers have done their duty, the time is arrived when moral and religious instruction must go forth to reclaim the people from the error of their ways' (see Johnson, 1976, p. 50).

For these writers, as for Oakeshott, the contemporary school in no sense represents an arena in which disinterested initiation into the conversation of mankind is promoted. But these writers, unlike Oakeshott, represent the school as an instrument of political manipulation provided by the state in order to secure the vested interests of dominant social groups, though there is a plausible case that the interests of business and the interests of government regarding the proper purposes of education have come to coincide closely (see Wolf, 2002, pp. 98–130). The concern of the school, according to this viewpoint, is not with the propagation of beliefs favourable to the pursuit of a common social purpose but with beliefs favourable to the vested interests of the rich and powerful. Moreover by its role in vocational selection, these writers would argue that the school further serves the interests of dominant social groups. This is because academic success correlates highly with social class background (see *ibid.*, pp. 168–200) with the result that the school system tends to eliminate young people from working class backgrounds. By providing such indirect apprenticeship to influential occupations the school thereby serves to maintain middle- and upper-class economic and cultural hegemony. Indeed such commentators make the claim that it is not just the school as an institution, but the curriculum itself, which is exploited in the interests of the agencies of social and political control. Here, for example, is a statement from Kevin Harris, one of many academics who have made successful careers from scourging the system. Curriculum content is, argues Harris in *Education and Knowledge: The Structured Misrepresentation of Reality*:

> a form of intellectual and political manipulation ... a carefully selected corpus of what has been deemed, by certain power figures, to be the most important and worthwhile knowledge that educands should have, and should carry with them into adult life. (Harris, 1979, p. 148)

According to Martyn Hammersley and Peter Woods, who are clearly singing from the same hymn-sheet, many sociologists have come to see the curriculum:

> not as something legislated by the nature of knowledge but rather as the product of struggle between groups promoting different subjects or different conceptions of a particular subject, and also as reflecting the class structure of the society. (Hammersley and Woods, 1976, p. 2)

A post-modern view of the indoctrinatory role of schooling of a similar character can be derived from the work of Jacques Lacan.

> Schools make an important contribution to society by reproducing the *status quo* in its intellectual and cultural variant ... providing significant ideological services to a capitalist society ... (T)he culture of the school is...transmitted through pedagogic practices, validated by the political power of the state. These prac-

tices, in combination, provide students with a language that defines them and their place in the social system ... In reality a litany of traditional values and beliefs are recited to them, which seek to define what is good and bad, who is intelligent and stupid, and what good manners ought to be in the classroom. (Blake et al, 1998, p. 125)[6]

In a similar post-modern vein is the spirit of Michel Foucault, well captured in the words of George Steiner. According to Foucault, writes Steiner,

Knowledge, praxis themselves, as defined and transmitted by a pedagogic system, by the instruments of schooling, are forms of power ... even the more radical modes of instruction are conservative and charged with the ideological values of stability. (Steiner, 2003, p. 4)

Though the ideological dispositions of these writers are very different from Oakeshott's, their critical spirit is akin to his. I do not propose to pass judgment on the general argument of Oakeshott and of these writers that publicly–sponsored schooling is designed to promote in pupils conformity to socially approved values. Even if we accept that it is plausible, I would question the assumption that schools are successful in securing this conformity. Such a view is inconsistent with the role attributed by Oakeshott to freedom and reflective consciousness as postulates or presuppositions of human personhood. As shall be demonstrated later in this volume, Oakeshott's writings also draw attention to the practical and logical limits of what we can induce others to do, let alone to believe. School authorities that seek to secure the conformity of young people to particular beliefs may find their efforts counter-productive. If only from the contra-suggestibility that can characterise puberty, adolescents my well reject beliefs that are foisted upon them.

But even if it were conceded that schools have been made to serve external interests, this concession does not entail that the school must always serve such interests. However powerful these interests may be, Oakeshott can still assert ideal of the school and of education free from their malign influence. In principle, therefore, the terms of his concept of the school do not preclude the possibility that the state could use the school to promote genuine education rather than the values of con-

---

[6]   These implications of Lacan's work are represented in this fashion by the authors for the purposes of commentary rather than uncritical endorsement.

sumerism. Indeed, as has noted earlier in the chapter, Oakeshott even believes that governments can acquire 'extensive control over the education of their subjects, over the curriculum of schools and the appointment of teachers … without imposing considerations hostile to the educational engagement and to the idea "School"' (Fuller, 1989, p. 80). Yet he does assume that state control normally leads to an illiberal form of vocationalism and this assumption reflects the lack of nuance that is a feature of his conceptual repertoire. Publicly-supported education should not be associated with narrow vocationalism. In many countries state-funded schools strive to provide exactly the kind of educational experiences that Oakeshott espouses. Many of the experiences referred to in this and other chapters take place in this context and exemplify the activity of liberal learning.

In concluding this chapter I wish to return to the possible charge against Oakeshott that his conception of the school is exclusivist. In principle it most certainly is not but access to educational institutions often requires significant state involvement and I have serious reservations about Oakeshott's begrudging attitude towards this involvement. State intervention is an expression of the interest of the community in ensuring maximum access to the intrinsic and positional advantages of education. The law of the market and the vagaries of philanthropy are highly unlikely ever to assure the full benefits of education (or of health care) to the population at large. It is one thing to tolerate private schooling but it is naïve to think that private agencies will assume responsibility for the education of the poor and the hard to teach. Without public support Oakeshott's model of liberal learning as articulated throughout this volume will not become the legacy of every citizen in our society. In Chapters 11 and 12 Oakeshott's theory of civil life will be shown to be compatible with the form of interventionism necessary to the provision of such support.

The two chapters that follow will explore the content of Oakeshott's curriculum of liberal learning and the contribution of this curriculum to human flourishing.

Chapter Four

An Elitist Curriculum?

Oakeshott's philosophy of the curriculum is developed in many different writings and this chapter aims to draw together the various strands of his thinking in order to appraise its value and limitations. The treatment of Oakeshott's theory of curricular experience opens with an account of some models of curricular organisation that he rejects. The manner in which the curriculum is organised in terms of his language/literature distinction is then explained and an account is given of the design and content of the curriculum as Oakeshott envisages it at different levels. In appraising Oakeshott's philosophy of the school curriculum questions arise about the plausibility of the language/literature distinction, about Oakeshott's treatment of specialisation and about his attitude towards practical subjects. Yet the curricular priorities in Oakeshott's writing are defended and the charge of elitism is once more rebutted. The curriculum that he advocates is in principle the patrimony of everyone irrespective of class origins.

Rejected Models of Curriculum Design

Readers will recall the argument of the previous chapter that Oakeshott believes strongly that education proper accommodates only one kind of curricular idiom, i.e, a considered and orderly programme of studies based on the languages of human understanding and of art. He rejects models of the curriculum based on any purpose other than that of the initiation of young people into these languages. These ulterior purposes belong to what is called in Chapter 3 the assimilationist project involving the substitution of socialisation for education. Concern with the interests of the supposedly less able has led to two versions of socialisation which seek to subvert the traditional curriculum. In the preceding chapter the first one was considered, i.e., a curriculum based on the putative vocational needs of the 'less able'. In order to identify its limitations, I shall rehearse it briefly. This kind of curriculum is generally justified on the grounds that some children would neither want nor be able to profit from genuine education. The vocationally oriented curriculum is promoted as offering the most appropriate initiation or apprenticeship to their future condition in life to those children whose intellectual capacities are assumed to be limited. What are the consequences for young people who follow this vocational curriculum? In the first place, it excludes them from participation in, and enjoyment of, any cultural heritage beyond what is supposed to be relevant to their world of practical experience and thereby limits the possibilities for personal, intellectual, and cultural development open to them. Secondly, as Alison Wolf (2002) has so ably demonstrated, young people who have not followed the traditional academic curriculum will also find that the vocational opportunities open to them are limited because they are excluded from pursuing careers in the high status professions. This outcome is well dramatised in Frank McCourt's memoir on his career as a teacher in New York. He suggests to one of his students in a vocational and technical school that she consider going to college and he is sharply taken to task by the guidance counsellor. McCourt is reminded that he is not teaching in a 'feeder school for colleges. These kids go into the trades ... They're not ready for college' and rebuked for 'giving kids ideas they shouldn't have' (McCourt, 2005, p. 110). And, as I shall argue below, a curriculum that is properly educative in a broad sense does not have to be at all elitist.

The second rejected model of the curriculum is one based on elements of contemporary culture. This curriculum, what might be called the tabloid curriculum, is based exclusively on a version of contemporary culture supposedly shared by everyone and derives from a misconceived endeavour to promote integration between social classes. According to advocates of this view, as Oakeshott represents it, the traditional curriculum is elitist and not sufficiently accessible to young people from backgrounds of social disadvantage. Therefore this curriculum is said to alienate these young people from formal education. The achievement of integration between social classes and the interests of social equality is said to require that this elitist culture be excluded from the school curriculum so that no citizen should feel excluded from intellectual and cultural pursuits appreciated only by a minority. Oakeshott uses the following quotation (characteristically unattributed) to illustrate what he considers typical of the aim of one such alternative curriculum. This aim is to promote '"flexible, exact and sensitive speech, creative writing, a cultivation of the living arts, an appreciation of the mass media and a concern for world affairs"'(Fuller, 1989, p. 85). Though Oakeshott does not make explicit his objections to curricula of this nature, the following two criticisms are consistent with his views. Firstly, these curricula must be seen as being without firm epistemological foundations and as being without roots either in the life of the community or in publicly recognised traditions of knowledge. Secondly, such curricula fail to offer definable, identifiable, and bodies of knowledge and skills which can be taught and learned. Quite reasonably, Oakeshott would wish to claim that, ultimately, a curriculum must offer the pupil substantive, identifiable bodies of knowledge and skill that can be taught and learned. These must be derived from the languages of human understanding in such a manner as to reflect genuinely the nature of these languages. Only a curriculum of such a nature is, Oakeshott would argue, epistemologically coherent and properly educative.

Introducing the Language/Literature Distinction

Underlying Oakeshott's positive curricular proposals is a distinction that he makes between what he calls the 'language' and the 'literature' or 'text' of a mode of thought (Oakeshott 1981, pp. 308/309). This distinction, which shall be revisited in this book, allows him to distinguish between different kinds and levels of education and should be considered more a conceptual tool than an epistemological truth. By language he means the 'manner of thinking' appropriate to a particular mode of experience, and by a literature or text he means 'what has been said from time to time in a "language"' (*ibid.*, p. 308). The literature consists in the facts, information, discoveries, conclusions, or disclosures provided by the appropriate explanatory language. A textbook of geology, for example, contains some part of the current state of geological knowledge, but this compilation need make no reference to the way in which geologists came to establish this knowledge. The textbook represents the literature or text of geological knowledge, while the investigatory procedures whereby geologists have established this knowledge represent the language of the discipline.

Stages of Curricular Experience

Turning next to the stages of curricular experience as described by Oakeshott we find early education involves, literally and metaphorically, a preparation to read the literatures of knowledge (*ibid.*, pp. 305–7). In primary school, children learn reading, writing, and arithmetic, to play musical scales and simple pieces of music, and they also begin to study foreign languages. Such activities involve much mechanical exercise to improve the children's dexterity at them. Here too Oakeshott makes the extreme claim that the content of what the children read and of what they write is not important; it is enough that they become able to recognise and reproduce words (*ibid.*, p. 305). It would be untrue to think that Oakeshott believes that this is all that children's early education should consist of. He explicitly acknowledges the place within the school curriculum of the activities of singing, drawing and dance, pointing out that they prepare the way for the next stage of education.

In Oakeshott's account of the matter no sharp division exists between the early and the second stages of education. It is through a gradual and imperceptible transformation that children progress to the second stage. At this stage the children begin to read the literatures of knowledge and to understand the information that these contain. To the pupils therefore the languages of mankind represent repositories of information about humankind and the world. In Oakeshott's similes, the world of learning 'appears much more like a stock of ideas, beliefs, perceptions, images and so on, than a capital'(*ibid.*, p. 305). From the foregoing it is clear that for Oakeshott the curriculum at second level should be non-specialist in nature. It should be 'without significant orientation' (*ibid.*, p. 315) and not concerned to cultivate 'individual talents and aptitudes' (*ibid.*, pp. 305–6). As school is the only institution specifically concerned with initiation into our cultural inheritance, it is, Oakeshott believes, appropriate that it should provide for its pupils the full range of this inheritance. In his view the ends of neither vocational nor university education are served by prematurely exposing young people to specialist studies.

Organisation of Curricular Experience

With regard to its organisation, it is hardly surprising to find that Oakeshott rejects the idea of organising the curriculum on what is supposed to be applicable to the practical lives of the pupils (Fuller, 1989, p. 58). By its nature, the curriculum has no direct bearing on the business of practical everyday life. The organisation of information in terms of the explanatory languages themselves as pursued in universities is, however, ruled out by Oakeshott as being too sophisticated for most school pupils. For these reasons Oakeshott claims that the organisation of knowledge in terms of school subjects is best. These subjects are not modes of thought as these are to be found in universities, yet they express their information, not as inert facts, but rather as components of rule-governed systems. Unfortunately Oakeshott provides no examples of what he means, but the following illustration is probably true to his intention. History in school can be presented to pupils as a self-contained chronological sequence of related events, i.e., as a system that allows facts 'to reveal their rule-like character ... as tools to be used in ... understanding' (*ibid.*). Yet, presented to school pupils, these facts do not have the problematic, provisional status which they have for historians. School pupils cannot be expected to be aware of the whole context of contingently related events that contribute to a particular situation, or of the different shades of emphasis and interpretation given to these events by different historians. Normally, school pupils do not have to establish the facts by working on original documents nor do they usually study the problems of historical interpretation as explored by the philosophy of history.

Oakeshott (see *ibid.*) also sees pedagogic advantage in the presentation of knowledge in forms other than those offered in terms of his languages of human understanding. Geography and current affairs represent such organisations of information which are commonly found in school curricula. This is because geographers expresses their information in the practical language of 'common names' (Oakeshott, 1978, p. 170) rather than in the quantitative terms of pure science. For this reason geography must be counted a form of natural history rather than a science. With regard to current affairs, Oakeshott would want to argue that the status of this field of knowledge falls short of that of pure historical inquiry. This is because the information component of current affairs is expressed in a combination of the practical language of 'common names' and the language of pure historical inquiry. Accordingly, both geography and current affairs constitute classificatory forms of knowledge that are situated ambiguously between the world of practical experience and the worlds of scientific and historical understanding.

Oakeshott's Philosophy of the School Curriculum: An Appraisal

Here I wish to make some comments on Oakeshott's philosophy of the school curriculum. Firstly, the plausibility of the language/literature distinction needs to be examined.

The Language/Literature Distinction

In order to adjudicate on the plausibility of the language/literature distinction, it is necessary to know at what point study in terms of the literature, i.e., contents, of a discipline becomes study in terms of its language, i.e., procedures. As Oakeshott does not provide epistemological criteria for determining the point at which, within each discipline, an individual begins to operate in terms of the language rather than in terms of the literature, I shall try to develop the metaphor here. Firstly a distinction might be made between the purpose involved in teaching a subject on prudential grounds and that involved in teaching the same subject on specifically educational grounds. In teaching a subject on prudential grounds, our aim is to help the learners manage the practical aspects of living in society. In this way we might, for example, justify the teaching of basic geography and historical facts. The instruction involved here could clearly be called education in the literature of the subjects concerned.

On the other hand, teaching a subject on educational grounds means teaching it in order that the learners become enriched by this study. Whilst engaged in such learning, pupils will almost certainly go beyond the stage of mere knowledge of its literature because even to read for oneself the literature of a subject requires a knowledge of its language.

The achievement of a learner who reads with genuine understanding, and who shows evidence of such understanding,
must be counted an achievement within the language rather
than within the literature of the discipline. Even at second
level to achieve mastery of a subject as a rule-governed system,
a learner must show an ability which goes beyond mere
knowledge of facts. A pupil at senior cycle writing on such
themes as, for example, 'The origins of the First World War',
'King Lear as a tragedy', or 'The rise of capitalism', or trying to
solve a problem in calculus or in organic chemistry must be
said to be working in terms of the disciplinary languages of
history, literary criticism, mathematics, or science. Indeed, a
pupil in primary school doing a project in history or on the
environment must also be said to be working in terms of the
relevant languages. Even to read the literature on these topics
requires some knowledge of the language of the discipline in
which it is written. Doing a project, writing an essay, or offering a solution to a problem must clearly be counted as achievements in managing the appropriate languages. Any
significant outcome of an educational nature in learning
means then achievement in terms of the language of the area of
knowledge concerned. Consequently, the language/literature
distinction, although useful as a tool in curriculum design,
cannot carry the decisive weight which Oakeshott ascribes to
it.

The Issue of Specialisation

Lack of precision in this language/literature distinction contributes to the problem of determining what Oakeshott counts
as specialisation. To what extent would Oakeshott wish any
form of specialisation to be excluded from the school curriculum? Closer reading of the relevant text reveals that the object
of his criticism is not specialisation *per se* but a form of specialisation in which the range of study is 'arbitrarily restricted
without either an increase in depth or any specific orientation'(Oakeshott 1981, p. 306). This claim needs to be examined
in some detail. In the first place it is hard to believe, as
Oakeshott implies, that anyone would actually advocate the
arbitrary restriction of a range of subjects without any regard
for a learner's aptitudes or interests. Even where pupils are
discouraged from pursuing their enduring interests because
of the career value of other subjects, this could hardly be called

arbitrary restriction. In so far as he is not attacking a seriously defended position, then Oakeshott's target here is a straw man. Secondly, it is hard to see how restriction of the range of studies would not produce some increase in depth. What he means, perhaps, is that school pupils are too immature to pursue studies in depth, but such a claim is highly questionable and in need of defence. Moreover, unless provision is made for some degree of specialisation then young people who do not proceed to university will be deprived of the opportunity to gain significant familiarity with any of the languages of mankind.

By 'specific orientation' what Oakeshott seems primarily to have in mind is vocational orientation. Quite reasonably he applauds the tradition whereby vocational education is 'undertaken from its beginning' and not preceded by a sort of 'pantomime' learning in secondary school (*ibid.*, pp. 306–7). Apart from the cultural impoverishment which such specialisation would entail, Oakeshott would probably also wish to say that the imposition of significant vocational orientation upon a school curriculum could commit young people, prematurely and almost irreversibly, to particular career paths when they are much too young. And if vocational preparation were introduced as a major consideration in curriculum design, it might, I suggest, prove very difficult to determine where this process should end. Linking the school curriculum to career aspirations would mean that a pupil who hopes to become a carpenter would spend most of his time doing woodwork or that one hoping to become an accountant would spend her day studying business related subjects. Such courses of study would be very limited and limiting, but it is at least clear what counts as appropriate activity for aspiring carpenters and accountants. In other cases it would be much more difficult to determine what would be appropriate vocational subject matter in a school curriculum. Certainly adapting the school curriculum to provide training for future lawyers or psychologists would entail great changes in what we expect of such a curriculum. Indeed we could find ourselves in a situation where schools function as university faculties in miniature. And this is a situation which many others, together with Oakeshott, would rightly deplore.

That Oakeshott's curriculum allows for some degree of specialisation is, in fact, consistent with observations elsewhere in his work. In the early article 'The B.B.C.' (Oakeshott, 1950/51), he considers the impact of broadcasting on school education. Its influence, he argues, is conducive to the

> encouragement of one of the less good products of contemporary education: the extensive mind, curious, interested, pseudo-sympathetic, preferring many contacts to few intimacies, preferring fact to thought and crowded with a disordered array of imperfectly realized images – the quiz mentality. (*ibid.*, p. 550)

And later in 'A Place of Learning' Oakeshott criticises the idea of a general education which, in aiming to be comprehensive, succeeds only in being superficial. 'Here learning amounts to little more than recognition; it never achieves the level of an encounter' (Fuller, 1989, p. 32). But, as Oakeshott would probably agree, an education which precludes any form of specialisation would remain at the level of recognition and never achieve the status of an encounter with the languages of mankind.

Uncertainty with regard to Oakeshott's position on specialisation is due to the lack of fine detail in the elaboration of his argument. As Oakeshott has never set himself the task of working out a comprehensive philosophy of curriculum, it is hardly surprising to find unresolved issues in his work. As regards specialisation, if all he wants to exclude is arbitrary specialisation and premature vocational specialisation, then his argument is reasonable. If, however, he wishes to exclude any form of specialised pursuit from the curriculum, then he must be criticised. Young people who leave school without some genuine feeling for, and a familiarity and identification with, some educational pursuit or pursuits are hardly likely to acquire these later in life. Life may indeed offer Birkbeck Colleges, which R.S. Peters refers to as 'that marvellous institution for those who come to discover as mature students the subjects which really interest them' (Peters 1974, p. 14). But few are those who can afford to return to such institutions. Moreover, in our youth, our 'resources of time and energy' (Fuller, 1989, pp. 101, 127) to devote ourselves to learning are probably greatest. Later in life we become 'committed to so much that … (we) cannot easily throw off' (*ibid.*).

This takes me to my main point of criticism of Oakeshott's curriculum, namely, its neglect of practical learning.

Affirming the Practical

Oakeshott's epistemology is too negative towards accommodating the language of practical life within the school curriculum. By this is meant general education in the practical aspects
of living as well as the teaching of practical subjects. The concern of education in the practical aspects of living is to improve
the skills and to increase the knowledge necessary to cope with
the tasks of everyday survival in society and includes health
education and what is usually studied in home economics.
Now Oakeshott can be understood to concede to the school, on
prudential grounds, a role in providing some instruction in
this area. For example, on the grounds that 'politics is every-
body's business' (Oakeshott, 1981, p. 316), he accepts that
political education has a place in the school curriculum. Nevertheless, the kind of curriculum advocated by Oakeshott
would seem inhospitable to the provision of education in the
practical aspects of living. There are, however, important
arguments against the rigorous exclusion of such education
from school.

No single family or community agency has at its disposal
the expertise or resources to organise learning on all the complex knowledge and skills that bear on survival in contemporary society and the school is in the best position to organise
this learning. Furthermore, young people from backgrounds
of social disadvantage are least likely to enjoy access to much
of the complex knowledge in such areas as diet, drugs and sex-
uality. In terms of social equity then there is a case for providing these young people with this kind of instruction in schools.
Of course, this should be in addition to, and not in place of, initiation into standard areas of the school curriculum.

With regard to the teaching of practical subjects, the scheme
of Oakeshott's curricular priorities notion would not seem to
be hospitable to the inclusion of such non-theoretical activities
as woodwork, metalwork, and other craftwork in the school
curriculum. He does not address himself directly to consideration of their place in education but there appears to be a tension in his work regarding their status. Quite rightly, as noted
in the Chapter 2, Oakeshott rejects the rigidity of the Greek distinction between arts and crafts (Oakeshott, 1995, p. 33). The
negative attitudes towards the activity of making derive from
the Greek philosophical and educational tradition. At the
heart of this are both an identification of rationality with rea-

soning, and also an underestimation of the rationality required by activities that require physical interaction between the agent and the environment. Oakeshott recognises the rationality in every episode of distinctively human conduct, from tying one's shoe lace to solving a problem in nuclear physics, and condemns the 'intellectualist disposition' (Oakeshott, 1975a, p. 89) that identifies only those actions that are preceded by a separate act of conscious reasoning as exercises of intelligence. Though not concerned with propositional reasoning, participation in practical activities involves the exercise of intelligence or rationality. For example, unlike solving an equation or giving an interpretation of an historical event, designing a tongs to withdraw an egg from boiling water does not result in mathematical or verbal propositions. Nonetheless, making the tongs is an exercise of human intelligence. One lesson that Oakeshott and Ryle have well taught is that the exercise of intelligence is not co-extensive with theoretical reasoning and that both thought and action are expressions of human intelligence (Ryle, 1973a). By sharing predicates such as 'careful', painstaking', 'attentive', clever', 'accomplished', the activities of reasoning and doing go through the same 'logical hoops' (Ryle, 1969, p. 60) and can therefore be said to be analogous at least in these respects. Practical/manual subjects and academic/theoretical subjects equally provide a context for the exercise of rationality.

In spite of this, Oakeshott does not seem to confer upon practical activities much of a role in the world of 'play' and by extension in the school curriculum. The epistemological separatism in his distinction between theoretical and practical activities leads him to neglect the playfulness to be derived from engagement in skilled manual activity. The rigidity of this distinction raises a criticism of Oakeshott's educational thought, perceptively diagnosed over 30 years ago by Josiah Lee Auspitz in respect of his general philosophy. This is a tendency to work with too rigid and restricted a conceptual repertoire, a tendency addressed elsewhere in this volume. Auspitz identifies the source of Oakeshott's 'over-economy of concepts' (Auspitz, 1976, pp. 266) in his having 'insufficiently multiplied essences' (*ibid.*, p. 288). Underlying this tendency is what I call his dichomotomising impulse, that is, the allocation of experience in an oppositional or either/or way to one of two categories. This generates an epistemological separatism that is unsustainable in the form in which he presents it. In the context of the argument being made here, the distinction between theoretical and the practical pursuits is not at all as clear-cut as he characterises it and that the relationship between them can be conceptualised in more nuanced ways.

Practical pursuits should not be identified with a crude instrumental 'language of appetite' (Fuller, 1989, p. 41) because they can have purely aesthetic dimension that contributes to the 'quality' rather than to the brute 'fact of life' (Oakeshott 1989, pp. 71, 83, 89, 91).[1] Despite his criticism of the Greek distinction between arts and crafts, Oakeshott is insufficiently alert to the joy and great playfulness of overt interaction between beings and their material environment. For human beings, writes Margaret Donaldson, 'joy in the immediate involvement of the body in skilled activity comes early and spontaneously' and although it is not 'reflective', it is 'by no means an unthinking joy' (Donaldson, 1987, p. 127). Affirming the joy and pleasure to be found in this relationship has little to do with the world of 'work' in a narrow sense of 'toilsome activity ' (Oakeshott, 1995, p. 30) and everything to do with the personal enrichment that should characterise a liberal education. The educational benefits that can be a feature of engagement in practical activities allow us to speak of what P.D. Walsh refers to as a 'liberality of making' (Walsh, 1993, p. 162). As well as giving us the opportunity to engage in play and to delight in the involvement of our bodies in skilled activity, craft subjects offer a context for the exercise and cultivation of such qualities as concentration, perseverance and willingness to take pains. Intellectual virtues, such as respect for truth, fair-mindedness, honesty, clarity and consistency in argument, which are characteristic of theoretical pursuits, find counterparts in virtues that are called upon in the exercise of craft skills. Among these are 'effectiveness, economy and good workmanship' (Walsh, 1993, p. 164), a 'passion for a kind of accuracy, for doing the job really well without falling into the trap of fussy perfectionism' (Smith, 1987, p. 198).

Identity creation, '(l)earning to make something of ourselves' (Oakeshott, 1981, p. 30) or learning to make 'the most or the best' (Fuller, 1989, p. 47) of oneself or *Bildung* can also

---

[1]   The distinction between the quality and fact of life is made by A.N. Whitehead (see Whitehead, 1926, p. 80) and is used by R.S. Peters (see Peters, 1972, p. 110).

assume an embodied quality. As argued in Chapter 1 this is a possibility suggested in Oakeshott's writing but, unfortunately, its implications are not explored. Engineer Mike Cooley gives the following telling illustration of this process. Cooley (Cooley, 1997, p. 59) shows vividly how his experience of working under the guidance of an inspirational engineering teacher in Tuam, Co. Galway contributed to his making 'the most of or the best of himself' (Fuller, 1989, p. 47) by enabling him 'to recognize himself in the mirror of the human achievements which compose his inheritance' (*ibid.*, p. 48). With a lathe as his only piece of equipment, Cooley asked the teacher for help in designing and building a steam engine. The close-grain cast iron required for the cylinders was not available in Tuam but they managed to locate an abandoned fly-wheel in an old sawmill and from it cut the pieces of iron necessary to make the steam engine which Cooley still has to this day. This incident represented part of Cooley's education in coming 'to recognize himself' (*ibid.*) in the mirror of human achievement composed by 'a craft tradition articulated through a sensitive education system' (Cooley, 1997, p. 60). Some people, writes Cooley, misconceive a craft tradition as 'simply the transmission of manual dexterity, whereas it is actually the transmission of a great culture, of how to organise yourself, how to get materials, how to plan things' (ibid). Interacting with the material world also provides a context in which human beings can express the 'fundamental human urge to be effective, competent and independent ... and to act with skill' (Donaldson, 1987, p 113). Autonomy, as noted previously, embraces more than the capacity to make informed and unconstrained life choices.

In brief, I would argue that for some young people practical activities may offer the most appropriate vehicle for creative expression, and for others these activities may represent the only area in which they can engage in significant self-expression. In spite of this affirmation of the practical, I would, nevertheless, argue that, as a principle of curricular discrimination, theoretical pursuits must ultimately have priority over practical pursuits and for this reason I would defend Oakeshott's priorities in curriculum design.

Priorities in Curriculum Design

This is because theoretical pursuits normally have a more intimate connection with human understanding and consequently with human identity. Oakeshott is correct in drawing attention to the enriching potential of literate culture for everyone irrespective of social class background. Literary and historical studies make a special and vital contribution to the development of human self-understanding. It is the actual content of these areas rather than any qualities their study may engender that endows them with this primacy. For this reason these subjects have been well described as 'identity or person-constitutive' (Carr, 2003, p. 12). In particular, the store of literature which we acquire during our schooldays shapes and informs our imagination and sensibility. What we learn at school can and normally does contribute in a significant and positive manner to making us the kind of persons we are. What we learn at school also has the potential to offer a world of joy and delight, of captivating excitement, enchantment and wonder. It is sensitivity to the positive features of our cultural heritage that is at the heart of Michael Oakeshott's idiom of curriculum design. Maybe there is some exaggeration but there is also a powerful truth in Simone's Weil's claim that '(a)cademic work is one of those fields containing a pearl so precious that it is worth while to sell all our possessions, keeping nothing for ourselves, in order to be able to acquire it' (Weil, 1973, p. 116).

Since the 1960s especially there has been a tendency to denigrate the academic dimension of the curriculum. A character in Ian McEwan's novel, *The Child in Time*, expresses an extreme version of this attitude.

> By forcing literacy on to children between the ages of five and seven, we introduce a degree of abstraction which shatters the unity of the child's world view, drives a fatal wedge between the world and the thing that the word names. (McEwan, 1988, p. 76)

With our 'busy intrusive books', we 'wrench' from our children 'an unforced, intelligent empathy' with life (*ibid.*, p. 77). There is a sense in which academic work is perceived in the manner in which the activity of the grammarian is described in Browning's poem 'A Grammarian's Funeral' as one who misguidedly forsakes ordinary living for scholarly endeavour. 'Dead from the waist down./....The man decided not to Live but Know' (Louchs, 1979, pp. 219–22). The speaker of this poem would certainly not share Oakeshott's notion of scholarly activity as 'play'.

In taking issue with aspects of this denigration of the world of the written word, I wish to draw on other literary examples.[2] These memorable lines from Wordsworth's 'Personal Talk' capture very well how books can enrich our lives.

> Dreams, books are each a world; and books we know,
> Are a substantial world, both pure and good:
> Round these, with tendrils strong as flesh and blood,
> Our pastime and our happiness will grow.
> (De Selincourt, 1974, p. 382–3)

Close to the spirit of the Oakeshottian curriculum too is the sense of adventure that animated Ursula Brangwen, heroine of *The Rainbow* by D.H. Lawrence as she embarked on her studies at secondary school. Feeling at last that 'she was going to inherit own estate', she 'trembled like a postulant when she wrote the Greek alphabet for the first time' (Lawrence, 1977, pp. 266/7) The physical elevation of the school on a hill is matched by the metaphorical notion of a summit to be scaled that is very different from the grammarian's mountain.

> There was always the marvellous eagerness in her heart, to climb and to see beyond. A Latin verb was virgin soil to her: she sniffed a new odour in it; it meant something, though she did not know what it meant. But she gathered it up: it was significant. (*ibid.*, p. 267)

Learning the rudiments of algebra and that '$x^2-y^2 = (x+y)(x-y)$' made her feel 'that she had grasped something, that she was liberated into an intoxicating air, rare and unconditioned … (i)n all these things there was the sound of a bugle to her heart, exhilarating, summoning her to perfect places'(*ibid.*). Approaching the end of her schooldays some of the 'magic' in her beginner's textbooks had disappeared but there still remained much excitement in learning. The 'cold absoluteness' of mathematics 'fascinated' her' (and) … the very sight of the letters in Algebra had a real lure for her' (*ibid.*, pp. 333/4). At times too she found 'a poignant sense of acquisition and enrichment and enlarging' (*ibid.*) from her other subjects. On one occasion 'when with her blood, she heard a passage of

---

[2] The use of literature in educational discourse is used to powerful effect by Duke Maskell and Ian Robinson (2002, pp. 36–56).

Latin, and she knew how the blood beat in a Roman's body; so that she felt she knew the Romans by contact' (*ibid.*, p. 334). She also 'enjoyed the vagaries of English Grammar, because it gave her pleasure to detect the live movement of words and sentences' (*ibid.*). Information gathered through the study of science was also capable of stirring 'unfathomable passion in her' (*ibid.*) Having learned that 'in the tiny brown buds of autumn were folded, minute and complete, the finished flowers of the summer nine months hence, tiny folded up, and left there waiting, a flash of triumph and love went over her' (*ibid.*). This is a powerful dramatisation of the world of learning as enrichment and of 'play' in Oakeshott's sense.

Yet this vision of learning will be perceived as elitist and exclusive by some people and the final section of this chapter returns to a theme raised in Chapter 3 regarding the charge of elitism in respect of Oakeshott's thought.

The Charge of Elitism

As noted in Chapter 1 Oakeshott's philosophy of the curriculum contains none of the social divisiveness of the epistemology of the conservative theorist, G.H. Bantock, who argues that different social groups can be distinguished on the basis of their capacity for consciousness and that the school curriculum should be designed to take this into account. But Oakeshott's philosophy of the curriculum can give rise to a charge of elitism. This charge is articulated, for example, even by such a careful philosopher as John White (2007) where it is prompted by a particular suspicion of Oakeshott's use of the metaphor of 'conversation'. He finds that the notion of conversation 'evokes the wide-ranging, unfocused atmosphere of an upper class dinner party' (ibid., p. 26). To base a criticism on suspicion of a metaphor is unfair and it is misguided to associate the notion of conversation with the 'upper class'. The charge of elitism is also seriously at odds with Oakeshott's strong conviction that the conversation of mankind is the patrimony of everyone regardless of social class background and that initiation into this emancipatory conversation is the right of every citizen and not just that of a cultural or social aristocracy. Though Oakeshott's views on liberal education were formed at a time when only a minority completed second-level schooling, the curriculum that he advocates has in principle the same purchase in the context of almost universal current participation rates at this level in the UK (see Wolf, 2002, pp. 1–7). In 'A Place of Learning' he insists that the invitation to become educated is extended equally to, for example, the child of 'a Neapolitan slum' as to the child of 'the better off' (Fuller, 1989, pp. 39, 40). Oakeshott's curriculum is therefore not elitist and indeed his passionate commitment to making available to everyone the curriculum traditionally restricted to the well-to-do reflects that of Jean Jaurès. As ready noted, Jaurès, like Oakeshott, argues that the children who will be future workers of the soil or labourers in factories should not be dis-inherited of the joys of art and of the beauty of great works of literature (Jaurès, 2006, pp. 26–7). Jaurès, though, is probably more sensitive than Oakeshott to the pedagogical issues that arise in teaching such children.[3]

In a very recent context, the fertility of Oakeshott's meta-phor of education as initiation into a conversation is invoked to telling effect in an essay by Maxine Greene on the future of the American public school (Greene, 2005). She suggests that the Oakeshottian conversation can be interpreted broadly enough to include colonialist, female and working class voices as well as popular and folk arts (*ibid.*, pp. 161–3). These voices and expressions of culture can indeed have a place in the school curriculum, although this does not have to at the expense of more traditional content. But it is necessary to find a way of making traditional content accessible to young peo-ple from backgrounds of socio-economic disadvantage. This is necessary both in order to enable such young people to join in the conversation that is conducted in the language in which this content is inscribed and also to enable them effectively to challenge the social order wherein conditions of social depri-vation are tolerated. Only by gaining access to the language of high status knowledge and discourse will the socially disad-vantaged come to exercise political control in their societies. I propose next to demonstrate that it is possible to provide access to the cultural heritage to be found within the tradi-tional areas of the school curriculum (literature, languages, history and science) to students from disadvantaged backgrounds.

---

[3] Whether what Oakeshott (and Jaurès) accept as great works of literature are themselves vehicles of cultural imperialism (see Lawn, 1996, p. 276) is a large question that beyond the scope of this volume.

Here is an account by Gervase Phinn of a teacher giving a lesson based on a novel set during the Second World War to a group of non-academically inclined learners.

> She used well chosen illustrations and probing questions to develop understanding of ideas and motives ... She encouraged the boys to explore character in greater depth, whilst sensitively supporting the less able, helping them to stay interested and involved by the use of questions matched to their abilities and interests. She required them to justify a point of view, refer to the text, relate to their own experiences and examine the use of language.
>
> The atmosphere in the classroom was warm and supportive, and the boys responded well to the teacher, clearly enjoying her touches of humour ... (She) had a real empathy with, and respect for, the pupils and ... had high expectations of their success. She encouraged, directed, suggested, questioned, challenged and developed the pupils' understanding in an atmosphere of good humour and enjoyment. (Phinn, 2000, p. 164)

The positive attitudes of the teacher are also reflected in the actual classroom environment. This 'was wonderfully bright and attractive with appropriate displays of posters, photographs and artefacts which gave the pupils a feel for the period in which the novel was set' (*ibid.*). Striking in Phinn's characterisation of the classroom is the reference to warmth and good-humour—the latter occurring in the comments of the principal and in the reference to laughter and fun in the reminiscence from Oakeshott cited in Chapter 3. Regrettably these concepts are not sufficiently foregrounded in educational discourse.

On leaving this class, however, Phinn, heads for the final lesson of the day through the school hall. There he finds two aggressive groups of boys shaping up to one another for a fight. So intense is their aggression that Phinn intervenes, much to the surprise of the boys and also of their teacher, who stands up to inform him that he has, in fact, been watching a rehearsal of *Romeo and Juliet*. He spends the next half an hour watching 'the most gripping opening' of the play he had ever seen (*ibid.*, p. 167). Even for young people who come from backgrounds of real poverty the potential of art to give the highest aesthetic pleasure is striking. The schoolmaster in Brian Friel's play, *The Home Place*, remarks on the effect of singing the wonderful melodies of Thomas Moore. According to this teacher the music 'liberates them briefly from their poverty ... A fleet and thrilling mayfly ... When they sing they fashion their own ethereal opulence and become a little heavenly themselves' (Friel, 2005, p. 40).

Here is another example taken from Jeanne Benameur's novel *Présent?* which is a thinly disguised fictional account of life in a school in a French ghetto area. The teacher of literature articulates a view that will resonate with many other teachers.

> Yes, he knows the syllabus! He knows also that the only syllabus that matters is the one that gets under their skin, makes their blood beat, makes them feel that the life of a human being is something great and that this greatness is to be found in texts. That's what literature is. (Benameur, 2006, p. 78) (my translation)

Franco-American author, Nancy Huston, reflects with admiration on the work done by teachers of literature in disadvantaged areas in France who, by managing to relate literature to real life, succeed in arousing in young people a passion for reading (see Truong, 2007, p. 73). The following is a telling vignette by Benoît Floc'h (2007) of the kind of work done by committed teachers in this context. Floc'h describes a project with very disadvantaged junior cycle second-level pupils in a French school designed to improve their literacy skills and also to awaken in them a sensitivity *'aux règles et aux plaisirs de la langue de Molière'* ('to the rules and pleasures of the language of Molière') (*ibid.*, p. 64). As part of this project the student are assisted to write personal diaries and among the memoirs they are invited to study are Simone de Beauvoir's *Mémoires d'une Jeune Fille Rangée* and Charles de Gaulle's *Mémoires de Guerre*. The above examples demonstrate that a curriculum based on high culture, in other words, the kind of curriculum advocated by Michael Oakeshott, need not lead to the alienation of young people from their folk and class culture. It certainly informed the life of the taxi driver whom Oakeshott met in Dublin and who quoted a line from Virgil to him.[4]

These examples may seem somewhat aspirational and admittedly there can be no certainty about the effect of this culture on those whom we teach. At the end of his comic novel, *The Lecturer's Tale*, James Hynes's hero, Nelson Humbolt, is facing a class of largely working-class and disadvantaged students, and he wonders if reading *The Great Gatsby* will 'raise

[4]   In letter to me dated 23 June 1983 and now available on the Michael Oakeshott website. library-2.lse.ac.uk/archives/handlists/Oakeshott/m.html. Accessed 11 March 2007.

their pay' (Hynes, 2001, p. 386) or whether familiarity with *Wuthering Heights* will 'lighten the burden of a dead-end job …' (*ibid.*). His answer to himself is worth repeating. 'I'll never know, thought Nelson, and that's the hard truth of teaching. It's also, he reminded himself, the glory of it' (*ibid.*). I never cease to be impressed by how committed teachers can bring this culture to life in the worlds of even the most unpromising of students. In answer to the question posed in the title of this chapter, the content of Oakeshott's curriculum is not based on an elitist culture and it is by no means the exclusive preserve of those who have attended or who aspire to attend traditional universities.

This is an appropriate moment to turn to the character of the curriculum of higher education.

Chapter Five

The Gift of an Interval

This chapter follows the discussion of first and second level education with an analysis of Oakeshott's account of higher education, both in its university and vocational forms. In 1989, when *The Voice of Liberal Learning* (Fuller, 1989) was first published, Timothy Fuller in his fine introductory essay, put great emphasis on Oakeshott's writing on university education and compared this work favourably with the work of Allen Bloom and E.D. Hirsch. Oakeshott's essays achieved nothing like the popular and academic exposure of the work of Bloom and Hirsch at the time but his work on the nature of university education has since attracted increasing interest (see, for example, Crawley, Smeyers, Standish, 2000).

In this chapter I propose therefore to identify the positive features of Oakeshott's idea of a university education and also to draw attention to certain inadequacies in its conceptualisation, as well as to certain dangers in its underlying values. The chapter has two principal sections. The first explores the distinction between university education and vocational education. The rigidity of the distinction that Oakeshott draws between the two, which derives from his epistemological separatism, is shown to be unsustainable in the extreme form in which he represents it. The second section addresses his account of university education in some detail. Some of the general features of the university as an institution are considered and the design and structure of the university curriculum are then elaborated. Special attention is paid to its two principal aims, that of coming to appreciate the contribution of the different disciplines or modes of thought to human knowledge and that of learning to master one of these disciplines for oneself. The chapter concludes by raising two questions that will be explored in more detail later in this volume. The first question concerns Oakeshott's attitude to the role of disagreement and critique as a feature of a university education. The second question addresses his attitude to access to university education and considers whether this form of education is the preserve of a social and academic elite.

University Education and Vocational Education Distinguished

Before expanding and applying this distinction, already outlined in Chapter 2, it will help to rehearse it briefly. According to Oakeshott it is the aim, point or rationale of applied, as opposed to non-applied, studies that marks the distinction between vocational and university education. In vocational education the aim is to use our learning in a transaction within the world of practical experience; in that what is learned must be useable we can speak of it as instrumental learning. On the other hand, the learning involved in university education has no extrinsic purpose; what is learned is learned for the sake of the interest which it offers on its own account, with no purpose other than that of contributing to further learning.

> Doctrines, ideas, facts and theories which are invested elsewhere to yield practical profits ... in a university are recognized as temporary achievements, valued solely for their explanatory value, in an enterprise of understanding which is, in principle, both endless and autonomous. (Oakeshott, 1967, p. 137)

The importance of these achievements lies in what is called their 'reinvestment value' (Oakeshott, 1981, p. 311) in the pursuit of further learning. By contrast, vocational education is concerned with a specific and 'strictly circumscribed body of knowledge that does not significantly look outside itself' and is thereby incapable of earning for us an 'unconsumed interest' (*ibid.*, p. 308). And, although there is probably 'a component of learning' in every 'notable' exercise of a vocational skill, the major task of learning is over once we can in fact practise the skill (Fuller, 1989, p. 43). In elaborating his account of the respective nature of vocational and university education, Oakeshott makes use of his well-known distinction between the 'language' and the 'literature' or 'text' of a mode of thought (see Oakeshott, 1981, pp. 308/9). This distinction, which was examined in the preceding chapter, must therefore be revisited in order to develop it in this context. By language he means the 'manner of thinking' appropriate to a particular discipline or mode of understanding, and a literature or text refers to 'what has been said from time to time in a "language"'(*ibid.*, p. 308). The literature consists of facts, information, conclusions, discoveries or disclosures provided by the appropriate discipline or explanatory language. A geology text book, for example, contains some part of the current state of geological knowledge, but this compilation need make no reference to the way in which geologists came to establish this knowledge. The text-book represents the literature or text of geological knowledge, while the investigatory procedures whereby geologists have established this knowledge represent the language of the discipline. In vocational education, as Oakeshott represents it, students learn only to read the literature, most usually of science, whereas in university education they learn to think scientifically (see *ibid.* p. 309/9). Unfortunately Oakeshott fails to expand on this distinction, but the following elaboration is probably true to his intention. In designing a bridge, engineers use the findings about the tensile strength of different materials that scientists have established, but they need not know how these conclusions were arrived at, nor need they know why it is that the materials have these particular qualities. Developing this metaphor, we could say that engineers learn only to read the language as represented in particular texts, but they do not learn how to write or speak the language concerned.

As used to discriminate between vocational and university education, the language/literature distinction has certain inadequacies. In the first place, not all the literature used in vocational education consists in findings, conclusions, or results derived from enquiries within the disciplines. In the respect of most vocational skills, as indeed Oakeshott himself points out, there normally exist what he calls 'technical literatures' (*ibid.*, p 319) by which he means texts containing practical theories or guidance for aspiring practitioners. Such technical literatures consist in inductive generalisations derived from successful practice within the activities concerned. Texts of technical literatures might have such titles as 'The Art of Teaching', 'The Art of Nursing', 'The Practice of Accountancy', or 'Engineering Skills'. Whereas the aim of theorising within the terms of the explanatory languages is to establish true propositions, the aim of the theories to be found

in these technical literatures is to help the individual to practise the relevant skill.

Here it is perhaps worth pointing out that, in some occupations, the relationship between vocational technical literatures
and explanatory languages is much clearer than in others. The
technical literature used by the engineer, for example, draws
quite directly from the explanatory language of science, particularly from that of physics. The technical literature available to the teacher or student teacher, on the other hand, is
more indirectly related to the languages of psychology, sociology, and history. Oakeshott's account of the relationship
between technical literatures, explanatory languages and
skills requires more nuance than he seems to appreciate.

In the later article, 'The Definition of a University',
Oakeshott would appear to qualify somewhat the exclusive-
ness of the language/literature distinction. In this essay he
acknowledges that students learning a vocational skill may
recognise that the literature which they are using is the 'product of enterprises designed to enlarge our understanding of
ourselves and the world' (Oakeshott, 1967, p. 136). But this is
still an unsatisfactory account of the relationship between literature and language in vocational education. The learning
involved in vocational preparation for certain occupations
requires much more than a mere recognition of the depend-
ence of the conclusions in the literature on achievement within
the explanatory languages. Even to read and understand the
literature of a subject assumes a significant mastery of its disciplinary language. The information in much vocational literature would just be unintelligible to someone who did not have
a grasp of the language from which it is derived. Without a
thorough knowledge of the language of physics, for example,
a person would be unable to make sense of a textbook on engineering. Moreover, it is hard to imagine that someone could be
a good engineer without being able to manage the explanatory
language of physics. Indeed an individual engineer may well
demonstrate a greater mastery of the language of physics than
a graduate with a degree in the subject.

There is also more to vocational learning than mere mastery
of a literature and even of its particular language. As Paul
Standish quite rightly argues, vocational education 'inevitably
involves theory, practice, pleasure and function' (Standish,
2005, p. 67). In designing a bridge or a road, much complex

knowledge is required that goes beyond the physics of bridge design. This knowledge involves consideration of the effects of the bridge on community life and as well as aesthetic elements (*ibid.*). Nor is intellectual excitement the preserve of the students who work on purely theoretical problems. The 'peculiar turbulence' that is excited by an intellectual problem, followed by the 'intense absorption' as we endeavour to pursue it, is as likely to be promoted by research in engineering or medicine as by research in pure science (Standish, 2005, p. 65). George Steiner also questions the erection of too rigid a distinction between pure and applied knowledge. For example, the 'borderline' between 'the geometries required by the surveyor or hydraulic engineer and the addictions of the number theorist' is 'always contingent and open to revision' (2003, p. 15).

I have worked with student teachers and also with students who are studying humanities without any prior vocational purpose and it has always seemed to me that Oakeshott's distinction between vocational and academic learning is too rigid. To demonstrate that there is no necessary conflict between learning pursued in different contexts, the example of the fictional experience of Ursula Brangwen in *The Rainbow* as a student at a College of Education is again revealing. Unprepossessing as was the building that housed her college, with little of the beauty of a college in Oxford or Cambridge, for her it was a 'remote' and 'magic land' (Lawrence, 1977, p. 430). In it was to be found a 'reminiscence of the wondrous, cloistral origin of education' (*ibid.*). The everyday world, which Oakeshott calls the world of work as opposed to play, was 'remote, remote', while the 'whispering' walls of the institution 'whispered all the while with reminiscence of all the centuries' (*ibid.*, p. 431). Here 'time faded away, and the echo of knowledge filled the timeless silence' (*ibid.*). She listened with 'joy, almost with ecstasy' to the 'black-gowned priests of knowledge, serving for ever in a remote, hushed temple' holding 'the beginning and the end of the mystery' of learning 'in their keeping' (*ibid.*).

She delighted in her studies, even in the study of education. 'Curious joy she had of the lectures. It was a joy to hear the theory of education, there was such freedom and pleasure in ranging over the very stuff of knowledge, and seeing how it moved and lived and has it being' (*ibid.*). Her engagement in the study of French and botany is associated with happiness, joy, love and even thrill. 'How happy Racine made her! She did not know why. But as the big lines of the drama unfolded themselves, so steady, so measured, she felt a thrill as of being in the realm of the reality' (*ibid.*). When it came to the study of botany, writes Lawrence, 'How she loved to sit on her high stool before the bench, … carefully mounting her slides, carefully bringing her microscope into focus, then turning with joy to record her observation, drawing joyfully in her book … (*ibid.*, p. 432). As noted in Chapter 4, Ursula was to become greatly disillusioned by her studies, following her perception of the salience of the credential effect of examination results and their connection to the 'single motive of material gain' rather than to 'the religious virtue of knowledge' (*ibid.*, p. 435). Despite this, botany remained:

> the one study that lived for her. She had entered into the lives of the plants. She was fascinated by the strange laws of the vegetable world. She had here a glimpse of something working entirely apart from the purpose of the human world. (*ibid.*, p. 436)

As Lawrence illustrates imaginatively, the presence of a vocational aim need not detract from the quality of the educational experience enjoyed by students. This raises again the previously mentioned criticism of Oakeshott's educational thought, namely, a tendency to work with a conceptual repertoire that is too rigid and restricted. In this case, I hope to have shown that the distinction between vocational and academic education is not at all as clear-cut as he characterises it and that the relationship is susceptible of being expressed with far greater nuance.

With these reservations registered, it is then appropriate to turn now to a closer consideration of Oakeshott's idea of a university education.

The University as an Institution

Distinguished by the notion of learning pursued for the sake of the interest that it offers on its own account, university education is the kind of education for which the Oakeshottian school curriculum has been a direct and an appropriate preparation. Like the school, the university for Oakeshott is a 'place apart' from the concerns of the world of practical experience. Consequently the claim according to which the historical function of the universities was to provide professional training for clergy or for a ruling class is firmly rejected. So too is the claim that the contemporary university serves to provide training in advanced or particularly complex skills (Fuller, 1989, pp. 92/3). As with education at primary and secondary levels, university education has no function in the sense of having a purpose extrinsic to the initiation of students into the educational conversation (Fuller, 1989, pp. 96, 103). Oakeshott argues that the manner of learning represented in a university was not designed to accord with some preconceived plan or premeditated purpose. As a particular institutional expression for the activities of teaching and learning, the university emerged over time and developed traditions which came to be valued and maintained for the manner in which they sustained and contributed to the pursuit of learning (*ibid.*, pp. 127–8).

Accordingly it is Oakeshott's view that the future occupational role of its students is of no concern to the university. Although it is possible to determine the number of practitioners of a particular vocational skill which society might require, it is, he argues, inappropriate to ask how many people should enjoy university (or school) education. On account of the profound and intimate relationship between becoming educated and becoming personally enriched, it is misguided to ask how many people should be educated. It makes as little sense for society to prescribe the numbers of educated persons as to prescribe the numbers who should be personally enriched

The University as a Community

Oakeshott does not consider that a university is the only arrangement which can provide education. A person would derive educational benefit from study under a private tutor, from a cultural tour under the direction of an informed and learned guide, or from the judicious use of a good library (Oakeshott, 1981, pp. 311–2). Nor is it through study alone that a person becomes educated. A university offers a full educational experience, not only through its curriculum of studies and programme of extracurricular activities, but also through its *genius loci* and through the opportunity it offers to be part of a human community.[1] For this reason Oakeshott stresses the

---

[1] As noted in Chapter 1, Oakeshott's argument here reflects that of Newman (Newman, 1901, pp. 145–8).

institutional nature of the university as a specific, localised community. Learning to become part of a university is like learning to participate in any traditional institution, such as the House of Commons or even a family business (Fuller, 1989, p. 99).

In a university we find three groups of people, students, scholars, and scholars-*cum*- teachers, corporately engaged in teaching and learning. Here, through conversation in this literal sense, all contribute their own voices to the metaphorical conversation of mankind, that is, the special conversation that is composed of the different aspects of human culture (see Fuller, 1989, pp. 38–9, 101, 126, 133–4, and Oakeshott, 1981, pp. 311–3). Each group is engaged in learning, scholars and scholar/teachers just as much as students. Some scholars devote all their time to learning and to the pursuit of knowledge, because they lack the sympathy required to be teachers. They provide the results and insights of their learning to their colleagues through their conversations and to the outside world through their publications (Fuller, 1989, p. 97). A distinction emerges here which will prove important when Oakeshott considers the content of the university curriculum. Teachers at a university are themselves exploring some aspect of their discipline, but they do not use what they are themselves exploring as the subject-matter of their teaching. There is a distinction between the role of scholars as explorers on the frontiers of knowledge and their activity as teachers. As scholars they are engaged in the pursuit of knowledge, but their primary concern as teachers is not to train potential successors to themselves in the world of scholarship. Rather it is to provide 'familiarity' (Oakeshott, 1967, p. 138) with the manner of thinking characteristic of their particular discipline or mode of thought (see also Oakeshott, 1981, pp. 312–13). As will be shown in more detail in Chapter 8, university teachers have a strangely passive role in respect of their students whom Oakeshott describes as 'spectators at performances' (Oakeshott, 1967, p. 139).

Consequently, Oakeshott's university student is not an apprentice scholar as most will not end up as historians, philosophers, scientists or literary scholars. Nevertheless, the education of the future diplomat, civil servant, trade union official, or school teacher is the same as that of the future scholar. What the undergraduate is offered above all is 'the gift of an interval' (Fuller, 1989, pp. 101, 127), an opportunity for 'the enjoyment of *schole* — leisure' (Fuller, 1989, p. 102; see also *ibid.*, p. 128 and Oakeshott, 1981, p. 315) before embarking on the business of earning a living. To enjoy leisure means to be 'freed for a moment from the curse of Adam, the burdensome distinction between work and play' in order to join in the educational conversation (Fuller, 1989, pp. 102, 128). While at university, students enjoy an opportunity to detach themselves from the everyday world of practical experience to suspend judgment on the world around them through the exercise of what Keats called '"negative capability"' (*ibid.*, p. 127).

This state of suspended judgment may sound implausible but it is one shared by David Denby in his wonderful account of the space that university studies allow students to personalise knowledge. Denby refers to the study of great writers as a process of 'role-playing and the trying on of selves' (Denby, 1997, p. 279).

> You read a persuasive argument and it filled your mind; you became an adherent of that text, swelling with it, enlarged by that implacably correct way of looking at world — for a week. You were a rationalist, an empiricist and skeptic, a Hegelian, a Marxist. Taking on one identity after another, you were, for a while, blissfully irresponsible. No one would burn you at the stake for the wrong opinion or for false enthusiasms. One advantage of living in an era that doesn't make ideas a life-and-death matter is that you can entertain many different ideas, retaining some, discarding others, mixing together what remained. Out of this early promiscuity, if you were smart and disciplined, would come something like intellectual experience and readiness for more. At the end of the year, you unconsciously retained that version of yourself that fit most tightly around your psyche. (*ibid.*)

In this way the learner is enabled in Oakeshott's terms 'to recognize himself in the mirror of the human achievements which compose his inheritance' (Fuller, *ibid.*, p. 48).

It is time next to consider in more detail the courses of studies offered by the university.

The University Curriculum

Firstly, as has already been pointed out, what is learned in a university is learned for the sake of the interest that it offers on its own account, rather than for the sake of the use to which it may be put. Even theology, law and medicine, studies that are directly related to professions, are included only because they represent branches of scholarship. Moreover, as apprentice-ship elsewhere has to be added to studies in these areas, what occurs in university is therefore a 'preludial' (Fuller, 1989, p. 125) form of education. Secondly, university education is an education in the great explanatory languages of human understanding, and not merely in the literature generated by these languages. The university student learns to manage these languages in order to gain an appreciation and an under-standing of what it is like to think within the terms appropriate to them (Oakeshott, 1981, pp. 313–4). University students do not simply learn to read the literature of knowledge but rather to manage the explanatory languages in which knowledge is pursued and to think in the terms appropriate to these lan-guages. The texts which they study are not repositories of use-ful information or advice. Hence, texts with negligible useable prescriptions have a place on Oakeshott's university curricu-lum. For this reason the student will study texts by such writ-ers as Aristotle, Descartes, or Adam Smith, not for the often long-superseded information that they contain, but rather to understand how philosophers, scientists, and economists thought in the past. Thus, by being taught to understand its characteristic explanatory manner of thinking, students learn to use, to manage, or to speak the language of their chosen dis-cipline. To acquire a facility in using such language involves the study of appropriate literature or text. A text is not treated as an organisation of information as it is in vocational educa-tion, but rather as the paradigm of a language. In university education the text is considered an expression of how a partic-ular explanatory language functions and this is something that cannot be taught on its own as an abstraction from sub-stantive texts.

In the determination of which disciplinary paradigms to include for undergraduate study, Oakeshott rejects the use of the current academic or research concerns of the teaching staff as these are not usually in an 'appropriate condition' (*ibid.*, p. 314) for study at this level. Instead the student is offered texts that represent clearer, less tentative paradigms of the manner of thinking in question. This is why the syllabus for Oakeshott's undergraduates will require them to study, for example, the English civil war, Aristotle, or mechanics, rather than the invasion of Iraq, the works of Michel Foucault or the latest theories in cosmic physics. In the determination of what should be taught this notion of the paradigm serves, therefore, as a purely pedagogic criterion, unconcerned with considerations of superficial contemporary relevance. Whatever texts are chosen have one property in common and that is their freedom from considerations of usefulness in the satisfaction of the wants of practical life.

Oakeshott suggests that there are two ways or organising this kind of study in a university (see *ibid.*, p. 314). The first offers a range of modes of thinking expressed in the various literary, historical, philosophical, and legal texts produced in Greek and Roman times. The second involves the study of a particular disciplinary language such as that of history, science, mathematics, literary criticism, or philosophy through whatever texts are available and suitable for study at undergraduate level. The human sciences of sociology and anthropology are admitted as somewhat attenuated branches of historical study. Psychology, on the other hand, in as far as it is concerned with quantifiable processes, is a natural, not a human science. But whatever a person is studying, the central aims of Oakeshott's curriculum are the same.

The first aim of Oakeshott's university curriculum is to teach the student to recognise and to distinguish between the different explanatory languages and to become 'familiar with the conditions each imposes upon utterance' (Fuller, 1989, p. 38). The second aim of this curriculum is to enable students to speak one of these languages, that is, to express themselves in terms of its characteristic manner of thinking in a manner which displays 'genuine understanding of the language spoken' (*ibid.*). Something more needs to be said about each of these aims.

(a) Understanding Different Voices

Regarding the first aim, it is necessary to ask how it is possible that students, who normally enjoy specialised initiation into a single language, can come to understand how their discipline fits into the map of knowledge and to appreciate how the other disciplines contribute to this map. This constitutes a particular version of a general problem in Oakeshott's epistemology that has been posed both by Bhikhu Parekh and Tariq Modood. Parekh wonders how Oakeshott can speak of conversation between voices where each uses a distinct, autonomous and self-contained language that shares nothing in common with the others (Parekh, 1979, p. 488, footnote 8). In the terms of Oakeshott's discursive universe therefore, as Modood argues, there would appear to be 'no point of contact for conversing' (Modood, 1980, p. 316).

In considering how such a point of contact might be promoted, Oakeshott scornfully dismisses the project of widening curricula to include a course or courses of 'integrating' (Fuller, 1989, p. 123) lectures. To be accessible to non-specialists, such course would be superficial and trivial. No 'sticky mess called "culture"' (*ibid.*, p. 98) can impose integration on the world of knowledge that he conceives as radically differentiated. Culture, I suggest, is best conceived as more like the very air that we breathe rather than an oxygen mask to be applied to make up a deficiency. Moreover, a culture is composed not of a 'set of abstract aptitudes' but rather of a conjunction of 'substantive expressions of thought' (*ibid.*, p. 32). And, just as it is impossible to speak without using a particular language, it is impossible to think outside the terms of the individual language of a specific universe of discourse. There exists, writes Oakeshott, no 'ideal non-idiomatic manner of speaking' (Oakeshott, 1981, p. 206). This means that people cannot join in the educational conversation between the languages of mankind unless they speak one such language for themselves. According to Oakeshott, therefore, integrated courses or general courses in culture are misconceived attempts to teach the 'art of conversation ... to those who ... (have) nothing to say' (Fuller, 1989, pp. 133–4).

Interestingly, and also somewhat ironically, Classics would be said to represent a model of integrated studies where a student may reasonably be expected to acquire familiarity with the different modes of thought—although readers would be very mistaken in assuming that Oakeshott recommends models of pedagogic integration for the disciplinary languages. He would have little patience with or sympathy for such interdisciplinary subject areas as Women's Studies, Black Studies, Equality Studies, Queer Studies, Critical Theory or Peace Studies. It certainly seems inconsistent on Oakeshott's part to reject such models of scholastic integration and, at the same time, find Classics an acceptable form of interdisciplinary inquiry. One major difference is between these forms of integrated studies is that Classics has been sanctioned by precedent. In fairness, perhaps, a further distinction between

Classics and contemporary interdisciplinary studies should be noted. In the study of Classics there exists a distinctive scholarly spirit that does not (at least yet) inform the study of issues of gender, race and human conflict. Oakeshott would probably want to argue that the presence of this spirit in the study of the Classics can become something like that which informs the study of a single discipline or explanatory language. Nevertheless, in so far as both the more contemporary and the classical areas of study represent forms of interdisciplinary enquiry, their epistemological status is quite similar, if not identical. Moreover, interdisciplinary courses do not have to be as ideologically driven as Gender Studies and Equality Studies. Stephen Prickett gives a persuasive account of the educational benefits of some of the interdisciplinary courses with which he was involved in his career. These included courses such as 'The English Romantics and their Society', 'Romanticism and Philosophy' and 'Landscape and Literature, 1650–1850' and the courses proved also as satisfying for the teachers as for the students (Prickett, 2002a, pp. 100–1). Ironically one of Oakeshott's contributions to curriculum design at university level has been his account of how the study of politics combines the study of history and philosophy (Oakeshott, 1981, pp. 301–33). Unfortunately his account of the university curriculum neglects this.

How then does he envisage that a student will come to understand and to appreciate the contribution of other voices to the educational conversation through the specialist study of one particular language or mode of thought? What Oakeshott believes is that the study in depth of one particular discipline will offer some perspective on other disciplines by virtue of the fact that each discipline when studied in this manner will necessarily reveal something of its 'limits' and its 'presuppositions' (Fuller, 1989, p. 134). Though here again he fails to provide more precise content to his argument, it seems reasonable to presume that Oakeshott means that any inquiry, pursued in depth, must demarcate subject-matter, elaborate method and establish criteria of relevance, truth and validity. Such a procedure will inevitably require some familiarity with the different contexts in which knowledge is pursued and, as a result, students will acquire an understanding of the place of their discipline on the map of knowledge and of how it can be seen as a 'reflection' of the 'whole' of human knowledge (*ibid.*, p. 132).

Mary Midgley makes a similar point when she argues that a thorough understanding of the presuppositions of any discipline will enable the student to 'relate' these presuppositions to 'those needed for other inquiries' (Midgley, 1980, p. 23). It is for this reason Oakeshott believes that each discipline, branch of scholarship or language of human understanding 'has within itself – when we drink deeply of it – a power to educate' (Fuller, 1989, pp. 100–1). Thus it is that 'no true and profoundly studied *techne* raises the distinction between acquiring a knowledge of some branch of learning and pursuing the general objects of education' (*ibid.*, p. 133).

The same point can be applied to vocational education, thereby undermining further the rigidity of Oakeshott distinction between it and academic education. The education of what Ido Weijers calls the 'responsible expert', requires that the person who learns a vocational skill acquires with it with a deep and extensive sense of its epistemological, social and ethical context (see Weijers, 2000, especially, pp. 130–3). This does not mean that incorporation of some version of 'general studies' into specialist education. What it does entail is rather 'a deepening and broadening of specialised education itself' enabling the students to 'articulate the principles embedded' within the practice and to 'subsume experience within a growing and more inclusive theoretical framework' (*ibid.*, p. 131). Weijers proposes what I have always felt was appropriate in education/*Bildung* of a vocational character, namely, making the studies more searching, more philosophically grounded and ensuring that they are informed by a rich sense of their historical and geographical context.

But, it may be argued, knowledge of the presuppositions and context of her or his own discipline or area of expertise does not, *ipso facto*, enable an individual to understand other disciplines. Assuming that a university does provide an opportunity for informal contact between students and teachers of different disciplines, how can they understand each other without a common language? Oakeshott does not address this issue directly and indeed he may consider that the problem of creating points of contact between the languages arises only if, like Parekh and Modood, we take an extreme and exaggerated view of the level of expertise required to converse in the metaphorical languages of mankind. The ability to use these languages is not restricted to university dons and their students but is to be found in embryonic, relatively undifferentiated form in the ordinary, everyday discourse of pre-school children. In this unschooled discourse lies the genesis of the sophisticated languages of science, religion, aesthetics, history, philosophy and of the moral life. Moreover, before engaging on a particular course of study, students will already, from their school education, have learned something of a more formal nature not only about their chosen disciplines, but also about other branches of scholarship (see Fuller, 1989, pp. 102, 127).

l also suggest that we should understand each of Oakeshott's languages as having a pedagogic as well as a discursive idiom. The discursive idiom is that used in the pursuit of knowledge, while the pedagogic is the idiom appropriate to teaching the discipline. In order to elucidate and to make accessible the character of their subjects, specialists will address their audience in the idiom of the teacher. In conversing with others from outside their discipline, those who wish to be understood will speak in this pedagogic idiom. And it is by means of such conversations in the literal sense that those disposed to do so may join in the metaphorical conversations between the great languages of mankind.

(b) Speaking for Oneself

What does Oakeshott have to say about the second aim of a university curriculum, that is, teaching students to make, in the appropriate language, statements of their own which display 'genuine understanding of the language spoken' (*ibid.*, p. 38)? Unfortunately on this matter there is a lack of definition and precision about what Oakeshott actually means. What he does, however, make clear is that facility in managing one of the languages of human understanding does not necessitate being able to make an original contribution to the world of knowledge. This, he writes, 'can only be a rare achievement' (*ibid.*). Precise clarification of what counts as genuine understanding might shed light on the following matters. For example, it might explain whether there is a difference in the kind of understanding of physics which can be expected from a graduate in the subject and that of a graduate in engineering. Provision of such clarification might also tell us something about how Oakeshott conceives the distinction between the level of understanding to be expected in history, for example, from an able student in the final year of secondary school and that to be expected from a university student of history. Perhaps, too, this clarification might explain in what sense a student of Classics, who has to deal with several universes of discourse, literary, philosophical and historical, can acquire a fluency in a particular language equivalent to that of the student of a single discipline. Doubtless, it would be unrealistic to expect of Oakeshott a graded taxonomy of levels of achievement in respect of all the languages of human understanding.

An attempt at such elucidation would, however, reveal ambiguities in Oakeshott's language/literature distinction. If what has been argued in this chapter with regard to this distinction is correct, achievement in reading and making use of the literature usually involves 'genuine understanding' of the language from which it is derived. Accordingly I suggest that Oakeshott's language/ literature distinction is useful to a degree but that in curriculum design, both at second and third levels, it will not carry the decisive weight that Oakeshott attributes to it.

In conclusion I wish to raise two aspects of Oakeshott's idea of a university education that are considered in more detail later in this volume.

Two Concluding Questions

The first question is closely related to the theme of finding one's own voice or speaking for oneself. This is the issue of the relationship, within his thought, between acquiring a cultural inheritance and developing a critical awareness of this inheritance. Oakeshott argues most emphatically that initiation into any of the languages of mankind must not be understood as initiation into static received doctrines. His conception of education as initiation into a cultural inheritance cannot therefore, in fairness, be described, as Fred Inglis implies, as a 'process of socialization into a given intellectual identity' (Inglis, 1975a, p. 41 and p. 47, note 15). A culture, writes Oakeshott, is 'not a doctrine or set of consistent teachings or conclusions about a human life' (Fuller, 1989, p. 28). Rather it is a 'conversational encounter' composed of 'feelings, perceptions, ideas, engagements, attitudes and so forth, pulling in different directions, often critical of one another' (*ibid.*) but not at same time, causing us 'to be dismayed by the inconclusiveness of it all' (*ibid.*,

p. 39). Ours is a culture which, he observes, accommodates 'not only the majestic metropolis of Augustinian theology but also the "greenwood" of Franciscan Christianity' (*ibid.*, p. 29). Oakeshott then conceives of our culture not as univocal but rather as plurivocal or, as Stephen Prickett put it, as a 'polyphony' (Prickett, 2002a, p. 85).

His conception of a cultural inheritance does, however, seem somewhat narrow. After all, our cultural inheritance accommodates more divergent and conflicting ideas, beliefs, and sensibilities than those of the Augustinian and Franciscan versions of Christianity. Even leaving aside the achievements of other cultures, western civilisation contains the ideas of Marx and Mill, the sensibilities of Jane Austen and D.H. Lawrence, of Marcel Proust and Jean Genet. It contains the atheism of Sartre and the religious conviction of Mauriac and the huge divergence in the management of church-state relations to be found, for example, in France, Britain, Germany and Ireland. Even within the Roman Catholic tradition it contains the versions of that faith articulated by Teilhard de Chardin, the Roman Curia, the German bishops, *Opus Dei* and the theologians of liberation. Perusing Oakeshott's writings, a reader may well wonder how such critics of civilisation as Marx, Nietzsche, or Freud are to be accommodated within his 'intellectual and moral inheritance of great splendour and worth' (Fuller, 1989, p. 71).

This leads to the question of critical inquiry in university – something that will arise again in the conclusion to Chapter 10. Oakeshott does say that staff and students in a university should be 'critical of one another' (Oakeshott, 1981, p. 310) and is very incisive in his treatment of the intellectual equipment necessary to engage in critique. To be critical 'it is not good enough to have a '"point of view" ... what we need is *thoughts*' (Fuller, 1989, p. 102). Nor is it enough, he argues, for a person to be 'in possession of an armoury of arguments to prove the truth of what he believes'; rather what is required is the intellectual capacities to put her or him 'beyond the reach of the intellectual hooligan' (*ibid.* pp. 102–3). This seems to me to be very acceptable but Oakeshott's metaphor of education as a conversation hardly implies a robust critical enterprise. In a conversation, insistence of the correctness of one's point of view represents 'bad manners' (Oakeshott, 1981, p. 201) and is inimical to the conduct of congenial social intercourse.

Accordingly, it is hard to see how a voice such as that of Paulo Freire, speaking with passion and anger on behalf of the poor and oppressed, would fit into Oakeshott's conversation. Oakeshott acknowledges that the educational conversation may have 'passages of argument' (*ibid.*, p. 198), but this conversation would not appear capable of accommodating systematic disagreement on moral, political, and religious matters. As Arcilla delicately notes, Oakeshott seems keener that students listen to, rather than join in, the educational conversation (Arcilla, 1995, p. 3). And my reservation here is that students who accept the invitation to be critical in order to challenge conventional moral and political values might find that criticism of certain values is in reality less than welcome within the academy. I am well aware that the 'discussion of ideologies' (Fuller, 1989, p. 122) can indeed be tiresome but the presentation of challenging argument does not have to be the preserve of self-serving ideologues of left and right. This leads to a final question concerning access to university.

Oakeshott stresses that the opportunity to develop a participant's fluency in one of the universes of discourse offered by the traditional university was not something which only one social class could appreciate, or something suitable only to a '"leisured class"' (Fuller, p. 128). The university student did not then, and does not now, belong to a 'leisured class' and access to university education does not depend now, nor did it depend in the past, 'on any definable pre-existing privilege or upon the absence of earning one's living in the end' (*ibid.*). In 'The Definition of a University' he eloquently expresses his conviction regarding the value of university education for anyone with the ability and the willingness to undertake it in the right spirit. '(W)*hen* I recall it, it seems to me so valuable an experience that I would not know how to deny it to anybody' (Oakeshott, 1967, p. 141). This comment goes some way towards modifying the following sweeping and unsubstantiated claim in the earlier article 'The Universities'.

> Anyone who has worked in a contemporary overcrowded university knows it to be an illusion that there was any large untapped reserve of men and women who could make use of this kind of university but who never had the opportunity of doing so. (Fuller, 1989, p. 129)

In 'The Definition of a University' Oakeshott would appear to have modified somewhat this view, writing that it does not fall to 'the lot of everyone' to be a student and that many who 'can recognize ... and even be excited by' the pursuit of knowledge 'do not and cannot actually participate' in this pursuit on a full time basis (Oakeshott, 1967, pp. 138–9). He would very much wish to admit to university such a person as the eponymous hero of Hardy's novel *Jude the Obscure* who is excluded on account of his class background. Nevertheless, as even such a sympathetic critic as R.S. Peters points out, Oakeshott remains remarkably unaware of the extent to which opportunity to avail of education, particularly at senior cycle in second level and at third level, is related to socio-economic background (Peters, 1974, p. 436; see also Falk, 1963, p. 69 and Kneller, 1984, pp. 225, 250; Moberley, 1950, pp. 207–8). Recent years have seen a huge expansion in the number of universities as well as in the number of students (see Wolf, 2002, pp. 168–199). Some 50% of the cohort of school leavers now attends university and what Oakeshott's response to this would be is uncertain but I doubt that he would be sympathetic to the view that I propose. I see no reason in principle why many, if not most, of these students cannot be 'excited' by the pursuit of understanding. I disagree with such stern critics of the contemporary university as Duke Maskell and Ian Robinson (Maskell and Robinson, 2002) in as far as they think that many of these young people have no place in a university because of their mediocre scholarly ability. I share their concern that the pressure to award degrees of a high classification is reprehensible but students whose intellectual ability is limited can derive profit and enrichment from university-level studies. These are the kind of students who feature in *The Lecturer's Tale*, Hynes (2001) mentioned at the end of the last chapter. At least in the Humanities, we should encourage such students, though their academic qualifications may be unimpressive, to become part of a post-school community and thereby to participate in the exploration of the great works of literature and in the study of history and philosophy. I concede that many will never make scholars but they have their lives and analytic abilities enhanced by their studies. To those who will say that this bestows on the university community more of the character of a book club or adult education class, I would reply that these too are versions of education that can offer models for the university. The 'gift' of higher education can take many forms and it is indeed a gift offered to everyone.

I would rather take the risk of being to generous in admitting students to university than to deprive anyone of the opportunity to profit from studying there.

At the heart of Oakeshott's conception of higher education has been shown to lie a distinction between vocational and university education. I have argued against the rigidity of this distinction on the grounds that the epistemological separatism on which it is based is not sustainable. This separatism is related to a more general separatism that is the subject of the two chapters that follow.

Chapter Six

Work and Human Fulfilment

As noted in the previous three chapters, Oakeshott is very hostile to the intrusion of a so-called vocational imperative into education. Vocationally-oriented education was originally designed for the poor and peasant classes in order to provide them with the skills to make them more socially useful as citizens, but with the emergence of industrial society he maintains that this orientation has been gradually extended to include all social classes. Contemporary society, he believes, emphasizes this orientation to such an extent that it has come to dominate thinking about education, particularly as all stages of education have fallen increasingly under state control. The first part of this chapter endorses, on strong practical grounds, Oakeshott's indictment of the attempt to assimilate school and university education to the world of work in order to increase productivity and employment. The 'ethics of productivity' (Oakeshott, 1967, pp. 141–2 and in Fuller, 1989, p. 111) are less 'plausible' (*ibid.*)than have been assumed by their advocates of recent decades and the notion of the school as a 'place apart' from the pursuit of 'barbaric affluence' (Fuller, 1989, p. 90) makes far more sense than its detractors appreciate.[1] In the second part of the chapter, I shall argue that Oakeshott's epistemological separatism leads to a view of work that is detached from experiences of satisfaction, pleasure and fulfilment and the development of autonomy.

---

[1] The expression 'the plausible ethics of productivity' appears in Oakeshott, 1967, pp. 141–2 and in Fuller, 1989, p. 111.

Education, Qualifications and the Economy: Keeping Work in Its Place

But firstly I should comment on what may seem like a very obvious issue. Why should access to education, particularly at university, be so highly prized and sought after? There are several reasons, all of which go to undermine Oakeshott's rather pious regret, mentioned in Chapter 2, that the attitude to the status of university degrees has had the unfortunate consequence of depressing that of other qualifications and of 'prejudicing the appearance of new ways of acquiring esteem' (Oakeshott, 1967, p. 141). The principal reasons have to do with employment possibilities. The proportion of managerial/professional/technical jobs is increasing and the employment opportunities in skilled crafts is declining, while openings in low-skill areas 'still exist in their millions' (Wolf, 2002, p. 48). Secondly, possession of academic qualifications correlates very highly with income, and consequently the more academic education a person enjoys, the more she or he is likely to earn (ibid, pp. 16–17). Analysis by Theodore Lewis (1997) of US Bureau of Labor statistics shows that 'those who are best educated will have the best options in the economy' (1997, p. 480). This analysis also gives support to the notion of education as a positional good, that was raised in the second part of Chapter 2, with the system of organised learning serving as a filter providing access to social advantage. The filering process is reinforced by the emphasis in schooling on determining the *relative* rather than the *actual* achievement of learners, that is, in establishing how successful learners are relative to others rather than focusing on the fine detail of what pupils actually know.

The association between academic achievement and prestige has been a long standing feature of human societies and it remains extraordinarily widespread. *Circa* 2000 BC an Egyptian father gave this advice to his son. 'I have seen how the belaboured man is belaboured – thou shouldst set thy heart in pursuit of writing ... behold, there is nothing which surpasses writing ...' (quoted in Donaldson, 1987, p. 84). The same refrain comes from modern China where the mother of young school girl, Ma Yan, has instilled in her daughter the 'desire to learn' (Haski, 2004, p. 54). Firstly, this is for reasons of very survival because, in 'the big cities, even going to the toilet requires being able to read' (*ibid.*, p. 45). Secondly, as the mother observes, it is because if Ma Yan does not study 'her future will be bleak. If she studies, she'll get a good job. People will look up to her, rather than looking down' (*ibid.*, p. 54).

Having said this, the exchange value of education can be exaggerated. A distinction must be made between being over-qualified and over-educated. People can never be over-educated in the sense that education normally enhances students' intellectual capacities and normally contributes to their overall self-confidence. Yet individuals can be described as over-qualified if they have a level of formal education or certification more than is necessary to perform a job. Experience internationally shows that where students have the impression that formal education guarantees particular jobs, failure to secure these jobs leads to frustration on their part or to the creation of huge numbers of underemployed. French sociologist, Marie Duru-Bellat, has incurred the wrath of the French establishment for her work on credential inflation and the frustrated expectations of students (Duru-Bellat, 2006; Perucca, 2006). According to her, exaggerated expectations of the exchange value of qualifications have led to corrosive credentialism in the minds of some students whereby the securing of a degree has become '*le moteur unique de la motivation*' (the sole engine of motivation) (Perucca, 2006, p. 23).

The consequences of providing education without exchange value for a large population in Mali are analysed by Peter Biddlecombe (1994, pp. 239/240). The local school-teacher remarks: 'I feel sorry for our students because we are educating them for nothing. No way will they ever get a job in Mali' (p. 239). Biddlecombe argues that increased provision of formal education has created dissatisfaction. 'Instead of creating an enlightened and civilised society they found it created nothing but problems' (*ibid.*). Though graduates felt that they deserved important jobs, their expectations could not be met because there were so few jobs to go around. The government was forced to increase recruitment to the public service with the result that most of its employees had no real work to do. As there was a great shortage of money to pay these graduates, the budget for salary was divided among an increasing number of workers 'until the over-educated employees were getting practically nothing to live on' (*ibid.*). '(I)n a country of philosophers' observes Biddlecombe, the government found that 'there were no plumbers' (*ibid.*) because those who received an education were unwilling to do manual work. Throughout West Africa, the author found many people with impressive university qualifications who were unable to find the kind of occupational outlets to which they felt these qualifications entitled them. There was a similar outcome in Egypt as a result of giving 'graduates first call on jobs in the public sector' which led, as Alison Wolf explains, to the creation of a 'vast and underemployed army of civil servants' (Wolf, 2002, pp. 39–40). This is consistent with the comments of Theodore Lewis that the Third World is 'filled with scholars' who disdain technical/practical education and who 'have abandoned rural agriculture, general education diploma in hand, only to become unemployment statistics in the cities' (Lewis, 1991, p. 104). The relationship between education and the economy needs further scrutiny.

Education and Employment

As Alison Wolf (Wolf, 2002) has demonstrated so persuasively, there is no compelling argument that a vibrant productive economy requires a *direct* relationship between the school curriculum and the world of work. The attempt to promote economic productivity directly through the curriculum is misguided because employment opportunities are related to the state of the economy rather than to the character of the educational system. Where there are jobs, the employment market adapts to the educated talent that is available in any society. The stories of Italy and Japan, both of which have enjoyed great economic success since the Second World War, illustrate this point very well. In a seminal essay in 1979, John Vaizey pointed out that the systems of education in both countries were 'vestigial in terms of providing people with skills, and ... the relationship between the employment system and the education system was singularly unarticulated' (Vaizey, 1979, p. 212). The experience of Italy and Japan demonstrates the fallacy of the view that vocationalising the school curriculum is necessary to economic development. In any case, if possession of skills of putative vocational utility became more widespread, this would simply intensify competition for a relatively fixed number of jobs. One particular danger of attributing unemployment to lack of educational qualifications is that unemployment comes to be attributed to lack of qualifications on the part of individuals rather than to structural inequalities in society. As research has long indicated (see, for example, Dale and Pires, 1984), employment opportunities may be more related to socio-political considerations rather than to technical qualifications. In other words, influence within the socio-economic hierarchy commonly plays a more decisive role in securing employment than qualifications.

Interestingly in the early 1990s, before the advent of the Celtic Tiger, concern to link education to the economy and employment was high on the socio-political agenda in Ireland. In a fairly extensive piece of research on the subject, the employers' organisation found that members simply did not put a high value on vocationally 'relevant' skills in the recruitment of school leavers and even of graduates. For example, in a survey of some 150 companies (Confederation of Irish Industry, 1990), only 18% and 15% of respondents respectively rated familiarity with computer systems and keyboard skills as very important. By contrast, oral communications were rated very important by 70% of the respondents, written communications by 58%, numeracy by 48%, enterprise/initiative by 46%, problem solving by 39%, foreign language skills by 26% and creativity by 22%. This research, which was borne out by other research studies shortly afterwards (see Lynch, 1992), confirmed the low value placed by employers on subjects of direct vocational relevance.

With regard to the relation between university education, the economy and employment, Desmond Ryan (Ryan, 2002) has perceptively analysed one of the melancholy ironies of government education policy towards universities in the UK from the 1980s. Those responsible for these policies, with their apparatus of control and monitoring, chose to ignore what manufacturing industry actually wanted from universities. What industry required of universities was, firstly, to educate their students and to allow industry itself provide appropriate training for graduates. This requirement tends to bear out the admittedly anecdotal evidence that even for those wishing to work in the information and communication technology industry, the study of philosophy may often provide more appropriate preparation than specialist studies in ICT or in computer science itself. Secondly, industrialists wished universities to engage in fundamental or pure research and allow industry use this research for its own purposes (*ibid.,* pp. 124–34). This wish reflects Mary Midgely's salutary reminder that the great discoveries 'that have made possible the astonishing technical advances of the last two centuries, such as those of Faraday and Clark Maxwell about electricity, have nearly all been made by people who were not actually directing their thoughts to practical applications' (Midgley, 1990, p. 291). All of this goes to show that the conception of the university as the engine that supplies 'human capital for use in the production sector'[2] is as misguided and as it is impoverished. The insight and intuition of Oakeshott are actually endorsed by the world of 'getting and spending'.

School and the World of Work

Returning to the school context, analysis by Alison Wolf (2002) of research findings in the UK and internationally demonstrates the significance of academic skills for employment purposes and reveals little evidence regarding the value of vocational and training initiatives. Though openings for traditional craft workers (plumbers, electricians, toolmakers, hairdressers) as well as for engineers are in decline, Wolf notes that there are many jobs still available in these areas (*ibid.*, p. 94). Having said this, the 'evidence on skills suggests that employers in the brave new "knowledge economy" are after just those academic skills that schools have always tried to promote' (*ibid.*, p. 37). High levels of numeracy and literacy are exactly what are required 'to just that expanding category of professional and technical jobs that we want for ourselves and our children' (*ibid.*, p. 86). On the basis of the above research it is clear that what is required for the world of work is a general education, together with the skills of accurate and effective communication, including the skills of literacy and numeracy. What these results show is the high value placed on the enabling skills which have traditionally been a concern of conventional schooling.

All of this research confirms what I learned myself from employers when I worked in the area of transition from education to working life over two decades ago. Above all, what the employers sought were willing, literate and numerate young people and any specialised training, below graduate level,

---

[2]   This quotation from Sausmann and Steel used in the Dearing Report is taken from Prickett (2002b, p. 184).

they were prepared to provide themselves. This helps to explain why the regimes of assessment for vocational training introduced by the British government have been a spectacular failure. The performance criteria specified by the bureaucrats who devised NVQs in the United Kingdom (see Wolf, 2002, pp. 72–9) produced qualifications that were 'unwanted and unused' (*ibid.*, p. 75). According to Wolf, the NVQ project was as misguided as the plans of Trollope's foolish Mr Jobbles who dreamed of the world divided into 'classes and sub-classes' and where even the grocer's assistant would not be allowed to 'carry out cabbages unless his fitness for cabbage-carrying had been ascertained' (quoted in *ibid.*). The irony is that the bureaucrats who felt that their system was practical found out that the real world of 'getting and spending' had no use for the scheme.

Why then do employers not seek a closer articulation between the school curriculum and the world of work? Quite simply it is because for the performance of many, if not most, jobs people do not need to learn very much of direct vocational relevance off the job—and certainly not in school. It is not a question of the school teaching the wrong or obsolete vocational skills; it is rather that there is no need for the school to teach any vocational skills. Accordingly, it can be plausibly argued that the main contribution of education to economic productivity goes little beyond the provision of mass literacy. Moreover, the standard sources on the relationship between education and economic productivity provide scant evidence to support the claim that higher levels of education among employees lead to greater productivity (Berg, 1970; Oxenham, 1988).

Many vocational skills are acquired on the job rather than in schools. Most of the skills necessary to employment, and not just the low-level skills of an office cleaner or a factory operative, are most appropriately, and also best, learned on the job (see Collins, 1979). Many low-level skills are, moreover, very highly specific so that, for example, learning how to operate one machine will not necessarily help a person to operate another in the same factory. Where it is not possible to learn skills on the job, training agencies rather than schools are the appropriate institutions to provide them.

The school is not at all a suitable arena in which to learn vocational skills because it would be unrealistic to expect schools to teach skills to a degree of specialisation which would be relevant to the workplace. Where specialist training is necessary in order to engage in certain tasks such as, for example, performing heart surgery, piloting aircraft, or driving heavy vehicles, the school is not the appropriate institution to provide it. We might also ask what sort of training the school could be expected to offer, for example, to prospective bus drivers without involving wasteful replication of the training provided by the driving schools of transport companies. It would therefore be impractical, as well as educationally restrictive, for school pupils to spend much of their time learning the skills required to drive heavy vehicles.

The general point can be applied to a particular area where the school/employment connection can be shown to be nothing like what its advocates imagine. This concerns the teaching of modern foreign languages in the English-speaking world (see Williams, 2000). Oakeshott condemns on educational grounds the encroachment of vocational considerations into the design of curricula in foreign languages (Fuller, 1989, p. 89) but I would wish to add that the attribution of a vocational rationale to language learning tends generally to be misguided. Typical are the claims that knowledge of foreign languages will open various employment opportunities. Yet there is a conspicuous lack of hard evidence that this knowledge will increase productivity and employment. To be sure, there are jobs available to young people with foreign-language 'skills'. There may be some truth in the claim (although I am very sceptical of it) that many companies invest in Ireland because 'they can find people with linguistic skills' (Russell, 1999, p. 7). I suspect that the only linguistic skill that attracts companies to Ireland is the availability of an English-speaking workforce. In any case, the principal job available to many people with competence in a foreign language is the contemporary equivalent of selling encyclopaedias — telemarketing.

Of course, this is not to deny the utility of a knowledge of foreign languages for certain purposes and it would be foolish to deny the usefulness of mastery of the languages of those countries to whom one is hoping to sell goods or services. Linguistic competence can therefore be very useful and sometimes crucial for business purposes. So what then is wrong with the vocational rationale for knowledge of foreign languages? If we are to limit the notion of usefulness to the sphere of work, it cannot plausibly be argued that such knowledge is necessary for most occupations. After all, most people, particularly within the English-speaking world, conduct their professional lives within their own speech communities and they have no reason to speak other than their mother tongue. And even if we were to accept the argument based on need, it is hardly possible to predict in advance which language may in the future prove of vocational utility to any particular pupil. And even if it were possible to do so in respect of individual pupils, this would serve to justify teaching the language in question only to this group; it would not justify teaching it to all pupils. On the grounds of utility alone, it is wasteful to subject all young people to the study of a language that they will never need to use.

More generally, there is no evidence to show that conferring upon the school a role in direct vocational preparation would improve the lot of the unemployed or the underemployed. After all, many countries have training agencies which offer such direct preparation for work. If these are not as successful as we would wish in equipping young people to secure employment, it does not seem logical to argue that schools would be any more successful. Even if we were to accept that the school curriculum should be directly related to the world of work, we would require evidence that particular school programmes of training in specific areas could help to secure employment for those unemployed. We would also need evidence pointing to job vacancies unfilled because of specific failures on the school's part to provide relevant training in identifiable areas, as well as evidence to show that there are people now in employment who would perform their jobs better if they had followed a curriculum of a more directly vocational character. Little enough research has been conducted into what is actually learned in schools, or on how long it has been retained, but it seems at least counter-intuitive that people would manage their vocational lives any differently or any better as a consequence of any changes of a direct vocational character to the school curriculum.

All of this goes to confirm that Oakeshott's resistance to replacing education with vocational aims has a sound practical rationale. There is, however, an aspect to Oakeshott's epistemology of work that needs to be addressed next. This was touched on at the end of Chapter 1 and now requires more considered attention.

Work, Play and Human Welfare

Oakeshott's epistemological separatism leads to a view of work that is detached from experiences of satisfaction, pleasure and fulfilment and the development of autonomy. This epistemological separatism does not accommodate the potential role of work in the literal sense as an important context through which human beings can find fulfilment, achieve and exercise autonomy and shape their identities.

Work and the Achievement of Autonomy

Here I wish to draw on a distinction in the work of John White, a philosopher of education deeply committed to autonomy as a value. White does envisage autonomy having a role within the context of work and makes a valuable distinction between autonomous and heteronomous work, although I would not take it as far as he does. What he understands as autonomous work is freely chosen and results in an end-product which is of substantial personal significance to the agent (White, 1997). In terms used by Havighurst (1964, quoted in Schofield, 1972, p. 155), autonomous work is always 'ego-involving' rather than merely 'society-sustaining'. By contrast, heteronomous work is not freely chosen and thus always involves a degree of constraint, although some heteronomous work may be of personal significance to the individual (White, 1997, p. 10). In terms of Oakeshott's distinction between work and play, heteronomous work is 'toilsome activity' (Oakeshott, 1995, p. 30).

Work of this character is essentially disconnected from the human person. This disconnection is captured in the reference in the Book of Job to 'pressed service' and 'hired drudgery', and to the worker who has 'no thought but his wages (Job 7: 1–4). There is a passage in *Zen and the Art of Motorcycle Maintenance* that gives a memorable sense of what is meant by the disconnection from what one is doing that characterises heteronomous work. The narrator encounters a group of mechanics who, although good-humoured and cheerful in their attitude towards him, are without commitment to their work. They were 'uninvolved' and 'like spectators':

You had the feeling they had just wandered in there themselves and somebody had handed them a wrench. There was no identification with the job. No saying. "I am a mechanic." At 5 p.m. or whenever their eight hours were in, you knew they would cut it off and not have another thought about their work. They were already trying not to have any thoughts about their work *on* the job ... . Or rather, they had something to do with it, but their own selves were outside of it, detached, removed. They were involved in it but not in such a way as to care. (Pirsig, 1994, p. 26)

This kind of work really does belong in a world that includes little more than than producing and consuming or what Wordsworth describes as 'getting and spending'. It is the world of people, described by St. Paul as those 'whose life is buying things' (*First Letter of St. Paul to the Corinthians*, 7: 30). In work of this nature the only 'incentives', as Simone Weil notes, are 'fear and gain'; it is to 'strive from necessity and not for some good' it is to be 'driven not drawn' in order merely 'to maintain our existence' (Miles, 1986, pp. 180–1). This is the view assumed in Oakeshott's characterisation of work as 'toilsome activity' (Oakeshott, 1995, p. 30) and it is not an uncommon view. In an essay where he pours scorn on Tolstoy's enthusiasm for manual labour, Somerset Maugham writes in a similar vein. 'There is nothing particularly commendable in work. One works in order to enjoy leisure. It is only stupid people who work because, when not working, they don't know what to do with themselves' (Maugham, 1971, p. 267).

Yet this attitude to work can be challenged and the lines of such a challenge can actually be found in Oakeshott's own writing. In a quite long and insightful footnote in *On Human Conduct*, he observes that the 'expenditure of energy entailed in a performance may itself be a satisfaction and not a cost to be set off against the yield of the performance' (Oakeshott, 1975a, p. 54, footnote 1) One implication of this point is that work can be conceived as having a play or pleasurable element. This element is captured in the remark of Émile Zola about the miller in his great story *L'Attaque du Moulin* (Zola, 1969, p. 87). Though retired, the miller continued work quite simply *'pour le plaisir'* (for the pleasure of it) — an attitude to work that is not all uncommon.

The satisfactions of work can assume an even more significant role in human life. Simone Weil goes as far as to claim that in work it is possible to find a 'mysticism' and a 'spirituality' whereby man can 'recreate his own life' (*ibid.*, pp. 178–9).

Much work can embrace a world described by novelist, Mary McCarthy, as 'beyond utility' (McCarthy, 1967, p. 26) and be invested with a quality of personal significance to the worker. Work of this character can provide a context for the expression of one's identity. The term 'professional' captures something of what is involved here. Being professional also says something about the quality of a person's skill and commitment —in this way we can speak of people being very professional in spheres not commonly considered 'professional' in the conventional sense—bus drivers, painters/decorators, postmen and women, restaurant staff and assistants in bookshops. Doing these jobs professionally means doing them with the required level of skill, and also with a care for the quality of service provided. In other words, the work is part of a *Bildung* through which identity is expressed. Alison Wolf (2002, pp. 143-5, 166, 276) draws attention to the identity-shaping dimension of an individual's occupation in Germany. The very word *Beruf* meaning occupation, is connected with the word *Berufung* which means calling or vocation, and it communicates a sense of exercising a vocation through which one expresses one's identity. Reflection on the full import of the terms 'vocation', 'calling' and also 'employment' and 'career' suggests that work can therefore connect with the deepest human aspirations. Vocational learning is indeed very much part of learning 'to make something of ourselves' (Oakeshott, 1981, p. 303)

Nor is conventional remunerated employment the only context in which people can find work. The activity can be understood in a broader sense and society needs to think imaginatively about its notions of work. There is much wisdom in the words written over a century ago by John Ruskin.

> We must not when our strong hands are thrown out of work look wildly about for want of something to do with them. If ever we feel that want, it is a sign that all our household is out of order ... You complain of the difficulty of finding work for your men. Depend upon it the real difficulty rather is to find men for your work ... Look around at this island of yours and see what you have to do in it. (Ruskin, 1893, pp. 19-21)

There never will be an end to the work that needs to be done—for example, in community and environmental service and in service to the young, the aged and the differently abled. For this reason, experience and intuition suggest to me that it would be better to subsidise work and to extend community employment schemes rather than waste money on many futile vocational training initiatives, a view also endorsed by Alison Wolf (2002, pp. 250–3). In this way people can enjoy the satisfactions conferred by work without wasting time on fruitless, unproductive training.

But whether or not 'ego-involving', or of substantial personal significance to the worker, or autonomous in White's sense, work makes a huge contribution to enjoying a sense of autonomy and achieving an identity and a sense of self-worth. Oakeshott does not seem to appreciate that through work, as well as through the pursuit of understanding, a person can come 'to recognize himself in the mirror of the human achievements which compose his inheritance' (Fuller, 1989, p. 48). Indeed, there is much evidence that many people would prefer to have a paid job rather than to enjoy the same income without having to work (White, 1997, p. 15). This highlights the difficulty in our culture of uncoupling the notion of work from notions of human dignity. Though this conjuncture may be a relatively recent development and may thus be historically and culturally contingent, yet the evidence suggests that the desire to find recognised employment is likely to remain an enduring aspiration of many people throughout the western world. My intuition is that this aspiration has roots in the very basic human impulse to be autonomous in dealing with the world both in the sense of being self-supporting and contributing to the welfare of the community, or in what Margaret Donaldson describes as the 'fundamental human urge to be effective, competent and independent' (1987, p. 113). The impulse to be effective in our dealing with our environment is related to children's desire to be independent. She refers to the example of a rather precocious child who when offered help with anything used to say 'Can man'ge' (*ibid.*).

Autonomy in the sense of being self-supporting also has a very significant communitarian dimension, showing that being autonomous and being community-minded need not be incompatible. There appear to be several strands underlying the wish to be self-supporting through employment. The aspiration embraces a pre-Enlightenment wish to contribute to the welfare and sustenance of the community to which one belongs; something of an Enlightenment impulse to achieve autonomy both by exercising responsibility for one's existence and also by accumulating as much wealth as possible for one-self; and a post-Enlightenment desire to seek as much security as possible in an uncertain world of economic change, human dislocation and ecological threat.

Unfortunately the kind of autonomy in the sense of being self-supporting is one which is overlooked by philosophers who treat autonomy as a capacity to make unencumbered decisions about life choices and about moral, political and religious beliefs. As already noted autonomy in this wider sense is intimated in the notion of *Bildung* that is implied in Oakeshott's writing. But Oakeshott does not appreciate that work can be part of our *Bildung,* and through work we can be enabled to create ourselves. This narrowness of vision in his understanding of work is another feature of Oakeshott's 'over-economy of concepts' (Auspitz, 1976, p. 266) and his tendency to overlook the nuance in human practices mentioned in the previous two chapters. Through work a person can come 'to recognize himself in the mirror of the human achievements which compose his inheritance' (Fuller, 1989, p. 48), and through work the individual can come 'to make the most or the best of himself' (Fuller, 1989, p. 47, Oakeshott, 1967, p. 130).

The burden of the arguments advanced in this chapter is therefore to call into serious question Oakeshott's view that the preparation of young people for work is necessarily anti-educational. As well as providing a context through which identity can be expressed and autonomy exercised, work and work-related learning are capable of yielding an *Arbeitsfreude* (joy in work) that can be experienced as a source of pleasure rather than as a chore, burden or disutility. These activities can offer profound satisfactions that contribute hugely to human flourishing. The contrast that Oakeshott draws between work and play that was reviewed in Chapter 2 is too stark and needs far greater nuance. It is a contrast that may not be at all strongly marked in the lives of people for whom work is one of the sources of satisfaction and even of enjoyment in their lives.

But Oakeshott's epistemological separatism has other negative implications and in the next chapter I propose to show this in respect of the teaching of literature.

Chapter Seven

Art, Life and the Study of Literature

The aim of this chapter is show that the distinction that Oakeshott makes between practical experience and experience in the other modes is not sustainable through a consideration of the relationship between aesthetic and practical experience. In challenging this theory of literary education and the philosophy of knowledge that informs it, the chapter shows in Oakeshott's work evidence of a more nuanced and defensible view of the role of literature in education.

The belief that literature can teach us something about life is intuitively plausible and I do believe that through teaching literature we also teach young people about life and thus contribute directly to their personal development. This connection between literature and life is even more salient where teachers use literary texts in the area of civic/political education, a practice endorsed by philosophers from Plato to the present day. Eamonn Callan (1997), for example, sees in literature an avenue to enable children to understand and appropriate their political traditions with 'generosity and imagination' (Callan, 1997, p. 122). In her book, *Poetic Justice: the literary imagination and public life*, Martha Nussbaum claims that the novel is capable of prompting 'empathy and compassion in ways highly relevant to citizenship' (Nussbaum, 1995, p. 10), and she actually envisages what seems to me a very questionable connection between this genre and 'the Enlightenment ideal of the equality and dignity of all human life' (*ibid.*, p. 46). Nussbaum, however, also shows how the reading of appropriate imaginative literature can contribute to the education of those studying law by sensitising them to the complex nature of human behaviour.

Yet there is a view of literary education endorsed by Oakeshott that would preclude a teacher from making a direct link between imaginative literature and life. Expressly denying that literature offers 'thoughts about the world in general and about the conduct of life' (Oakeshott, 1981, p. 243), he rejects the possibility that it can 'give a special kind of moral education' (*ibid.*, p. 240). This is because, for Oakeshott, the aesthetic marks a unique area of human experience that absolutely resists reduction to any other terms. This aesthetic theory is clearly very hostile to the use of literature with any kind of didactic intent. If it were sustainable, this theory would exclude any role for literature in moral or civic education and require an extremely formal approach to the teaching of literature.

A view of literary education hostile to any direct link between education and life is not peculiar to Oakeshott. It will help to dwell briefly on the work of a theorist of literary education who subscribes to the view advanced by Oakeshott and who invokes Oakeshott's authority in support of this view (Gribble, 1983, pp. 61, 168). Gribble takes to task those teachers of English who assume 'that literature is just a semi-fictional way of analysing moral and social problems'(Gribble, 1983, p. 158).

> In many schools, works of literature are used as adjuncts to social studies, and books allegedly 'about' old age, the environment, the family and so on are discussed. It is implicit in such courses that works of literature are viewed as sources of knowledge on matters of public or personal concern ... (*ibid.*, p. 5)

He criticises the 'way "topic-based courses" ... tend to draw on literature as merely a form of social documentary' (*ibid.*, p. 158) and gives as an example someone who presented *Romeo and Juliet* to police cadets 'as a study in juvenile delinquency' (ibid, p. 5). This practice derives from a view of truth in literature as 'the accurate portrayal of aspects of the world or of human life' (*ibid.*, p. 12). This view can lead many readers of literature to believe

> that they gain knowledge and understanding from works of literature ... It is common to find literature courses in schools organized around themes such as 'the family', 'authority', 'race relations', etc., and some teacher education programmes include courses such as 'Children in Literature'. One assumption of such courses is that the works of literature will develop knowledge and

understanding of the nature of authority, the family, children and so on. (*ibid.*, p. 12)

Gribble perceives great danger in the use of literature as what he calls '"source material"' in classes of 'social studies or social biology' (*ibid.*, p. 158). This is because it involves an attempt to 'tear the "thought" out of the delicate "organic" structure of a work of literature' and any such attempt will 'destroy' the aesthetic quality of the thought (*ibid.*). On account of the '"embodied"' nature and the 'intricate unity' of good literature, Gribble argues that we must never view it as 'a form of expression reducible to, and thus comparable with, other forms of expression or communication' (*ibid.*). Therefore he announces that his 'own tendency is to take the risks of some form of aestheticism' (*ibid.*, p. 155) rather than to accept that works of literature could be studied in other than aesthetic terms. By this he means that he would prefer to take an extremely formal approach (that is, a concern with form) to the analysis of literary texts rather than to give any impression that the thoughts or ideas of the writer can be considered on their own terms apart from their aesthetic embodiment. As we have seen Oakeshott's epistemological position supports this view and this now merits some closer attention

Oakeshott's Aesthetic Separatism

For Oakeshott, it will be recalled, experience offers itself in terms of discrete and autonomous modes: the mode of practice or practical living and the modes of scientific, historical and aesthetic experience. The notion of the practical as a distinct mode of experience serves to distinguish the ordinary world of human affairs from the scholarly and aesthetic/contemplative forms of understanding or experience. Ironically in *Experience and Its Modes*, first published in 1933, aesthetic experience is described by Oakeshott as an aspect of the world of practice. Here he writes that music, art and poetry and 'all that we mean by beauty' are ultimately 'wholly taken up with practical life' (Oakeshott, 1978, pp. 296/7). And so he concludes that the 'most thoroughly and positively practical life is that of the artist or the mystic' (*ibid.*, p. 296). But he entirely revises this view and, later, in the preface to *Rationalism in Politics*, he writes that the essay, 'The Voice of Poetry in the Conversation of Mankind', is a 'belated retraction' of the 'foolish' inclusion of mysticism and art in the practical mode of life (Oakeshott, 1981, Preface). In this essay he identifies aesthetic experience as a distinct and autonomous activity which consists in contemplating or 'delighting' in works of art. Poetic, by which he means artistic, experience consists in creating and responding to images simply and exclusively for the sake of the delight they give us. Creating and enjoying works of art are solely and exclusively experiences in responding to images of delight. In an apposite metaphor he describes the 'poetic' as a 'dream enjoyed for its own sake' (Oakeshott, 1995, p. 32).

> The world for the poet is not material to be used for satisfying wants, it is something to be contemplated ... Poetic imagination is not a preliminary to doing something, it is an end in itself. (*ibid.*, pp. 32/33)

Therefore, we can say, that within the terms of Oakeshott's account of the matter, aesthetic experience, in an exemplary and pre-eminent sense, is characterised by its intrinsically valuable or non-instrumental nature. More so than with the scholarly forms of knowledge represented by science or history, art exists for its own sake or on its own account, rather than for any instrumental reason. 'A poem should not mean/but be', Archibald MacLeish's famous lines from *Ars Poetica*, would be an excellent epigraph for Oakeshott's theory of art.

We should note also a contrast between the delight that characterises aesthetic experience and pleasure, a term that belongs to the language of practical experience. In the language of practical experience, the pleasurable is contrasted with the painful and associated with desire as opposed to aversion. In the world of poetic experience even the pity and fear prompted by the depiction of a tragic situation such as that of King Lear provoke aesthetic delight rather than feelings of sadness. Pleasure is also associated with entertainment, distraction, or diversion that belong to the world of practical endeavour rather than to that of art. For Oakeshott the world of aesthetic experience is absolutely discrete, self-sufficient, and autonomous and offers neither 'wisdom' nor 'entertainment' (Oakeshott, 1981, p. 237).

As this is a fairly severe theory of aesthetic experience, it is not surprising to find that Oakeshott acknowledges that the enjoyment of such experience is an uncommon occurrence. All departures from practical experience are, he writes, 'excursions into a foreign country' (Oakeshott, 1978, p. 296; also 1981, p. 222), but access to the universe of aesthetic experience is particularly difficult to achieve. It is described as 'a momentary release, a brief enchantment' and as 'a sort of truancy, a dream within the dream of life, a wild flower planted among our wheat' (Oakeshott, 1981, p. 247), and 'every backward glance' to the world of practical experience is 'an infidelity at once difficult to avoid and fatal in its consequences' (*ibid.*, p. 242). How, then, do we come to 'absolve ourselves' (*ibid.*, p. 143) from the world of practical activity and enter the world of aesthetic experience? The mode of practical experience includes what Oakeshott calls 'ambiguously practical activities which intimate contemplation' (*ibid.*, p. 244). This includes any activity that we engage in for the pleasure of it rather than for an extrinsic purpose such as a reward, and it also includes relationships of friendship, love, and affection. These relationships are 'dramatic, not utilitarian' (*ibid.*, pp. 177, 244), and those involved are concerned only with enjoying one another's company and rather than with any considerations of usefulness. Oakeshott believes that the cultivation of moral character, where 'doing is delivered, at least in part, from the deadliness of doing' (Oakeshott, 1975a, p. 74; see also 1981, p. 245), also intimates the world of aesthetic experience. Our moral sentiments or achievements in what he calls 'self-enactment' (Oakeshott, 1975a, pp. 70–4) are 'private and self-sufficient' (Oakeshott, 1981, p. 245). By this he means that where an action does not have the positive consequences that we intend, our moral integrity cannot be impugned on this account. As regards the aesthetic mode of experience, Oakeshott argues that this finds embryonic form in those moments of lethargy where we take lazy delight in the images that flow into our minds. This is why memories can be a 'fruitful spring of poetic images' because when we are indulging in memories 'we are already halfway released from the practical world ...' (ibid, p. 232, n. 2). (He distinguishes between contemplating which involves dwelling upon a memory and simply remembering, which is a feature of the practical world.) The poetic mode is not, however, lethargic but asserts itself only when the urgency of practical desire and ambition have abated, when 'practical and scientific imagining have lost their authority' (*ibid.*, p. 222). Aesthetic experience is, therefore, a leisurely, 'non-laborious activity', it is 'playful and not businesslike' (*ibid.*, p. 221).

Art and the Languages of Human Inquiry

Oakeshott's account of the relationship between the world of aesthetic experience and the worlds of history and science is intriguing. He believes that it is mistaken to understand works of art as 'contributions to an inquiry into the nature of the real world' (*ibid.*, p. 230) and susceptible of being shown in some sense to be 'true'(*ibid.*, p. 229). He claims that the impulse of aesthetic, as well as scientific and historical, activity lies in wonder. The wonder experienced by the scientist or historian has, however, a restless quality that passes into curiosity, inquiry, speculation, and research. By contrast, the wonder associated with aesthetic experience provokes only 'delight' (*ibid.*, pp. 146, 216–23). According to his theory, creating or appreciating a work of art offers a satisfaction of a very different character from that associated with the construction of an explanatory account of human experience. Furthermore, unlike in the case of a piece of scientific or historical inquiry, a work of art provides no detachable conclusions that can be translated into the language of practical activity. (Here he is referring only to the results, outcomes, or conclusions of scientific and historical inquiries because he maintains that actual research in science and history cannot be translated into the language of practical life.) Quite commonly, scientific investigation yields results or information that can be exploited in devising technological inventions. Historical study can also furnish conclusions that can be detached from the activity of research that went into establishing them. For example, historically authenticated conclusions about the development of the institution of private property might be used to make a point in a political debate.

Works of art, by contrast, do not have a connection to the world of practical life. A work of art is absolutely divested of its aesthetic quality when introduced into the world of practice. A politician who, for example, accuses an opponent of 'vaulting ambition which o'erleaps itself' (Shakespeare, 1997c, *Macbeth*, Act 1, Sc. vii, line 27) is speaking the language of practical life rather than of poetry (Oakeshott, 1983, pp. 18–19, 38–9) because she is treating art as capable of yielding an outcome or end-product. When invoked in the engagements of practical living, the aesthetic integrity of an image is absolutely dissipated; what is left is 'merely what is unpoetic' (Oakeshott, 1981, p. 243). This is because in art, form and content, activity and outcome are absolutely inseparable; in art '*what* is said and *how* it is said' (*ibid.*, p. 246) are indistinguishable'. For this reason, as already noted, Oakeshott believes that literature cannot furnish us with detachable 'thoughts about the world in general and about the conduct of life' (*ibid.*, p. 243) or 'give a special kind of moral education' (*ibid.*, p. 240).

Unsurprisingly Oakeshott's view of art has been subject to much criticism. Colin Falck criticises Oakeshott's attempt to dissociate the cognitive from the affective aspects of aesthetic experience, and he argues that Oakeshott's view of poetry would apply only to such poetry as that of Mallarmé (Falck, 1963, p. 72). Howard Davis wonders whether one can impose 'a single form of experience on to such a heterogeneous and expanding "object" as art' (Davis, 1975a, p. 66). More to the point of this discussion he asks whether Oakeshott's universe of aesthetic discourse is 'sufficiently "stable" a Mode of Experience' (*ibid.*, p. 65). Davis's point is that it is hard to see how we can entertain the artistic expression of emotions, thoughts, and ideas without reference to the languages, both natural and metaphorical, of practical life from which they are constructed.

Regrettably Oakeshott fails to make sufficiently explicit the connection between the mode of practical experience and the modes of human understanding and of art. The discrete, autonomous, and disjoined nature of his epistemological categories makes it hard to discern how precisely he conceptualises the relationship between the world of practical experience and the other universes of discourse. In correctly identifying contemplative delight as a feature of aesthetic experience, Oakeshott then, implausibly and restrictively, seeks to make delight the sole criterion of the aesthetic. This raises once again the general problem with his epistemology in relation to his philosophy of art. It suffers from an 'over-economy of concepts', which comes from his having 'insufficiently multiplied essences' (Auspitz, 1976, pp. 266, 288).

Literature, Life and Truth

The separatism that seeks to make delight the sole criterion of the aesthetic is inconsistent with a common conception of the relationship between literature and life, and indeed, truth. Literature can prompt us to review critically beliefs and attitudes that we hold dear. Reading well, as Harold Bloom reminds with reference to the advice of Samuel Johnson, challenges us 'not to contradict and confute, nor to believe and take for granted ... but to weigh and consider' what we read in respect of how to make sense of the world and even to acquire knowledge 'not just of self and others, but of the way things are' (Bloom, 2001, pp. 21, 29).[1] In a famous passage, Jane Austen, for example, speaks of the power of the novel to communicate 'the most thorough knowledge of human nature' as well as the 'happiest delineations of its varieties' (Austen, 1987, p. 22). Indeed, it is due to what she can tell us about life that we find Jane Austen's novels being used as a guide to romance in the twenty-first century by Karen Jay Fowler in *The Jane Austen Book Club* (Fowler, 2005). In his novel/autobiography, *The Pupil*, Monk Gibbon makes a claim similar to Austen's. It is, argues Gibbon, the aspiration of '(s)erious novelists ... to make some contribution to the greater understanding of human nature' (Gibbon, 1981, p. 62). Such novelists seek to offer to their readers 'truth' rather than mere 'verisimilitude'; he describes them as the 'giants of their profession' whose 'insight is matched by their powers of invention' (Gibbon, 1981, p. 62). Marcel Proust also thought of himself as a searcher after truth. 'I very much wish to finish the work I've begun and to put in it those truths that I know will be nourished by it and that otherwise will be destroyed with me' (quoted in White, 2000, p. 31). Alain de Botton's (1998) book on Proust owes some of its popularity to the psychological truthfulness de Botton discloses in his work. Proust, he writes, 'offers us a picture of human behaviour that initially fails to match an orthodox account of how people operate, though it may in the end be judged to be a far *more* truthful picture than the one it has challenged' (*ibid.*, p. 108). Seamus Heaney endorses this conception of the relationship between literature and truth; he has written persuasively of the poet's 'truth-telling urge' (Heaney, 1988, p. xvi) and of the 'necessary function of writing as truth-telling' (ibid, p. 97). Novelist, Amy Tan, has a similar conception of the role of the imaginative writer. She writes in the hope, she explains, 'that I will discover what I mean by

---

[1]   The first quotation is taken by Bloom from Johnson and the second is Bloom's own.

truth' and she revises her work until what she has written 'feels true' (Tan, 2004, pp. 322–3).

Of course, affirming a relationship between literature and life and between literature and truth is not to be committed to a didactic view of literature. This is the view famously expressed by John Milton in his description of *Paradise Lost*, in the introductory lines of the poem, as an attempt to 'justify the ways of God to man'. Daniel Defoe expresses a similar view in the description of *Moll Flanders* as 'a work from every part of which something may be learned, and some just and religious inference is drawn, by which the reader will have something of instruction, if he pleases to make use of it' (Defoe, 1980, p. 30). The intention of its creator does not define the meaning of a work of literature and this meaning is never reducible to its author's proselytising intent.

Literature can also can a significant psychological impact on our lives. In a very interesting interview, literary scholar, Tzvetan Todorov, speaks of his conversion from a formalist approach to literature to one that envisages literature as offering readers illumination of their own lives. He condemns the formalism underlying the teaching of literature in French schools on the grounds that it neglects the impact of literature on the lives of students. Literature, he now believes, helps us to understand human emotions and speaks to us of ourselves and of our lives (see Dupuis, 2005).[2] Commenting on the effect of reading and writing fiction on her own psyche, Amy Tan captures this feature of literature dramatically. Fiction, writes Tan, has the power 'to startle my mind, to churn my heart, to tingle my spine, to knock the blinders off my eyes and allow me to see beyond the pale' (Tan, 2004, p. 322). As poet, Brendan Kennelly, puts it: 'Poems that work get to the root of your position, they insist on becoming central to your life and my even change it'(McSweeney, 1983, p.140).[3] Such poetry 'reads you' in the sense that it 'really forces you to look at yourself' operating like a 'time bomb in the guts of complacency'

---

[2] I have paraphrased the points made by Todorov in the interview in Dupuis, 2005. Indeed the remarks by Nancy Huston that I refer to in Chapter 4 are taken from a recent joint interview on the teaching of literature by Todorov and Huston (see Truong, 2007).

[3] This quotation is taken from part of an interview with Brendan Kennelly by Siobhán McSweeney (1983).

(Murphy, 1987, p. 54).[4] Another poet makes a similar point with specific reference to teaching. One aim of the good teacher of poetry, argues Michael Longley, is to explain to his pupils what a poem is 'doing to him, the teacher, spiritually, emotionally and intellectually' (McSweeney, 1983, p. 139).[5] As the teacher of literature in Jeanne Benameur's novel *Présent?* referred to in Chapter 4 explains, the syllabus must be one 'that gets under their skin, makes their blood beat, makes them feel that the life of a human being is something great and that this greatness is to be found in texts (Benameur, 2006, p. 78) (my translation).

In the context of teaching at third level, Azar Nafisi's *Reading Lolita in Tehran: A Memoir in Books* provides a compelling the account of the potential of literature to subvert our usual ways of understanding the world. Gathering a group of former students to read forbidden works of western literature, Nafisi demonstrates how encounters with fictional worlds encouraged the students in their opposition to the theocratic totalitarianism of Iran in the 1990s. '(M)ost great works of the imagination', writes Nafisi, are 'meant to make you feel like a stranger in your own home'(Nafisi, 2004, p. 94). They prompt us to question what we take for granted, especially 'traditions and expectations' where they appear 'immutable' (*ibid.*). She invites her students to consider the way in which great literature unsettles them, makes them 'a little uneasy' and invites them 'to look around and consider the world, like Alice in Wonderland, through different eyes' (*ibid.*) What a novel offers, she writes, is:

> the sensual experience of another world. If you don't enter that world, hold your breath with the characters and become involved in their destiny, you won't be able to empathize, and empathy is at the heart of the novel. This is how you read a novel: you inhale the experience. (*ibid.*, p. 111)

The image of inhaling experience could hardly be further from the aesthetic continence of Michael Oakeshott.

Literature also has a power to shape the civic imagination and literary images have a power to reach young people in a way that more theoretical and abstract argument may fail to and also to provide a source of imagined experience that can

---

[4]   These quotations from Kennelly are taken from Daniel Murphy (1987).
[5]   This is from an interview with Michael Longley in McSweeney (1983).

serve as an accessible and sustaining form of civic glue. This power is acknowledged in one of the standard justifications for the teaching of Greek and Latin. This was to gain access to the potential of the great literature of Greece and Rome to provide civic instruction. There is a wonderful short story by Rudyard Kipling (2000) entitled 'Regulus' that illustrates how both in theory and in practice Horace's great ode was taught in this perspective. The story shows how the poem actually provides the boys with images of courage and forbearance that they apply in their own lives. In the twentieth century, *Lord of the Flies* and *Animal Farm* are examples of well-known novels that, as well as being engaging works of literature, could also serve as vehicles of civic learning.

This defence of the relationship between literature and life is not based merely on the authority of distinguished writers. If literature and life are not related, then it is hard to see how the sensibility acquired through engagement with the world of aesthetic experience can inform and enrich the quality of practical experience. It is difficult to see how experience organised within the terms of Oakeshott's rigorously discrete epistemological categories can cohere in the sensibility and character of the human person. In particular, Oakeshott fails to explain how the sensibility acquired through engagement within the world of aesthetic experience can inform and enrich the quality of practical experience. Reading *Hard Times*, for instance, may provide aesthetic pleasure, but in some readers it may also provoke feelings of increased sympathy towards others and perhaps hostility to uncontrolled market economics. For readers who have these feelings, their encounter with the novel has implications for their moral lives. Nonetheless, it is in principle possible to appreciate works of art and make no connection between art and life and obviously people of aesthetic sensibility can be cruel and heartless in the manner of Gilbert Osmond in *The Portrait of a Lady* by Henry James or indeed of some Nazi officers, as mentioned Chapter 1. As noted there, the notion of *Bildung* serves to distinguish between the individual, who is merely cultured and cultivated, and the person who is genuinely educated in the wide sense of *gebildet*.

Though Oakeshott appears to want us to believe that what we learn in one mode can be 'completely evaded or forgotten' (Greenleaf, 1966, p. 95) within the other modes, there is also evidence that he seems aware of some relationship between aesthetic experience and the conduct of our lives within the world of practical experience. For example, he contrasts the quality of moral sensibility likely to be developed by young people in the English-speaking world through exposure to Shakespeare and that likely to be acquired by young French people through study of Racine (Oakeshott, 1981, p. 243). Moreover, in writing about education, he draws attention to the potential of literature to enhance and celebrate 'human self-understanding' (Fuller, 1989, p. 40). Unfortunately, however, he does not pursue the implications of these insights. The failure to make the connection between his aesthetic theory and education is quite surprising in view of Oakeshott's affirmation that his general epistemology 'springs from reflecting upon teaching and learning rather than from reflecting upon the nature of knowledge' (Fuller, 1989, p. 57). If he had dwelt on the implications of his remarks about education, this would have allowed him to clarify aspects of his theory of art and would probably have led him to temper its separatism. This illustrates a point that will be noted again — Oakeshott's thinking is often more subtle than it first appears in the sharp contrasts that he draws.

Means, Ends and Didactic Intent

How can we reconcile this eloquent testimony to the power of literature in education with the separatism of the aesthetic theory? It can seem unfair to apply an aesthetic theory to educational practice when it was not conceived with teaching and learning in mind. Yet I think that what animates his strictures about didacticism in art derives from a fear that the presence of didactic intent will have a corrosive effect on the life-enhancing purposes of literary education. The pre-eminent of these purposes is to nourish the imagination or, to adapt a phrase of Oakeshott's from a slightly different context, to introduce young people to a world of 'wonder and delight' (*ibid.*, p. 40). He rightly fears that didactic intent may subvert the properly educational purposes of teaching literature and reduce literary works to a means for purveying 'truths' in what he describes as '"lessons" learned' or as 'hackneyed and unrecognized quotes from Virgil, Dante and Shakespeare' (Oakeshott, 1983, p. 19, n. 3). What he seems to have in mind is something like the situation in China as described by Colin Thubron where everything 'politically and ethically — is *settled*' and where consequently works of fiction are conceived as *romans à thèse* and serve as mere 'instruments of education' (Thubron, 1988, p. 187). Indeed, in a western context, we even find the philosopher, William Galston (1991), echoing Plato's notion of literature as providing noble lies or moralising fables to induce allegiance to the polity on the grounds that children can best be brought to accept the 'core commitments' of a liberal polity through exposure to a 'pantheon of heroes' who offer to them 'noble, moralizing' narratives (Galston, 1991, pp. 243–4). This kind of didacticism is anathema to Oakeshott, as it is to most educators, and this is what he is rejecting in arguing that literature cannot 'give a special kind of moral education' (Oakeshott, 1981, p. 240). What he wishes to affirm is respect for the integrity of literary works and the necessity to maintain a certain pedagogic detachment or distance in teaching literature. By detachment or distance I mean the attitude that allows literature speak to the learners in its own terms, unencumbered by any proselytising intent or ulterior purpose on the part of the teacher. In achieving this detachment, much will depend on the manner in which literature is treated by the teacher. Pedagogic tact will be required to avoid an instrumental and reductionist approach and to ensure that the encounters that young people have with literary works are sensitive to their complexity.

In rejecting the encroachment of instrumentalism, something remains to be said about the relationship between means and ends in the teaching of literature. Literary education has multiple purposes and those that relate to life (enhancing understanding, sensitivity and tolerance, for example) are not extrinsic to teaching literature. In other words, they are not related to teaching literature in instrumental terms or in terms of using a means to achieve an end. To rehearse an argument made in Chapter 2, it is as inappropriate to speak in means-ends terms of benefits of literary study as it would be to speak of the activity of sailing as a means to the pleasurable end of enjoyment.

An understanding of the moral corruption that can be engendered by ambition, for example, is not the end to which watching a performance of *Macbeth* is the means, any more than an understanding of the beliefs and loyalties, the fears and commitments of Northern Irish Unionists is an end to which a performance of *Observe the Sons of Ulster Marching Towards the Somme* by Frank McGuinness is the means. In the same way, feelings of increased sympathy towards others, an appreciation of, and a sense of outrage at, the destruction wrought by misguided patriotism are not ends, results, consequences or effects which may or may not follow a sensitive reading of Frank O'Connor's short story 'Guests of the Nation' (O'Connor, 1968). To read the fictional 'Guests of the nation' is to come to a deeper understanding of the malign potential of national sentiment, just as to read Roddy Doyle's non-fictional essay, 'Republic Is a Beautiful Word', is to enter vicariously into the joys of generous-spirited patriotic feelings (Doyle, 1993). Though not all readers will react in the same way, responding to novels and plays actually means enjoying insights and having experiences. In using imaginative literature with law students, this is precisely what Martha Nussbaum (1995) aims to achieve. She makes the students aware of the complex patterns of motivations and circumstances that go to make up human behaviour and which may be present in the cases about which they will be called upon to make judgements in their future careers. In brief then responding to literature involves the enlargement of understanding and sympathy as a feature, rather than as an effect, result or by-product of our reading.

Literature and Imaginative Outreach

On account of its capacity to cultivate sympathy and what Oakeshott calls 'human self-understanding' (Fuller, 1989, p. 40), literature can make a significant contribution both to personal development and also to the shaping to civic sensibility. And if we read Oakeshott's aesthetic theory in the context of his writings on education, it is clear that he too accepts that literature can play a role in enhancing the imaginative outreach of the young generation. Literature offers what Oakeshott describes as 'images of a human self-understanding' (Fuller, 1989, p. 40) that extend beyond 'the narrow boundaries of the local and the contemporary', and beyond 'what might be going on in the next town or village, in Parliament or in the United Nations ...' (*ibid.*). Works of literature offer a store of images that may endure in the consciousness of young people long after most of what they have learned at school has dropped into the deep well of human forgetfulness. What we read becomes part of what we are and in this sense, as noted in Chapter 4, literature has been well described as 'identity or person-constitutive' (Carr, 2003, p. 12).

This concludes the analysis of the character and content of Oakeshott's curriculum. As noted earlier in this chapter, however, Oakeshott asserts that his general epistemology 'springs from reflecting upon teaching and learning rather than from reflecting upon the nature of knowledge' (Fuller, 1989, p. 57). The following two chapters deal with teaching and learning, the first addressing Oakeshott's treatment of the important issue of motivation in education.

Chapter Eight

The Discipline of Inclination

Another problem with Oakeshott's epistemological separatism is the difficulty of giving an account of the role of motivation in learning. This issue needs to be explored as part of a general review of his conception of the relationship between teachers and learners. In exploring the nature of this relationship with student teachers and graduate students of education, I refer to Oakeshott's writings in order to illustrate very dramatically the authoritarian view of this relationship. In Chapter 3 Oakeshott was seen to share Michel Foucault's hostility to the intervention of governments in our lives but, by contrast, some of his writing on the teacher-learner relationship could be taken to exemplify everything that Foucault finds reprehensible in this relationship. George Steiner captures very powerfully and succinctly Foucault's view of teaching as 'an exercise, open or concealed, in power relations' (Steiner, 2003, p. 4).

> The Master possesses psychological, social, physical power. He can reward and punish, exclude and promote. His authority is institutional or charismatic or both. It is sustained by promise or menace .... even the more radical modes of instruction are conservative and charged with the ideological values of stability ... (*ibid.*)

But it is not only Foucault who would take issue with Oakeshott's views — commentators on his work (Kneller, 1984, pp 225, 250-1; Peters, 1974, p. 436; Pitkin, 1974, pp. 280-1) direct particular criticism at his explicit and unfashionable assertion of the need for, and justifiability of, compulsion in the relationship between teacher and pupil. Even G.H. Bantock is taken aback at Oakeshott's disregard for the children's capacity for understanding what they are asked to learn

(Bantock, 1981, p. 56). This emphasis on compulsion and even coercion in the teacher-pupil relationship is communicated in the frequent reference to 'conditions of direction and restraint'[1] that Oakeshott takes to characterise this relationship. This purpose of this chapter is to examine the extent to which he envisages compulsion as a feature of the educational relationship that is, after all, designed to initiate young people into a world of 'wonder and delight' (Fuller, 1989, p. 40). What emerges is that, when he devotes more considered attention to issues of pedagogy, Oakeshott is obliged to accept the limits of authoritarian conservatism in conceptualising the relationship between teacher and pupil. Again more nuance is to be found in Oakeshott's thinking than in the dichotomies that are a feature of his more explicit theorising.

Paternalism and the Teacher/Pupil Relationship

Firstly, however, it is important to situate the discussion in the context of Oakeshott's general conception of the teacher-pupil relationship and of the place of paternalism within it. According to Oakeshott, the relationship between teacher and pupil is categorially unique and distinguishable from all others. As was noted in Chapter 1, categorially unique means that it pertains to a separate category from all other relationships such as those of buyer and seller, doctor and patient, lawyer and client. 'And while a teacher and his pupil may have a legal and a commercial relationship, they also have an educational relationship whose terms are neither those of law nor of commerce' (Oakeshott, 1983a, pp. 119/120). Teacher and pupil constitute *personae*, that is, persons who are related to one another in a 'specific formal relationship' (Oakeshott, 1975a, p. 59), with 'distinct and exclusive conditions' (Oakeshott, 1983a, p. 120). Formally and ideally school pupils are both 'recognized and recognize themselves pre-eminently as learners' and the pupil is in Oakeshott's words a 'declared learner' (Fuller, 1989, p. 24). The degree of conceptual precision in Oakeshott's talk of ideal relationships and of pupils who 'recognise' and 'declare' themselves as learners may suggest that the teacher/pupil relationship is in some way immune from

---

[1]   The expression 'conditions of direction and restraint' occurs in Fuller (1989, pp. 68, 72) and in Oakeshott (1981 p. 303) where he also uses the expression 'circumstances of direction and restraint'

the difficulties that are endemic to all personal relationships. Oakeshott appreciates this and, moreover, makes the observation, familiar to any who have taught, that the teacher/pupil relationship is probably more than other human relationships subject to 'latitudes and imprecisions' (Fuller, 1989, p. 47). What Oakeshott wishes to stress is that there exists, in principle, a particular educational relationship whose terms are peculiar to the *personae* of teacher and pupil. Education is, in his words, a 'specific transaction' or 'specific human engagement'(*ibid.*, p. 63).

Oakeshott highlights the necessarily personal nature of the teacher/pupil relationship. A teacher is someone who knows and 'studies his pupil' (*ibid.*, p. 47) and who enters into a direct relationship with him.[2] He is also the 'agent of civilization' (*ibid.*, pp. 46, 48) with a mastery of, and commitment to, some aspect or aspects of this civilization so that in him a part of a civilization is 'alive' (Oakeshott, 1989, p. 70). In a school, teachers who undertake to impart to their pupils some form of knowledge or understanding are the 'only indispensable equipment' (*ibid.*, pp. 69–70). Oakeshott envisages the teacher as a 'custodian' of part of a culture in whom 'an inheritance of human understanding survives and is perpetually renewed in being imparted to newcomers' (*ibid.*, p. 70).

Any educational relationship can be said to be unique and personal, but there is a fundamental distinguishing feature between the teacher/learner relationship in general and the teacher/pupil relationship in a school context. The latter is a relationship between an adult and a child, and Oakeshott makes a rigorous distinction between the world of the adult and that of the child. Though he does not directly address the question of the status of children relative to adults, his position on the issue is expressed by implication and in the form of *obiter dicta* on the matter. A good school, he writes, offers 'the gift of a childhood' (*ibid.*). In 'The Definition of a University' we find the literary but, one hopes, not literal description of the years of childhood as 'semi-conscious' (Oakeshott 1967, p. 140). In 'On Being Conservative', Oakeshott contrasts children who are *in statu pupillari* with adults on the basis that adults need not 'justify their preference for making their own

---

[2] Sometimes it is not possible to avoid gender-biased language that is characteristic of Oakeshott's writing.

choices' and need not acknowledge the 'superior wisdom' or 'authority' of other adults in managing their own lives (Oakeshott, 1981, p. 187). Elsewhere he observes that the authoritarian regime of Calvin's Geneva was 'perceptively' recognized by John Knox as being appropriate to a 'school' and rather than to 'an association of adult persons' (Oakeshott, 1975a, p. 285, note 1). For Oakeshott even the status of the university student is ambivalent. The university student is described as one who is 'neither a child nor an adult' (Fuller, 1989, p. 100) and who stands at the 'strange middle moment of life' (ibid). While at university, before they have to cope with 'inexorable demands of adult life' (Oakeshott, 1967, p. 141), students enjoy what he describes as 'the gift of an interval' (Fuller, 1989, pp. 101, 127).

Consistent with this view of childhood is Oakeshott's understanding of the teacher-pupil relationship as paternalistic. Clearly, he would have little sympathy with the designations of the teacher that have featured in the pedagogic rhetoric of recent decades – such as facilitator, enabler, coordinator of a learning system, learning manager or guide. The adult world is composed of 'mysteries' (Fuller , 1989, p. 70 and see also Oakeshott, 1975a, p. 59) into which children are initiated by a teacher who decides when the learner is 'ready to receive what he has resolved to communicate' (Fuller, 1989, p. 47). So when Oakeshott describes the pupil as partner in the educational transaction he is not thinking of a partnership of equals in the manner of business partners. Rather he is thinking of a partnership like that between a doctor and a patient, or between a lawyer and her client, in the sense that these relationships involve a shared recognition of a difference in knowledge and expertise (ibid., pp. 44–6). The pupil is partner in the sense of being the subject of the teacher's activity but she is in the process of being initiated into a possible future partnership in which pupil and teacher come to share knowledge. In the subordinate role which, according to Oakeshott, they necessarily assume, pupils may be subject to a 'discipline of inclination' (ibid.,p. 68) through the imposition of 'conditions of direction and restraint' (ibid.). The imposition of such conditions seems at odds with the spirit of the metaphor of education as a conversation which pervades Oakeshott's work (see especially Oakeshott, 1981, pp. 199–200, 304, 311–2). It could also be considered at odds with his characterisation of school pupils who 'recognize themselves pre-eminently as learners' (Fuller, 1989, p. 24).

To explore this tension in Oakeshott's conception of education, his account of what need restraining—the inclinations of children—needs attention.

Oakeshott's Conception of Inclination

According to Oakeshott, in the young child 'the self is inclination' (*ibid.*, p. 67), that is, 'undifferentiated appetite' (*ibid.*, p. 128) or 'energy' (Oakeshott, 1981, p. 104) in the pursuit of pleasure and in the avoidance of pain. This aspect of the self belongs in the world of practical living where everything is conceived *sub species voluntatis*, that is, in terms of 'desire and aversion' (Oakeshott, 1981, p. 206) or of its propensity to provide pleasure or pain. As young children develop awareness of their world, when they begin to be 'self-moved' (Fuller, 1989, p. 67), formless impulse gives way to inclination in the form of 'habits of desire and aversion' (Oakeshott, 1981, p. 206). Everything exists in terms of its propensity to be exploited or to be made use of to yield immediate satisfaction in the assuagement of occurrent/inclination/wants/desires. In coping with this world a kind of knowledge is required, but it is a *scientia propter potentiam*. We may improve upon this knowledge but, as it come naturally to us, 'we never lack the equipment for the engagement' (*ibid.*, p. 207). Oakeshott uses the term 'inclination' (Fuller, 1989, pp. 67, 72) to stand only for the disposition to seek assuagement of occurrent desires through immediate satisfactions, a disposition which we acquire without being taught. Oakeshott's narrow definition of inclination does not appear to include intellectual curiosity and seems inhospitable to a view of persons as 'naturally inquiring animals' (Midgley, 1980, p. 75). For example, in his review of Polanyi's *Personal Knowledge*, Oakeshott appears to be somewhat sceptical of characterising human beings as having a 'primordial drive' to learn about the world, or a 'desire for intellectual understanding' or an 'urge to satisfy (themselves) intellectually' (Oakeshott, 1958, p. 77). It is this scepticism with regard to the existence of intellectual inclinations which prompts such provocative assertions as at 'school we are, quite properly, not permitted to follow our own inclinations' (Oakeshott, 1981, p. 306). Our 'own inclinations' are not relevant to the teacher's task because, asserts Oakeshott, what the teacher has to 'impart ... is *not* immediately connected with the current wants or "interests" of the learner' (Fuller, 1989, p. 68).

But I am not persuaded that he means us to take these tendentious statements altogether seriously. Their extravagance suggests that they might be read as a wish to provoke politically correct liberals rather than as the expression of a considered opinion. Closer reading of his essays provides evidence of a more nuanced view of the intellectual motivation of children—although those who have criticised Oakeshott on this issue (Kneller, 1984; pp. 225, 250–1; Peters, 1974, p. 436; Pitkin, 1974, pp. 280–1) do not seem to have detected this nuance. In 'Learning and Teaching' (Oakeshott, 1989, first published, 1967), for example, he does speak of intellectual curiosity but seeks to characterise this curiosity in terms of 'a desire not to be ignorant' and of 'vanity' rather than in terms of the young person's positive 'desire to understand' (Oakeshott, 1989, p. 57). More reasonably in the later essay, 'A Place of Learning' (Fuller, 1989, first published 1975), we find acknowledgement that 'the intimations of what there is to learn' represent both an 'awareness of our ignorance' and 'a wish to understand' (Fuller, 1989, p. 22). The learner does not know the exact nature of the intellectual and cultural satisfactions that he is prompted to seek—indeed he cannot know this until he has learned what these satisfactions are, because these are 'satisfactions he has never yet imagined or wished for' (*ibid.*, p. 24 and also p. 69). Oakeshott wishes to draw a distinction between 'intimations of what there is to learn' (*ibid.*, p. 22) or 'intimations of excellence and aspirations'(*ibid.*, p. 69) by which the learner is 'animated'(*ibid.*) or 'moved'(*ibid.*, p. 24) on the one hand, and on the other hand, 'the inclinations he brings with him' (*ibid.*, p. 69) or 'the wants he may happen to have acquired' (*ibid.*, p. 24). But he fails to make clear the nature of the distinction between 'intimations of excellence and aspirations' and other inclinations and wants. Although they are different from inclinations to seek immediate satisfaction of physical desires, these intimations are also inclinations/wants/desires. Indeed, education is possible because there are different kinds of inclination and because human beings are willing to exercise 'choice and self-direction' (*ibid.*, p. 43 and Oakeshott, 1967, p. 130) in respect of the impulse to seek immediate, physical gratification, including indulgence in the 'laziness of mankind' (Oakeshott, 1950, p. 551). Accordingly, it can be argued that Oakeshott actually subscribes to a broader conception of inclination than would appear from some of his more provocative pronouncements.

Part of the problem with regard to Oakeshott's conception of inclination relates once more to the rigidity of his epistemological categories. Regrettably, he fails to make sufficiently explicit the connection between the genesis of the languages of human understanding and the intellectual curiosity that it is the business of the school and universities to promote. In *Experience and Its Modes* he says merely that 'science and history and philosophy ... must be thought of as, in origin and impulse, practical' (Oakeshott, 1978, p. 297). Accordingly, for Oakeshott, as noted in the preceding chapter, the genesis of the languages of human understanding is in the world of practical experience. Their genesis lies in human 'wonder' (Oakeshott, 1981, p. 223) at some aspect of the world, a wonder which is joined to a 'curiosity' (*ibid.*) to find out more about it and a 'restlessness' (*ibid.*, p. 221) to satisfy this curiosity. And it is a similar 'urge' (*ibid.*, p. 214), 'impulse' (*ibid.*, pp. 200, 203, 214) or 'inclination' (*ibid.*, p. 203) that lies at the heart of the intellectual curiosity of children and which enables them to make the transition from the world of practical experience to Oakeshott's various worlds of human understanding. With regard to university education, he writes of the pursuit of understanding in terms of excitement, enchantment, and of its propensity to captivate the learner. In 'The Definition of a University', he speaks of students being 'excited' by 'the great enterprises of understanding' (Oakeshott, 1967, p. 138) and he also speaks of the 'enchantment of the pursuit of understanding' (*ibid.*, p. 142) while the term 'captivate' appears in 'The Universities' (Fuller, 1989, p. 126). Education is possible, therefore, because there are different kinds of inclination than the desire to seek immediate satisfaction of physical desires, something of which Oakeshott is well aware.

But what then does he mean by his reference to education as involving the 'discipline of inclination'? The point Oakeshott wants to get at is that where children feel no 'intimations of what there is to learn', these 'intimations' must be engendered in them and come to supervene upon whatever are their occurrent wants, or desires. And even where young people experience 'intimations of what there is to learn', these intimations must submit to 'direction and restraint', that is, to the demands and discipline of formal education. Oakeshott argues that becoming subject to 'conditions of direction and restraint' is in itself an educative experience. The context of learning 'appears not only in what is learned but also in the conditions of direction and restraint which belong to any education' (Oakeshott, 1981, p. 303). How extensive is the compulsion envisaged by Oakeshott in the 'conditions of direction and restraint' that are required in order to secure the 'discipline of inclination'?

Oakeshott's Concepts of Direction and Restraint

In the essays on education we find an elusiveness about what might be involved in the imposition of 'conditions of direction and restraint'. Perhaps this is not surprising because, as has previously been remarked, such conditions could hardly be considered features of a conversation. From his comments in 'The B.B.C' (Oakeshott, 1950, p. 550) where he deplores a possible future situation in which 'ushers' might be employed to 'keep order' as pupils receive instruction through the mass-media, it is clear that for Oakeshott the maintenance of order is a normal part of the teacher's task. In 'The Study of "Politics" in a University', where he first mentions 'conditions of direction and restraint', the tone is uncompromisingly peremptory. 'We learn these things (dates and tables) at school because we are told to learn them ...' and with regard to

> individual talents and aptitudes ... if these show themselves (as they may) the design in school-education is not to allow them to take charge. At school we are, quite properly, not permitted to follow our own inclinations. (Oakeshott, 1981, p. 306).

In this essay, Oakeshott also makes the bold and confident assertion that the school curriculum contains significant elements such as multiplication tables and dates in history that 'must have the qualities of being able to be learned without necessarily being understood, and of not being positively hurtful or nonsensical when learned in this way' (1981, p. 306). What is taught must be learnable, he writes, 'without the point of learning it being evident to the learner' (*ibid.*, p. 316). At school, he argues, learning involves 'borrowing raw material the possible uses of which remain concealed ... . It is learning to speak before one has anything significant to say ... ' (*ibid.*, pp. 305–6). In asserting that pupils shall be *told* what they may or may not do Oakeshott obviously is not offering a very illuminating guide to educational practice. What should happen if the pupils refuse to obey, and even to listen, let alone to attempt to learn?

Closer reading of his essays does indicate somewhat of a retreat from the notion of simply telling pupils what to do. In the essay under consideration he also states that 'what is taught must be capable of being learned without any previous recognition of ignorance' on the part of the pupil' (*ibid.*, p. 306). '(W)ithout any previous recognition of ignorance' is certainly not synonymous with 'without necessarily being understood' or 'without the point of it being evident to the learner'. If we are to bring children to recognise their ignorance, then we must necessarily teach them the point of learning what we are asking them to learn. In 'Learning and Teaching' (Fuller, 1989 first published in 1967), the tone is certainly less authoritarian and Oakeshott shows awareness of methodological considerations not to be found in 'The Study of "Politics" in a University' (Oakeshott, 1981, first published in 1962).[3] Moreover, in 'Learning and Teaching', somewhat surprisingly, he makes no mention of the possible need for compulsion. The activities of the teacher are 'designed to promote' the 'initiation of a pupil into the world of human achievement, or into some part of it' (Fuller, 1989, pp. 46–7). This will require that the teacher introduce his pupils to facts which have 'no immediate practical significance' (*ibid.*, p. 57). By modifying the 'inertness of its component facts' (*ibid.*) the teacher must, however, 'make the information he has to convey more readily learnable' (*ibid.*, p. 58).

This shift in emphasis that is to be found in Oakeshott's essays continues in 'Education: The Engagement and Its Frustration' (Fuller, 1989, first published in 1971) where, unlike in 'The Study of "Politics" in a University', school education is the main focus of his attention. Though the expression 'conditions of direction and restraint' appears twice (Fuller, 1989, pp. 68 and 72), we nonetheless find evidence of an increasingly thoughtful, nuanced, and less authoritarian attitude. Here we read that education 'supervenes' (ibid, p. 68) upon the world

---

[3] It is surprising that his sympathetic commentator R.S. Peters (1974) does not give Oakeshott credit for this awareness.

of childish play and that, '(s)uperimposed' upon this world by the teacher, is a 'considered curriculum of learning to direct and contain the thoughts of the learner' (*ibid.*) Although we find the notions of direction and restraint in the words 'direct', 'contain' (which seems to mean 'restrain' as well as simply 'hold') and 'superimpose', we also find a methodological concern implied in the word 'considered'. Further on in the same essay the following definition appears: 'To teach is to bring it about that, somehow, something of worth intended by a teacher is learned, understood and remembered by a learner' (*ibid.*, p. 70). Reservations that spring to mind on reading the word 'somehow', which would offer a dangerous latitude in respect of method, are somewhat allayed by the elaboration which follows. A list of 20 typical teaching activities, such as hinting, suggesting, coaxing, encouraging, guiding, pointing out, excludes only any method which would 'belie the engagement to impart an understanding' (*ibid.*). Likewise the 14 itemised learning activities such as 'looking, listening' and 'submitting to guidance' are compatible with any activity that does not 'belie the engagement to think and to understand' (*ibid.*). These terms include no reference whatever to directing or restraining or of being subject to these. ('Submitting to guidance' is the closest reference to either.) Elsewhere in this essay, Oakeshott parodies the view of 'progressive' educators in a passage already referred to in Chapter 3. According to this view, education:

> is, and must be, children condemned to a prison-like existence in cell-like classrooms, compelled by threats to follow a sordid, senseless and rigid routine which destroys all individuality, dragooned into learning what they do not and cannot understand because it is remote from their 'interests' ... (Oakeshott, 1989, p. 73).

By these remarks Oakeshott implies that children ought not to be compelled, under threat, to learn. But what about those who do not want to learn or to be in school? Should such young people be compelled by threats to learn?

Unfortunately we seek in vain for an answer in the essays on education, consequently the nature and limits of Oakeshott's 'conditions of direction and restraint' remain unspecified. The degree of such 'direction and restraint' which might be considered compatible with imparting an understanding is open to very wide interpretation. Although it should be stressed that

Oakeshott has not set himself the task of elaborating in close detail a theory of education, nevertheless the repeated notion of 'conditions of direction and restraint' specifies a quality of compulsion that needs to be elucidated. Such elucidation is made even more necessary in view of Oakeshott's conception of education as a conversational encounter. By exploring the treatment of the themes of coercion and consent elsewhere in his work a clearer idea of what he has in mind emerges.

Force and Manipulation

Firstly, the consequences of interpreting direction and restraint or the promiscuous 'somehow' in terms of the use or threatened use of power, force, or coercion must be examined. Oakeshott defines such power or force as:

> the energy a man may intentionally exert to destroy, to manipulate or to overcome the resistance of an object (or of another man considered merely as an object), but in human affairs it stands for the ability to procure with certainty a wished-for response in the conduct of another (Oakeshott, 1975b, pp. 332–3).

Yet, as I explained in Chapter 1, Oakeshott argues that in principle, it is possible, even under the most extreme compulsion, to resist the author of such compulsion, as happens in the case of martyrs. In relations between persons in respect of 'the ability and the disposition of the respondent to perform the wished-for action ... certainty can never be absolute and power can never be irresistible' (*ibid.* p. 333). '(P)ower can never be "total", not even where it is attributed to a so-called "first cause"' (*ibid.*, p. 323). This formal freedom inherent in the nature of human agency, then, sets limits to what we may be made to do against our will by force or by the threat of force. In the educational context, therefore, moral considerations apart, the use or threatened use of physical force alone cannot guarantee learning in a situation where the pupil is absolutely determined to resist it. Where her will is unshakeably set against it, it is impossible to force a pupil to make an effort to understand something, let alone to understand it.

Though the nature of human agency sets limits to the power of a teacher to induce a pupil to learn by coercive means, this power can also be exercised by psychological manipulation. 'What cannot be compelled may yet be procured', writes Oakeshott (Oakeshott, 1949, p. 389) in another context, and at its most extreme such procuring or manipulation can take the form of brain-washing or hypnotism. Yet Oakeshott would want to reject as non-educative the learning that might result from the use of such processes. In so far as they constitute a subversion of the freedom presupposed in the notion of human agency, such processes clearly belie the teacher's 'engagement to impart ... understanding' (Fuller, 1989, p. 70). The use of such methods is manifestly incompatible with extending a young person's capacity to become autonomous, and thereby to exercise 'choice and self-direction in relation to his own impulses and to the world around him' (*ibid.*, p. 43). And it is also incompatible with the nature of education as a conversation.

Transactionalism

Apart from subverting her or his capacity to choose, there are limits, in principle, to the possibility of converting another against her or his will to one's designs. Moreover, in practice, the use of coercion alone is rarely an efficient or expeditious manner of securing the compliance of another to one's wishes. Oakeshott observes that as a matter of expediency it may be necessary to acknowledge the 'subjectivity of the other self' (Oakeshott, 1981, p. 209) in terms of an alliance of convenience. In this situation, others are recognized only as a means to our ends in an alliance in which moral considerations of right, duty, and obligation have no place. Failure to make this '*de facto* admission of the subjectivity' (*ibid.*) of the other person is not a moral failure but it may frustrate the successful achievement of our purposes. These alliances bear on all those transactions between people for the reciprocal satisfaction of wants, most conspicuously between individuals as buyers and sellers of goods or services, and most dramatically in the *quid pro quo* in the form of inducements or bribes. Relationship between people as instruments of one another's respective wants is what Oakeshott calls 'transactional association' (Oakeshott, 1983a, p. 121, 1975a, p. 112). It is 'relationship in terms of power' in as far as it is concerned solely with the relationship of persons to one another as 'seekers of substantive satisfactions' (Oakeshott, 1983a, pp. 121–2). This mode of human association can also take the form of those small acts of mutual accommodation whereby, for example, an individual desists from playing her radio early in the morning and her neighbour refrains from doing so late at night. In politics, of course, these accommodations are what is known as maintaining the balance of power, the phrase itself is an acknowledgement of the status of the relationship as being very literally 'in terms of power' (*ibid.*).

The conduct by teachers or school authorities of relationships with pupils in transactional or instrumental terms is most pronounced where pupils are offered inducements for successfully completing learning tasks, either of a short term nature such as a prize or of a longer term nature such as the possibility of getting a sought-after place at university. Inducements to learn can also take more subtle forms such as where teachers tell their pupils that success at learning will give pleasure to their parents. Used as instruments of power or expediency to get pupils to learn, the offer of inducements and the negotiation of accommodations of a transactional nature may conduce to successful learning. As with the use of threats, use of inducements is not in itself inimical to the acquisition of understanding, although it is clearly at odds with the notion of education as initiation into activities of an intrinsically valuable nature. In so far as teaching is an activity qualified by considerations of morality, the teacher's task cannot be conceived solely in terms of expediency. Teaching, as Oakeshott writes, is a 'moral transaction' (Fuller, 1989, p. 63). The task of the teacher is not simply to impose the most expeditious manner of promoting learning, she must also take into account the moral status of any conditions that she imposes. Accordingly any 'conditions of direction and restraint' must be morally justifiable if they are to be compatible with teaching of a genuinely educative character.

Education as a Moral Endeavour

This crucial point is also intimated in Oakeshott's writings. For example, he condemns any arrangement that would have 'persuasion and physical intervention (take) the place of rules of conduct' (Fuller, 1989, p. 73). In other words, as they involve 'neither more nor less than the beliefs of the respondent about the consequences to himself of compliance or non-compliance with the demand' (Oakeshott, 1975b, p. 333), transactional considerations (which is what is meant by 'persuasion' in the foregoing) and the use of coercion (physical intervention) do not enjoy the status of moral demands. (This is not to imply that the use of such tactics has no moral significance – the use of these tactics in teaching can be subjected to moral appraisal and criticism.) To acquire moral status in themselves, the demands of the teacher must be subject to non-instrumental or moral qualifications. And where these demands, together with the 'conditions of direction and restraint' that they may entail, are moralised we introduce the notions of authority and obligation, rights and duties.

Unfortunately Oakeshott does not address himself to a consideration of the notions of authority, obligation and consent within the teacher-pupil relationship and again it must be stated that he never set himself the task of elaborating a comprehensive theory of this relationship. It is probably fair to conclude that Oakeshott is aware that there are practical and moral limits to the degree of compulsion compatible with the 'discipline of inclination'. He must, however, be criticised for his elusiveness about the degree of constraint compatible with the teacher-pupil relationship, as well as the manner in which this constraint may be imposed. In seeking to exonerate Oakeshott from charges of extreme authoritarianism, we must acknowledge that the teacher-pupil relationship sometimes assumes an unnecessarily stark quality in his writings. Though he characterises school pupils as recognising and declaring themselves 'as learners' (Fuller, 1989, p. 24), Oakeshott is still reluctant to recognise young people as moral agents in their own right with a stake in their own education who are both willing to learn and also capable of understanding why they are being asked to do so. This reluctance is also consistent with Oakeshott's general undervaluing of the child's experience and insensitivity to the significance of the present. After all, educational experiences are not mere metaphorical 'raw material' (Oakeshott, 1981, p. 305). Unless children understand the point of what they are doing or why they are doing it, unless a task is in some way a live one for them, then we are talking of a harsh version of schooling rather than of education.

Oakeshott is passionately concerned that the experience of education should be for young people an *entrée* to a world of 'wonder and delight' (Oakeshott, 1989, p. 40).[4] If, however, it took the form advocated in some of his extreme statements, education could seem to some young people a repressive and confusing imposition to which they are subjected by an alien and alienating school system.

This leads to another aspect of his pedagogy namely, the actual dynamics of teaching and learning and this will be the subject of the next chapter.

---

[4] In a letter in response to an early piece on his work (Williams, 1983), Oakeshott writes most eloquently and persuasively of his concern that young people should enjoy the *entrée* to the world of 'wonder and delight' that he and his school contemporaries (of all social classes) enjoyed. See Oakeshott (1983b) Photocopy of letter from Oakeshott to Kevin Williams, library-2.lse.ac.uk /archives/handlists/Oakeshott/m.html. Accessed 11 March 2007.

Chapter Nine

The Dynamics of Teaching and Learning

How then does Oakeshott envisage teaching and learning occurring? For all that it is rich and suggestive, his pedagogy contains many loose ends and puzzling elements of which some, as shall emerge, have been noted by others. Somewhat surprisingly, though, in an excellent essay drawing attention to the positive features of Oakeshott's conception of teaching, Anthony O'Hear does not refer to any problems associated with it (O'Hear, 2005, pp. 44–8). I hope that in reaching a fuller understanding of Oakeshott's pedagogy, an enhanced under-standing of the concepts of teaching and of learning them-selves will be reached. Before exploring these concepts, Oakeshott's analysis of the nature of skills has to be teased out because his account of the activities of teaching and learning is set in the context of his analysis of the nature of skills or of the activity of knowing. Obviously theory of knowledge and the-ory of learning are intimately related because, as Ryle explains, knowing is the 'achievement' word which corre-sponds to the 'task' word learning (Ryle, 1973a, pp. 143–7). Like Ryle (*ibid.*, p. 299), Oakeshott puts great emphasis on the relationship between epistemology and theory of learning. The significance of this relationship is conveyed in his obser-vation that what he has to say about the nature of skills 'springs from reflecting upon teaching and learning rather than from reflecting upon the nature of knowledge' (Fuller, 1989 p. 57).

As this chapter involves some particularly fine-grained exe-gesis of Oakeshott's work, readers may find helpful some signposts to the various sections. Firstly, the language/litera-ture distinction will have to be revisited once more in order to demonstrate the inadequacy of knowledge of rules (or, in

Oakeshott's term 'technical knowledge') *alone* in the actual exercise of a skill. Facility or fluency in the exercise of a skill will be seen to require what he calls 'practical knowledge'. The nature of this practical knowledge will be explored, together with the notion of a personal style or idiom characteristic of performers who are particularly accomplished in their exercise of a skill. Next follows Oakeshott's account of the activities of teaching and learning and this is shown to derive from the distinction between kinds of knowledge. This is reflected in the distinction between two kinds of teaching, namely, instructing and imparting. Imparting means the communication of judgement. Oakeshott envisages the imparting of judgement as taking place according to an apprenticeship model but, in his account of this model, crucial omissions are identified.

First then some of the fruits of Oakeshott's reflections on the nature of knowledge require examination.

The Language/Literature Distinction Revisited

Crucial to his analysis is a distinction between the knowledge of an activity that can be put into words, or articulate knowledge, and 'complete'(Oakeshott, 1981, p. 19, fn. 1), 'concrete' (*ibid.*, pp. 24, 26, 29), or 'genuine' (*ibid.*, p. 33) knowledge that is manifested in the practice of the activity itself (*ibid.*, pp. 19–33). Oakeshott's language/literature distinction is again relevant to this issue so it needs to be rehearsed briefly before developing and applying it in this context. Every human skill or ability, from mowing the lawn and swimming to the activities of the scientist and historian, can be understood as a metaphorical language of human achievement, so every skill can also be said to offer a literature. The literature consists in what might be called the propositional ingredient of knowledge—what, in 'Learning and Teaching', Oakeshott calls '"information"' (Fuller, 1989, p. 51). Theoretical activities, as already noted, which are propositional of their nature, offer a literature that consists of the results of the relevant enquiries. This literature consists of the detachable propositions or items of information that result from enquiries in, for example, science or history. Accordingly, it would include formulae in science or mathematics or dates in history, in short, whatever facts are authoritatively established as a result of enquiries conducted in the appropriate disciplinary languages.

Practical activities such as swimming or cabinet-making do not, of course, offer a literature in this sense. The purpose of these activities is to realise certain practical goals and not to produce propositions. Yet every skill, whether of a practical or theoretical nature, is capable in principle of yielding its own 'technical literature' (Oakeshott, 1981, p. 319). The term 'technical literature', which arose in Chapter 5, embraces what he previously called 'technical knowledge' or 'knowledge of technique' (*ibid.*, p. 7) and refers to the rules that govern skills. 'Technical knowledge' in this sense might be better described as disjunctive knowledge since this expression draws attention to the character of such knowledge as disjoined from knowledge in use (see Looker, 1965, pp. 304–6).

Care must be exercised not to confuse disjunctive knowledge, that is, the formulated rules that inform an activity and theoretical or propositional knowledge. The latter derives from theoretical enquiries and is, of its very nature, propositional. Confusion between the two concepts is to be found in R.J. Looker's essay on Oakeshott, where Looker speaks of a scientific hypothesis as 'technical knowledge' (*ibid.*). A scientific hypothesis is an example of theoretical or propositional knowledge and not of disjunctive knowledge. In fairness to Looker, though, Oakeshott might at times be understood as wishing to reduce the status of hyopothesis in science to that of 'technical knowledge' (see Oakeshott, 1981, pp. 99; Fuller, 1989, pp. 142–4; and Watkins, 1952, pp. 334–5).

In his discussion of 'technical' or disjunctive knowledge Oakeshott stresses that knowledge of rules alone does not enable an individual to practise a skill. He further observes that such knowledge is most conspicuously inadequate in the exercise of those abilities which have human beings as 'their plastic material, arts such as medicine, industrial management, diplomacy ... the art of military command ... (or) political activity' (Oakeshott, 1981, p. 9). And to these might be added the art of teaching. As generalisations retrospectively derived from prior performances, rules are incapable of telling an individual what to do in any particular situation; rules then are 'afterthoughts, not categorical imperatives' (Fuller, 1989, p. 56). In the exercise of any skill, rules must be applied, and there is always a gap between propositional knowledge of rules and the ability to apply them. Moreover, even where individuals can apply the rules, they are not considered to possess a skill unless they can practise it in a way not specified by the rules. Rules, writes Oakeshott, 'require interpretation in respect of persons and circumstances' (*ibid.*, p. 55). Knowledge of child psychology or even of useful practical injunctions will not in itself enable a student teacher to control a rowdy class and hence to teach the children anything. Furthermore, to be a teacher, the student must be able to apply her knowledge to an indefinite number of situations which could not, in principle, be exhaustively provided for in the rules. No cumulative number of discrete actions or items of information makes up a skill. The need to be able to adapt one's competence to an indefinite variety of tasks means that there is always a gap between the ability to perform a finite number of operations and the possession of a skill. The nature of a skill is such that it requires us to be able to advance beyond instructions and previously performed tasks and to adapt what we have learned to new situations.

Practical Knowledge

Disjunctive knowledge alone, therefore, cannot in itself constitute what Oakeshott calls 'complete', 'concrete', or 'genuine' knowledge. By these terms is meant the actual ability to exercise a skill through mastery of its language as well as its literature. To possess such knowledge an individual must also come to acquire what Oakeshott calls 'practical' or 'traditional' knowledge (Oakeshott, 1981, p. 8). To refer to this aspect of knowledge he also uses the terms '"know-how"' (*ibid.*, p. 9), 'taste' (*ibid.*, p.10), and 'connoisseurship' (*ibid.*, pp. 10, 11, 24) — which is also called 'the connoisseurship of knowing how and when to apply [rules]' (*ibid.*, p. 103). 'Judgement' is the term favoured in 'Learning and Teaching', but he also uses 'knowing how' a few times and 'connoisseurship' (see Fuller, 1989, pp. 51–60).

Practical knowledge' is the ability to realise performances not specified in previously formulated rules. 'Technical knowledge' becomes 'practical knowledge' when a person can exercise a skill without consciously adverting to the rules which govern it or when, in Pascal's words, such rules are observed '*tacitement, naturellement et sans art*' (Oakeshott, 1981,

p. 20). This occurs where, for example, a person who has learned to swim or to drive a motor car can practise these skills without being overtly and concurrently conscious of which movements she is making or is next about to make. Throughout Oakeshott's writings we find resistance to 'making conduct self-conscious' (*ibid.*) because self-consciousness is at odds with genuine facility in the exercise of a skill (*ibid.* and also pp. 35, 66, 75, 76, and Fuller, 1989, pp.118–9). The quality of performance which Oakeshott has in mind is what might be called fluency, a quality which can be applied to facility in metaphorical as well as actual languages. Fluency is an attribute of skilled performances where there is a possibility of self-conscious adherence to rules but where rules are no longer consciously applied.

The belief that 'practical knowledge' is can be fully converted into propositions regarding ends to be pursued and rules to be followed to achieve these ends is what Oakeshott calls 'rationalism' (Oakeshott, 1981, pp. 11–13). The critical debate regarding what he understands by rationalism in this context raises one of the puzzling elements in his theory of teaching and learning. For example, in his review of *Rationalism in Politics*, Julian H. Franklin identifies the following ambiguity in Oakeshott's characterisation of the defect of rationalism (Franklin, 1963, p. 812–3). Rather than the belief that 'practical knowledge' can be fully formulated as 'technical knowledge', at times Oakeshott appears to associate with rationalism a manifestly bizarre and silly refusal to admit that practical experience is necessary in order to acquire skills. Even if the real target of Oakeshott's criticism is the rationalist's belief regarding the reducibility of all knowledge to propositions, Bernard Crick reasonably asks whether any reputable thinker ever thought that such 'technical knowledge' constituted the whole of knowledge (Crick, 1963, p. 71). Oddly enough, Franklin himself seems to defend a version of this view, arguing that a rationalist might well show that the 'objective content' of a skill could 'in principle at least, be reflectively analysed into formal rules and maxims' (Franklin, 1963, p. 813).

Franklin's rationalist is right in so far as any exercise of a skill provides further rules that can be assumed to the whole body of rules relating to that skill. At a certain point these rules must become confusingly prolix and even then they will not specify what a person should do in an indeterminate future situation. As just noted, it is impossible to devise in advance a comprehensive set of strategies that can prescribe for every future performance. The practice of an activity always goes beyond even the most exhaustive body of precepts. What Peter Winch calls the 'slippery slope' (Winch, 1980, p. 55) of infinite regress awaits anyone who tries to convert executive or 'practical knowledge' (the knowledge required actually to exercise a skill) into disjunctive or 'technical' knowledge (propositions regarding how to exercise the skill).

The irony is that the spirit of monitoring and measuring that pervades the discourse of educational policy makers is infused by this kind of rationalistic spirit. Chapter 3 drew attention to the tendency of our times to try to convert the open learning that traditionally characterised university studies into a closed system with everything as tightly prescribed as moves in chess (see Standish, 2005, pp. 54–5). Requiring rigid specification of aims, objectives, and outcomes with a regime of assessment based on these, everything is based on the 'fact that what teachers and learners are required to do will be fully specified' (*ibid.*). A similar regime was also applied to vocational training by the bureaucrats who devised NVQ performance criteria in the United Kingdom (see Wolf, pp. 72–9) mentioned in Chapter 6.

The Tacit Dimension

Significantly, Franklin uses the term 'objective' when speaking of that component of knowledge that can be expressed in the form of propositions. This characterisation points to the existence of a more elusive subjective, personal, or what Oakeshott calls a 'tacit', or 'implicit' component of knowledge (Fuller, 1989, pp. 53–4). The term 'tacit' appears in the previously quoted remark of Pascal's where a skilled performance is described as one in which rules are observed '*tacitement, naturellement et sans art*'. Here though Oakeshott is beginning to go beyond even the notion of fluency and into the area of the personal 'idiom' (*ibid.*, pp. 56–61) peculiar to accomplished practitioners of a skill or what he called earlier 'style', 'artistry' and 'insight' (Oakeshott, 1981, p. 11). He also refers to 'judgement' as 'the tacit or implicit component of knowledge' (Fuller, 1989, pp. 53–5). This could be the judgement of an historian or of a detective that the truth does not lie in the direction in which a conventional reading of the historical or forensic evidence might indicate. It could also be the judgement of a military general or of a chess player that leads her or him to use a ploy that proves successful but which, in terms of conventional strategy in war or at chess, is unorthodox. Oakeshott's notion of personal style also embraces the notions of feeling for, and identification with, an activity that may come to partner mere competence or facility in the practice of the skill in question. This sensitivity to the conjunction of knowing and feeling in the accomplished exercise of a skill is expressed in the contrast that he draws between the technique of military command which, during wartime, was readily acquired by the intelligent civilian and the knowledge that the regular officer possessed and which derived from an education 'in the feelings and emotions as well as the practices of his profession' (Oakeshott, 1981, p. 34, fn. 2). Elsewhere this aspect of personal 'style' and 'judgement' is associated with possession of the 'intellectual virtues' and with 'the ability to feel and to think' (Fuller, 1989, pp. 60–1).

There appears to be an inadequacy in Oakeshott's notion of personal style and this leads him in places to conflate the possession of flair and insight in the exercise of a skill with mere competence at it (see Duncan, 1963, pp. 114–5). Such inadequacy in conceptualisation reflects the rather undiscriminating nature of Oakeshott's conceptual repertoire or the 'over-economy of concepts' that sometimes characterises his work (Auspitz, 1976, p. 266) and which has already been referred to in previous chapters. The inadequacy in question, one of several puzzling elements in his theory, derives from Oakeshott's failure to distinguish between the different senses in which he uses the term 'judgement' (see Peters, 1974, pp. 443–9). Oakeshott speaks of judgement with regard to the use of any concept that is a feature of all language acquisition. It is the judgement involved in making any discrimination whatever among phenomena and which he came to call recognition or identification (see Oakeshott, 1975a, pp. 3–6). In the context that concerns us here judgement is used to refer both to the judgement necessary to exercise a skill in non-routine situations, the literal paradigm of which is the judgement exercised by a judge in a court of law, and also to the judgement that is necessary in the particularly accomplished exercise of a skill. Although the terms of 'idiom' and 'style' point to the distinction between flair and mere competence, Oakeshott never succeeds in making it sufficiently explicit. The conceptual borders between the two are blurred but the distinction between the two can be of great importance in many spheres. Teacher educators, for example, commonly distinguish between students who show flair and those who are merely competent in their teaching.

But beyond even the notion of flair lie the notions of the creative, the innovative, and the original. Oakeshott fails to address himself directly to an exploration of these concepts and this omission in his work has prompted even such a sympathetic commentator as J.W.N. Watkins to speak of the 'unduly restrictive theory of imagination' (Watkins, 1952, p. 334) that leads Oakeshott to stress tradition to the detriment of the novel. Watkins is possibly too severe on Oakeshott here. This is because what Oakeshott, quite reasonably, wants to emphasize is that the innovative, creative, novel, and original can emerge only from within the traditions of a practice. If I am right in my reading of what is implied in Oakeshott's work regarding creativity (see Oakeshott, 1981, pp. 102–3; and Fuller, 1989, pp. 142–6), he believes that innovation can make sense only in terms of some recognised practice. The genius of Joyce, Stravinsky, or Picasso, for example, was manifested, not in their introducing alien and incomprehensible innovation, but rather in their moulding existing traditions in an original and creative manner.

An account of the relationship between tradition and creativity that seems to me to be consistent with the spirit of Oakeshott's writing is given by Jay Parini in his observation on the work of Seamus Heaney (Parini, 2005). In Heaney's work are found echoes of Anglo-Saxon poetry, as well as of the work of Gerard Manley Hopkins, Yeats and Robert Frost (*ibid.*, p. 66). But the 'mature voice of Heaney'

> has swallowed up, and digested, these precursors; but they remain part of him, ingredients of his own voice. His originality — like the originality of all great artists — is a product of the way he has been able to use what went before him, to absorb and extend a particular tradition, making himself part of it. (*ibid.*, p. 67)[1]

---

[1]   There is a further interesting dimension to Parini's makes comments because they arise in a discussion of the art of teaching where the author goes on to

Within any practice there are limits to what we are prepared to count as innovation and beyond these limits lie the eccentric and the incomprehensible. Moreover, in seeking a solution to a problem that is genuinely novel and without precedent, we must have recourse to the resources of the activity or the practice that provided the context in which the problem has arisen. It is only through our familiarity with the resources of the practice in question that we can find solutions. But in any activity, in science, in politics or in architecture, for example, it takes a person of genius to find them.

At this point it is necessary to explore how Oakeshott envisages knowledge being acquired

Instruction

The distinction between disjunctive/articulate knowledge or information and practical/executive knowledge or judgement is reflected in a further distinction between two kinds of teaching, namely, instruction and imparting. The concept instruction needs therefore closer examination. Instruction is teaching 'in the simplest meanings' of the words, and it constitutes only the 'meanest part of education in an activity' (Oakeshott, 1981, pp. 11, 92). Involving the communication of inert facts as items of information and the provision of directives relating to the performance of particular actions, it is that aspect of teaching to which Ryle applies the term 'teaching *that*' (Ryle, 1973b, p. 110). What Oakeshott seems to have in mind is what Ryle, in the same collection of essays in which 'Learning and Teaching' first appeared, calls drilling (*ibid.*, p. 109). Drilling is a useful term because it communicates the notion of teaching both verbal and non-verbal routines of a mechanical nature. Just as army recruits are drilled in parade ground exercises, pupils are drilled (rather than instructed) in such routines as reciting the multiplication tables and spellings.

As instruction is limited to telling that something is the case or that something should be done, there are only very few educational tasks for which such teaching is appropriate. Besides the alphabet, spelling, tables, and perhaps dates in history and geographical names, there is little in the school curriculum

make a comparison between what Heaney has done and what teachers have to do in learning to find their own pedagogic voices.

that can be communicated as simple propositions. Even where the term had some currency, in the expression 'religious instruction', it normally referred to the teaching of principles rather than to the promotion of a mechanical knowledge of catechism. Little significance can be attached to the ability merely to recite doctrine because the mere recitation of propositions without some understanding of the meaning of what one is saying is a fairly trivial achievement. Oakeshott shows this awareness by saying that the teacher, as instructor, must exercise his pupils in the information so that it:

> may be recognized in forms other than those in which it was first acquired, and may be recollected on all the occasions when it is relevant. That is, the instructor has not only to hear his pupils recite the Catechism, the Highway Code, the Capes and Bays, the eight-times multiplication table and the Kings of England, but he has also to see that they can answer questions in which this information is properly used. (Fuller, 1989, p. 59)

Imparting and the Teaching of Judgement

The notion of making appropriate use of information leads very quickly into the kind of teaching to which Oakeshott applies the term 'imparting' rather than instruction. Rather than the communication of facts, he understands imparting as the communication of judgement. What does he have to say about the imparting of judgement? In the first of two useful negative observations, Oakeshott reminds us that there is no abstract aptitude called 'judgement' which can be acquired apart from the context of its exercise in the performance of particular tasks (*ibid.*, pp. 56–7, 59–62). As it makes no sense to speak of teaching judgement in the abstract, teaching judgement involves therefore the teaching of specific skills. The point seems lost on those policy makers who wish young people to be equipped with such attributes as critical thinking and flexibility acquired in a decontextualised way. Secondly, he rejects the idea that to teach a skill we must first convert 'our knowledge of it into a set of propositions . . . and that in order to learn an activity we must begin with such propositions' (Oakeshott, 1981, p. 91). Again this is puzzling because it is hard to believe that anyone would think that, in order to learn a skill, we must begin by learning propositions about it. But here he is no doubt thinking less of a theory of learning and more of a tendency to conceive of teaching and learning as being of this propositional nature. (Certainly it was the tendency in the old fashioned grammar book method of teaching foreign languages.) Although formulated rules have a 'pedagogic value' (*ibid.*, p. 92), this does not mean that a skill can be taught by instruction in any determinate number of propositions or facts; learning judgement cannot be reduced to the acquisition of 'technical knowledge'.

With regard to the teaching of judgement/practical knowledge we find a definite shift over time in Oakeshott's attitude towards the matter. In *Rationalism in Politics* he writes that 'in the simplest meanings of these words ... practical knowledge can neither be taught nor learned, but only imparted and acquired' (*ibid.*, p. 11). But later, in 'Learning and Teaching', he writes that '"judgement" may be *taught*; and it belongs to the deliberate enterprise of the teacher to teach it' (emphasis Oakeshott's) (Fuller, 1989, p. 60). But the account of the manner in which this 'deliberate enterprise' is managed requires much further elaboration in Oakeshott's theory. Judgement, argues Oakeshott, is acquired by the learner's 'imitating the example' provided by the teacher's performances in 'a concrete situation' (*ibid.*, pp. 60–2 for this recurrent phrase). It must, he writes:

> be imparted obliquely in the course of instruction ... It is implanted unobtrusively in the manner in which information is conveyed, in a tone of voice, in the gesture which accompanies instruction, in asides and oblique utterances, and by example. (*ibid.*, pp. 60–1)

Teaching by example is very important in Oakeshott's pedagogy and he condemns those who would disparage it 'as an inferior sort of teaching' that generates 'inflexible knowledge because the rules of what is known remain concealed . . .' (Fuller, 1989, pp. 61–2). By contrast, observing an exemplar at work, emancipates 'the pupil from the half-utterances of rules by making him aware of a concrete situation' (*ibid.* p. 62). He goes on to recall his own experience of learning from the example of his gymnastics instructor in the army. What he owed to him was not due to 'anything he ever said but because he was a man of patience, accuracy, economy, elegance and style' (*ibid.*). There is a strikingly similar account of a positive response to army training by Jay Parini in his book entitled *The Art of Teaching* (Parini, 2005) mentioned earlier. Parini refers to Kenneth Dover, his teacher at the University of St. Andrews who, like Oakeshott, was impressed by the example of good teaching that he experienced in his army days. In the army, writes Dover, 'a remarkable amount of careful thought had gone into methods of instruction and training' (quoted in Parini, 2005, p. 62). The 'clarity of exposition' of 'a disappointingly large number of university lecturers' he remarks 'fell far short of the standard of the standard expected in gunnery schools' (*ibid.*).

Oakeshott's high valuation of the place of example in teaching may be considered rather *passé* but it is also shared by George Steiner who makes some pertinent comments about it. Steiner envisages the teacher as exemplar of the skill to be learned and he refers to this kind of teaching as 'enactment'; it is 'ostensible' because it shows' the learner what is to be learned. In Latin *dicere* meant to show and later came to mean 'to show by saying'. The Middle English words token and techen imply '"that which shows"' and in German *deuten*, to 'point to' is intimately linked to the word *bedeuten*, 'to mean' (Steiner, 2003, p. 4). Yet for all that imitating the example of a teacher may be a very good way of learning judgement, it is not, as will become clear, the only way to do so and the teaching involved need not be as oblique and arcane as Oakeshott suggests.

Oakeshott's Model of Apprenticeship

Part of the difficulty with Oakeshott's account of the teaching of judgement lies in the ambiguous manner in which the term is used. As already explained, there are two kinds of judgement relevant to the acquisition of skills. In the first place, judgement can refer to the competent exercise of a skill in non-routine situations and, secondly, it can refer to the style or idiom peculiar to the particularly accomplished skilled practitioner of a skill. The essential thesis of Oakeshott's pedagogic theory is that the acquisition of judgement of both kinds involves the learner's following the example of a teacher. What he proposes therefore is an apprenticeship model of learning whereby the learner works 'alongside the master' (Oakeshott, 1981, p. 33). The master provides him with an 'opportunity not only to learn the rules, but to acquire also a direct knowledge of how he sets about his business (and, among other things, a knowledge of how and when to apply the rules)' (*ibid.*, p. 92).

This model of learning next needs to be applied to acquiring a skill. On this matter Peters points to a distinction, which is ignored by Oakeshott, between different kinds of skill (Peters, 1974, pp. 447–9). This is a distinction between skills such as typing, driving, or swimming which have a simple, specifiable goal, and those such as teaching, social work, historical research or wood carving which have more complex goals where the notion of success is less definable. It is manifestly at odds with common sense to argue that the judgement required in the exercise of a skill with a determinate goal can be acquired only through apprenticeship to someone proficient in the practice of that skill. For example, people can and do learn to type, to service their motor cars or to swim by the trial and error method of doing it themselves without the mediation of instructors, although they may well have recourse to the 'technical knowledge' inscribed in books and manuals. They will probably learn more quickly and more efficiently with the help of a teacher but the presence of a teacher cannot be said to be a condition necessary to learning such skills. (This, of course, is not to deny that, without such apprenticeship, learners are likely to make serious mistakes.)

In acquiring more complex skills such as teaching, diplomacy or medicine, the opportunity to observe and imitate the practice of skilled performers is obviously desirable and conducive to effective and economical learning. But it cannot be shown that these aspects of apprenticeship are a condition necessary to the acquisition of such skills. However undesirable it may be in practice, there is no reason in principle why, once she has some grasp of what is required, a person cannot learn even such complex skills as these without recourse to the model performances of others. In fairness to Oakeshott, it must be said that he is not unaware that people can teach themselves even complex skills. In 'The Definition of a University', for example, he rejects 'the prejudice which attributes all learning to teaching – especially in a university, where to be a pupil and to be taught is not at all the only path to learning' (Oakeshott, 1967, p. 132 and see also Fuller, 1989, p. 44). The possibility of self-teaching is also suggested in the observation derived from Aristotle that 'we come to penetrate an idiom of activity in no other way than by practising the activity; for it is only in the practice of an activity that we can acquire the knowledge of how to practise it' (Oakeshott 1981, p. 101). Strangely enough, in this passage there is no reference whatever to the teacher's role in providing a model for the learner to imitate. Here too, Oakeshott mentions the importance of the notion of practice in learning, but unfortunately he fails to elaborate on the crucial role that this practice has in the learning of a skill (see Peters, 1974, p. 446).

With regard to judgement in the sense of a personal style or idiom, Oakeshott seems to confuse the activity of detecting the style peculiar to a skilled performer with that of acquiring such a style for oneself (*ibid.*, p. 448). In neither case is the actual personal experience of 'working alongside the master' in principle necessary. Though Oakeshott would probably concede this, the point is not clear from his writings. In the absence of a teacher, a learner may very well learn to detect the idiosyncratic style of a historian or a philosopher by reading her books, or learn to identify the personal style of a cabinet-maker by examining work she has done, or she may learn to identify the style of golf stroke peculiar to a particular player through watching him on television. Subsequently, without the personal intervention of the learning model, by assiduous practice, the neophyte may come to incorporate something of the other's style into her own performance. Once more though this is puzzling because Oakeshott would hardly approve of too much mimetic, of too much assimilation of another person's style. Such imitativeness would be inconsistent with the proper insistence in his conception of education on 'enabling the pupil to make the most or the best of himself' (Fuller, 1989, p. 47).

Defects in Oakeshott's Model of Apprenticeship

As characterised by Oakeshott, therefore, the apprenticeship model in accordance with which judgement is imparted and acquired is incomplete. In his anxiety to stress the personal nature of teaching on the apprenticeship model, he neglects essential features in the mechanics of the engagement. Most puzzling of all is Oakeshott's attribution to the teacher of a strangely passive role. What he seems to have in mind is a model of apprenticeship learning based on the university practice of medieval times whereby students were admitted merely as spectators to the great debates between Masters and

Doctors. In *Rationalism in Politics*, medieval undergraduates are described as 'spectator-learners of a mystery' (Oakeshott, 1981, p. 312) and in 'The Definition of a University', he refers to contemporary students as 'spectators at performances' (Oakeshott, 1967 p. 139). But the *disputatio* is not a teaching situation. In the *disputatio*, the role of the disputants is primarily polemical rather than pedagogic and, consequently, they exercise no direct pedagogic function in respect of the student spectators. Accordingly, the relationship between students and disputants is not in fact an apprenticeship relationship at all. In Oakeshott's model of the apprenticeship situation, therefore, the idea of supervised initiation into a skill of a learner by a teacher is not referred to. His version of apprenticeship would appear to accommodate only the attenuated notion of a learner imitating the teacher's example.

Wishing to resist the reduction of teaching skills to instruction in propositions, Oakeshott neglects that feature of apprenticeship whereby the learner gets a chance to practise a skill under the critical direction of a teacher proficient both at the activity and at initiating others into it. Judgement, which is made manifest as knowledge only in practice, is also best learned through gradual supervised practice. In his resistance to the idea that the teaching of skills can be reduced to instruction in propositions, it could reasonably be argued that the notion of supervised practice is assumed in Oakeshott's theory of learning. The observation just quoted that 'we come to penetrate an idiom of activity in no other way than by practising the activity; for it is only in the practice of an activity that we can acquire the knowledge of how to practise it' (Oakeshott, 1981, p. 101) is consistent with such a theory. But Oakeshott fails to make this explicit and his theory of apprenticeship is unfortunately therefore defective in this crucial respect.

In fairness, Oakeshott never set himself the task of providing a comprehensive pedagogy, that is, a theory of learning and of apprenticeship. Moreover, in his discussion of the teacher's role, he assigns to the teacher a very active pedagogic office that goes a long way to compensate for deficiencies in his concept of the master in the apprenticeship situation. Perhaps it is this that prompts G. F. Kneller to suggest that Oakeshott's main contribution to philosophy of education lies in the area of teaching and learning (Kneller, 1984, p. 227). In

'Education: The Engagement and its Frustration', Oakeshott points explicitly to those features of teaching and learning of which he fails to take due cognisance in his comments on apprenticeship and in his analysis of the concept of 'imparting'. In the previous chapter, the wide range of activities associated with teaching and learning was noted. In place of the oblique activity of imparting, teaching is now identified with some 20 activities, including 'urging, coaxing, encouraging, guiding, pointing out, . . . demonstrating, exercising, testing, examining, criticizing, correcting, tutoring, drilling' (Fuller, 1989, p. 70). And learning is seen to consist, *inter alia*, in 'submitting to guidance . . . asking questions, discussing, experimenting, practising ... and so on' (*ibid.*). Significantly, this more enriched understanding of the dynamic of the pedagogic engagement is to be found when he is writing of the teacher/pupil relationship in the school context. It is worth noting that this understanding emerges when his writing is unencumbered by his tendency to work with the sharply contrasting categories of instruction and imparting represented in an oppositional or either/or way. As pointed out in the previous chapter Oakeshott's thinking tends to be more subtle than it can appear from his more explicit theorising. At times his theorising can come across as tendentious and more like a party manifesto than the expression of a considered view. So when he does reflect directly on teacher/pupil relationship without reference to his over-sharp distinctions he provides a much richer pedagogy. At heart of this pedagogy is a personal relationship between a teacher and a learner.[2]

---

[2]   Oakeshott's view also reflected in George Steiner's *Lessons of the Masters* (2003). This volume has much to say on teaching that is reminiscent of Oakeshott's treatment of the subject. I am struck by the openness shown by Steiner towards the possibilities of the interactivity offered by electronic texts (pp. 32–3, 180–1), a development that was not available in Oakeshott's lifetime. But for all the potential of elearning, Steiner gives priority to the 'ideal of lived truth' that is embodied in 'orality, of face-to-face address and response' (*ibid.*, p. 8). In the concentration camps, he writes, some rabbis and Talmudic scholars were known as '"living books"' (*ibid.*, p. 32) whose memories offered texts of consolation to other inmates. By contrast the 'written word does not listen to its reader. It takes no account of his questions and objections' (*ibid.*). He reports a former student writing of the lessons given by French philosopher, Alain. In his classes, he writes,'"We were not attending an exposition of the ideas of Plato and Descartes ...we were in their presence. Without intermediaries"' (Steiner, 2003, p. 106). A similar impulse animates Oakeshott's pedagogy.

This leads to another important pedagogical question with regard to Oakeshott's philosophy. His philosophy of learning does allow for a positive interaction between tradition and creativity, but the thorny question of the relationship between tradition, autonomy and critique in the moral and political spheres needs next to be considered.

Chapter Ten

Conformity and Dissent in Teaching and Learning

How then does Oakeshott conceive of the relationship in the moral sphere between tradition on the one hand and autonomy and critique on the other? Several critics (Kneller, 1984, pp. 226; Pitkin, 1974, pp. 280–4; 249; Wood, 1959, pp. 661–2; Benn and Peters, 1959, pp. 317–8) are convinced that Oakeshott subscribes to a conception of tradition that excludes the possibility of critical reflection on prevailing traditions of moral and political conduct. As has been noted in chapter 5, Fred Inglis implies that education for Oakeshott involves a 'process of socialization into a given intellectual identity' (Inglis, 1975a, p. 41 and p. 47, note 15). The perception of Oakeshott as promoting an uncritical appropriation of tradition is shared by others. For example, John Searle, who is an erudite, measured and quite sympathetic commentator, takes Oakeshott to task for his neglect of 'the critical purpose of education' and suggests that his ideal of an educated person 'looks a lot like the ideal of a First Class Honours BA in Classics or History' from Oxford of the 1950s (Searle, 1990, p. 41). This kind of person 'does not look as if he would produce any intellectual revolutions, or upset any intellectual apple carts' (*ibid.*). Underlying Oakeshott's views may not be 'exactly conformity' but it is an 'acceptance of the rules of the various discourses' (*ibid.*). It is surprising that Searle, a deservedly eminent philosopher, seems to believe that acceptance of the 'rules of various discourses' implies an uncritical view of life. In addition, Searle's comments appear in an extended treatment of *The Voice of Liberal Learning* where Oakeshott explicitly refers to education as an 'engagement of critical self-understanding' (Fuller, 1989, p. 26). Being self-critical implies at least some level of critical detachment from the traditions of which one is part.

Two very severe indictments of the neglect of social critique in Oakeshott's work come from Michael Matthews (1980) and Joe McCarney (McCarney, 1985, pp. 400–11). Matthews claims that underlying the essay 'The Voice of Poetry in the Conversation of Mankind' (Oakeshott, 1981) is 'the world view which inspired the English ruling class to carry on their (*sic*) conversational diplomacy with European fascism in the 1930s' (Matthews, 1980, p. 160). Unsurprisingly this tendentious, extravagant and false statement is not supported by any arguments. McCarney, by contrast, does elaborate on the grounds for his hostility towards Oakeshott. His criticism arises in the context of a trenchant denunciation of Richard Rorty for the latter's appropriation of Oakeshott's metaphor of the 'conversation of mankind'. As noted in Chapter 4, John White (2007) associates the metaphor with elitism but McCarney goes even further, perceiving its use as evidence of an ideological collusion by Rorty with the political right. McCarney then continues to reprove Rorty in an idiom that is as misguided as it is racist in respect of Oakeshott. 'Why', he wonders, 'should a sophisticated, contemporary Mid-Westerner assume the persona of a fake eighteenth-century English gentleman?' (McCarney, 1985, p. 400). The answer, he alleges, lies in Rorty's endorsement of Oakeshott's conservative ideology that informs the metaphor. Underpinned by notions of 'aesthetics' and 'etiquette', this metaphor, argues McCarney, is 'precious and vapid' (*ibid.*, p. 400) and 'sponsors a contemplative acceptance of the perennial riches of the human condition' (*ibid.* pp. 400–1). This version of 'acceptance' is clearly inimical to any critical endeavour. But this charge is very unfair and misguided. In the first place, Oakeshott's notions of freedom and reflective consciousness that were explicated in Chapter 1, assume that all human conduct necessarily involves reflection about our actions because, without reflection, we are speaking merely of behavioural process rather than of rational conduct. Reflection on our actions assumes the provision of reasons for acting as we do and this means that, at least in principle, we must be able to defend our conduct against criticism from others.

In the second place, careful perusal of his writings reveals further why this attribution to Oakeshott of an uncritical traditionalism or unquestioning 'acceptance of the perennial riches of the human condition' (*ibid.* p. 401) is unjustified. As this point is very important and, indeed, the criticism is one that I have heard students and philosophical colleagues make of Oakeshott, I propose to take some time to rebut it comprehensively. In 'The Universities' can be found the somewhat impatient assertion that 'nobody would be so foolish as to deny the value of a critical attitude towards things . . .' (Fuller, 1989, p. 115.). Quite explicitly in the essay 'The Political Economy of Freedom', in an observation which has escaped the attention of his critics, Oakeshott disparages the form of traditionalism which 'consists in merely doing what was done "last time"' (Oakeshott, 1981, p.p. 48/9). This is why he insists that 'a morality in which reflection has no part is defective' (*ibid.*, p. 73). In fact, Oakeshott makes the quite questionable claim that even the most habitual form of moral conduct develops an element of 'selective conformity' (*ibid.*, p. 62) to tradition. Alas, recent history provides sad evidence of fundamentalists and fanatics whose moral convictions allow for no deviation whatever from rigid standards of conduct.

There is a linguistic point here that needs clarification. For Oakeshott the term 'habit' refers to conduct that is normal, customary or traditional. In this sense, habitual conduct is to be distinguished from that which is self-conscious. On the very first page of *Rationalism in Politics*, the terms 'traditional, 'customary' and 'habitual' are used as synonyms (Oakeshott, 1981, p. 1). With its connotations of referring to an automatic, unreflective and reflex response, use of the term 'habit' is misleading and liable to give rise to misunderstanding (see, for example, Winch, 1980, pp. 61–5). Oakeshott, in fact, shares the view of custom that Shakespeare (1997b) puts into the mouth of Coriolanus. If what is conventionally done were to be accepted as the sole criterion of moral value, if it were the case that '(w)hat custom wills, in all things should we do't', the result would be that:

> The dust on antique time would lie unswept,
> And mountainous error be too highly heaped
> For truth to o'erpeer. (Act 11, Scene iii, lines 108–111)

In 'The Tower of Babel' (the version in *Rationalism in Politics*) Oakeshott also lists some of the disadvantages of a form of moral life consisting merely in a '*habit of affection and behaviour*' or the 'unreflective following of a tradition of conduct' (Oakeshott, 1981, p. 61). Some of the confusion regarding the matter is dispelled in *On Human Conduct* where, as was shown in Chapter 1, Oakeshott speaks of the moral life as a practice (Oakeshott, 1975a, p. 60–81) and as a metaphorical 'language of moral converse' (*ibid.*, p. 59). Adaptability and flexibility are written into the very notions of practice and language.

What Oakeshott does find undesirable is the subjection of every act and institution to persistent and frenetic critical scrutiny. '*(C)easeless* criticism never did anyone or anything any good; it unnerves the individual and distracts the institution' (Fuller, 1989, p. 115). Oakeshott's view on the role of critical reflection on moral values is very well articulated in *Experience and Its Modes*:

> It is one thing to say that there is a kind of reflection, that there are modes of thought, which will paralyse moral sensibility and make a man less, rather than more capable of conducting his life, but it is quite another to say that the less a man thinks about how he is acting the more satisfactory will be his way of living. (Oakehshott, 1978, p. 303)

Oakeshott's critics have failed to appreciate that even his earlier conception of tradition is one that allows for, and accommodates, modification, and change as a matter of course. In the title essay of *Rationalism in Politics*, he describes tradition not as rigid and fixed, but as 'pre-eminently fluid' (Oakeshott, 1981, p. 31). And in 'The Tower of Babel' he writes of an 'elasticity' (*ibid.*, p. 64) that lies 'at the heart of every traditional way of life' (*ibid.*, p. 65). After all, where a situation is genuinely novel and without precedent (as, for example, with embryo research), it is to the resources of our moral tradition that we must turn in seeking a response. And it is largely through our familiarity with these resources that can find such a response (see *ibid.*, pp. 126–7). As participants in a tradition of moral life, we have recourse to resources that allow us to cope with changing circumstances. Among these resources is, of course, the possibility of critical reflection on our actions.

There is a third reason why the charge against Oakeshott of uncritical traditionalism is unfounded. The tradition of moral conduct which he describes is one that also accommodates moral deviation. Such deviation, he argues, may be an expression of the 'freedom and inventiveness at the heart of every traditional way of life', and may spring from 'a sensitiveness to the tradition itself', while at the same time 'remaining faithful' to it (*ibid.*, p. 65). These qualities are characteristic of the individual who represents Oakeshott's ideal moral character type. In elaborating on this character type, he makes it quite clear that this individual is in no sense a mere conformist (see Oakeshott, 1961, pp. 151–70 and Oakeshott, 1975a, pp. 234–42, 275–9).

Oakeshott's Moral Ideal

Far from being an advocate of moral conformity, Oakeshott subscribes passionately to the ideal of personal autonomy or individuality, and he offers an illuminating account of the historical emergence of this ideal. It is worth exploring this moral ideal and its counterpart of the '"anti-individual"' or of the '"individual *manqué*"' (see Oakeshott, 1961, pp. 158–70 and Oakeshott, 1975a, pp. 275–9) both because it is rich and resonant and also because it provides some of the texture of lived moral experience that is often absent from discussions of the moral life.

Oakeshott identifies three forms of moral conduct which, in his essay, 'The Moral Life in the Writings of Thomas Hobbes', he calls 'first, the morality of communal ties; secondly, the morality of individuality; and thirdly, the morality of the common good' (Oakeshott, 1981, p. 249). Each register of moral sensibility has a corresponding understanding of the appropriate office and task of the activities of government. The different forms represent dominant tendencies in the evolution of European moral consciousness and these have been, of necessity, somewhat artificially extrapolated by Oakeshott from actual history. Communal morality identified good conduct with appropriate observance of one's role and duties in the life of the community. Moral expectations were prescribed and circumscribed by the individual's position in the feudal social hierarchy. Conditions of medieval life made the expression and the assertion of individuality very difficult, as any manifestation of non-conformity risked being interpreted as treason or heresy (see Oakeshott, 1961, pp. 152–3).

Feudal conditions of social organisation were gradually modified and a new social order emerged in which the individual's status as lord, vassal or serf was no longer automatically assumed. In conjunction with the evolution of this new social order, Oakeshott argues that there also emerged a new and different kind of understanding of human nature. This was expressed in terms of general culture in what we call the Renaissance, and it took a specifically religious form in the Reformation. Calling into question the theological assumptions underlying the communal organisation of the feudal social order, an awareness of moral identity in terms of individual personality revealed itself. This awareness first took hold in Italy which, in the memorable words of Burkhardt, at the end of the thirteenth century 'began to swarm with individuality', where 'the ban laid upon human personality was dissolved', and where 'a thousand figures meet us, each in his own special shape and dress' (quoted in Oakeshott, 1961, p. 153).

According to Oakeshott people responded in two ways to the challenge posed by demands of this new social order. Some welcomed the opportunity to create a personal moral identity for themselves, while others were satisfied to assume the attenuated moral identity of what Oakeshott scathingly dubs the '"individual *manqué*"', '"the anti-individual"' or even more dismissively, '"the mass man"' (*ibid.*, 1961, pp., 151, 161). This kind of personality rejected the challenge to exercise moral autonomy that followed the dissolution of the medieval social order. Freedom and its consequent responsibility were unwanted burdens which such individuals felt unable or unwilling to assume. They felt unhappy and insecure without the support of the feudal social order which prescribed their social and moral duties. Among the dominant personal qualities of this kind of character were (and still are) pusillanimity, lack of confidence, and also envy and resentment at those who derived satisfaction from the exercise of their freedom. According to Oakeshott what this character type sought was a morality which would at once assuage her or his insecurity and curtail or proscribe the activities of the person who found happiness in a private sphere of action. Though it was not possible to reconstitute the feudal order, the anti-individual sought a form of morality which would reflect, as far as possible, the medieval 'morality of communal ties' (Oakeshott, 1981, p. 249). The outcome of these efforts was what Oakeshott variously calls a morality of the '"common good"' (Oakeshott, 1975a, p. 277), '"the social good"', '"the good of all"'

(Oakeshott, 1981, p. 250) or the '"public good"' (Oakeshott, 1961, p. 165).

A contrary conception of human nature and of morality is expressed in the character of the individuals who embody Oakeshott's positive moral ideal. These individuals responded to the moral challenge which followed the dissolution of the medieval social order by forging for themselves a moral law — an *auto-nomos*, namely, a self-made law, making of each individual a 'law to himself' (Oakeshott, 1961, p. 153). Associated with the character of autonomous individuals was a profound self-understanding, together with a confident command of personal resources (Oakeshott, 1975a, p. 237). But the moral character of this person is very different from that of moral eccentrics who, in the idiosyncrasy of their moral choices, might also be considered a kind of law unto themselves.

Throughout Oakeshott's work we find a resistance to any identification between an *auto-nomos* and mere subjectivity or idiosyncrasy. As noted in Chapter 1, he resists excessively subjectivist accounts of human conduct. He rejects therefore the subjective ethic of 'trivial liberations' and its 'banal individualism' which would justify the easy indulgence of desires of the moment (Oakeshott, 1975a, 241–2). In merely exploiting the freedom to indulge occurrent inclination, a person is not really subscribing to any moral law at all (see ibid and also pp. 51–2, 75). By contrast, the values to which individualists subject themselves represent a law (*nomos*) in that what they choose to submit themselves to are public, perhaps traditional, ideals which are transmitted in a 'language of moral converse' (Oakeshott, 1975a, p. 64), a language that demands reasonableness and consistency from those who use it. Yet their ethic is personal in that their commitment to these values is their own (*auto*) and so, in this sense, their ethic can be said to be subjective. Oakeshott reserves particular scorn for the notion that conscience represents a supreme moral criterion, what he calls 'the fashionable so-called morality of conscience' (Oakeshott, 1975a, p. 75). In one of his earliest published works he argues that knowledge must necessarily be a personal acquisition but that standards of truth and falsity are public, and not a matter of mere private choice (Oakeshott, 1927). 'Free action' he writes, 'is not moral action unless it is also wise . . . . and we have other standards of truth and falsehood, than those of mere personal insight' (*ibid.*, pp. 10/11). If 'mere personal insight' or opinion were the criteria of rationality in moral discourse, then genuine argument would be impossible. In *Experience and Its Modes*, he puts the counter argument well, pointing out that '(i)f anything were a matter *mere* opinion, then there could be no difference of opinion' (Oakeshott, 1978, p. 254). Again, his point here is that moral judgment is a personal matter in that no one else can, in principle, decide for us what we should consider right or wrong. Yet moral judgments are objective in that they must be based on beliefs that are factually correct, and also subscribe to standards of sincerity and consistency.

It was the transformation of the feudal social order that offered individuals the freedom to personalise their moral identities. The responsibility that was the necessary concomitant of this freedom did not have to be regarded as a burden, since the exercise moral freedom could itself be a source of satisfaction and happiness. For morally autonomous individuals, 'choosing and acting', he writes, were considered 'not as costs incurred in seeking enjoyments but as themselves enjoyments, the exercise of a gratifying self-determination or personal autonomy' (Oakeshott, 1975a, p. 236; see also Oakeshott, 1981, pp. 186). For Oakeshott the person who came to cultivate and enjoy this freedom was the personification of Montaigne's ideal of the man who '"knows how to belong to himself"' (Oakeshott, 1981, p. 290). Another striking Gallic expression of the individualist virtues cherished by Oakeshott is to be found in many of the songs/poems of the twentieth-century troubadour Georges Brassens. Among the personal qualities of people who know 'how to belong' to themselves are a suspicion of the herd instinct, resourcefulness, a firm but modest sense of their own worth, and a willingness to accept responsibility for the character that they have created for themselves.

Some of the texture of the notion of autonomy characterised by Oakeshott is captured by Irène Némirovsky (2006) in her novel, *Suite Française*. Hubert, a young man of seventeen has run away to fight the Germans and during this time learned much about life and about words such as '(d)anger, courage, fear, love' which previously were abstract concepts but 'now he knew the real meaning of these words' (Némirovsky, 2006, p. 147). As a result he feels 'better now, stronger, and very confident. He would never see the world through anyone else's eyes again. But more than that, anything he might love and believe from now on would come from himself, and no one else' (*ibid.*). This shows very well that the capacity for autonomous thought and action is a combination of cognitive, affective, moral and character elements.

The exercise of one's capacity for self-direction can also be understood as an important virtue (Oakeshott, 1975a, pp. 238–9). The version of personal integrity proposed by Oakeshott takes due account of the demands of other selves, conceived as autonomous sovereign ends in themselves. In his essay on Hobbes, he describes such a morality as 'the art of mutual accommodation' (Oakeshott, 1981, p. 250) between many individuals, each pursuing her and his own version of fulfilment or happiness. In their freely chosen actions, individuals express their integrity, that is, their authentic nature, or the moral core of the human personality. Memorably Oakeshott describes a person's integrity as the quality of 'knowing how to be loyal to himself' (Oakeshott, 1975a., p. 75). His example of an expression of integrity is Luther's famous '*Ich kann nicht anders*' whereby Luther resolves to act in the face of a public phenomenon, the corrupt state of the Church, in terms of personal moral values (*ibid.*, p. 238). Perhaps the exemplary appeal in literature to an individual's integrity is Polonius's celebrated exhortation to his son in *Hamlet* (Shakespeare, 1997d).

> To thine own self be true,
> And it must follow, as the night the day,
> Thou canst not then be false to any man. (Act I, Sc. iii, lines 78–80)

There is, however, a potential for disastrous human consequences in too passionate a striving for autonomy and self-realisation. In Isabel Archer, heroine of his great novel, *The Portrait of a Lady*, Henry James dramatises this character trait. Isabel makes a very unhappy marriage because she had a misguided perception of her capacity to make autonomous choices and thereby successfully to achieve complete self-realisation. As Oakeshott observes, the ideal of acting according to the virtue of authenticity or integrity can fall victim to the same 'corruption which every disposition recognized as a virtue' is susceptible (Oakeshott, 1975a, p. 238).

All of this goes to show that Oakeshott is no defender of moral conformity. Indeed, his view would not be incompatible with that of the narrator in *The Good Soldier* by Ford Madox

Ford. 'Conventions and traditions . . .' he reflects, 'work blindly but surely for the preservation of the normal type; for the extinction of proud, resolute and unusual individuals' (Madox Ford, 1987, p. 214). Oakeshott does not advocate the uncritical acceptance of traditional patterns of conduct in the moral and political sphere, and his ideal character is very much an autonomous human being. The exercise of choice with regard to moral commitments and conduct, it will be recalled, is an expression of the 'freedom and inventiveness at the heart of every traditional way of life' (Oakeshott, 1981, p. 65). It is suspicion of debate and argument, rather than of differences in moral and political beliefs, that characterises Oakeshott's writing. A reader of his work gets a strong sense that he finds the notions of argument, and even debate, in morals and politics somewhat uncongenial. To understand the reasons for his reservations about debate and argument in the moral life, it will be helpful to consider his account of civic life.

Civic Life and Civic Learning

There is a clear parallel between Oakeshott's accounts of moral and civic life. The treatment of the latter is based on a distinction that he draws between two different styles of political activity. The first of these Oakeshott calls the ideological and the second of which might be referred to as the 'ecological' (Fuller, 1989, p. 154).[1] The ideological style of politics, like the 'morality of the Rationalist' (Oakeshott, 1981, p. 35), is based on the self-conscious pursuit of ideals and the application of rules. For the political rationalist therefore politics consists in the implementation of a pre-meditated ideology that specifies ends thought to be desirable and fit to be pursued. This ideology is implemented by means of applied or 'technical knowledge' of a scientific nature, for example, by the use of economics or psychology (Fuller, 1989, pp. 141, 145). The form of education appropriate to this understanding of politics is instruction in an accepted ideology, or in the intellectual skill

[1]   'Ecological' is a more accurate term that 'traditional' as Oakeshott tells us that he has abandoned the term '"tradition"' as 'inadequate to express what ...(he) wanted to express' (see Oakeshott, 1976, p. 364). This is why Hanna Pikin writes that '(m)ore profoundly than anyone since Burke [Oakeshott has] developed for us a vision of society that might today properly be called "ecological": an awareness of the complexity and delicacy of the interrelationships among institutions, customs, and ways of life' (Pitkin, 1976, p. 301).

of devising and learning to defend one for oneself, together with instruction in the technique of implementing it. Needless to say Oakeshott rejects totally this conception of political education. His reasons for rejecting the 'ideological' style of political education are similar to those he uses in rejecting the reflective form of moral life based on vague, general ideals. In this form of education, which is based on a failure to appreciate the culturally embedded nature of political ideals and principles, instruction in the composition or acquisition of ideologies assumes greater importance than imparting a knowledge of how to behave. Without concrete knowledge of how societies conduct political affairs, such instruction will make no sense to learners. Where successful it would endow them with no more than the ability to recite a non-understood catechism. Even instruction in the ideology that informs current political practices and institutions is of only limited pedagogic value. There will always be a gap between propositional knowledge of rules and principles and the ability to apply them in concrete circumstances. And this knowledge can only be acquired through practical experience of political activity.

By contrast, the ecological style of political life has its roots in participation in a political culture and consists essentially in exploiting the resources offered by our current patterns of political behaviour to alter or to conserve laws and social institutions (see Oakeshot, 1975a, pp. 163, 184 and 1976, pp. 361–2). In this version of political life, individuals engage not in the pursuit of ideologies but rather in 'the pursuit of intimations' of their traditions of political behaviour (Fuller, 1989, p. 148, pp. 155–8). Engaging in politics means exploring, exposing, and pursuing the 'intimations' or 'flow of sympathy' (*ibid.*, p. 149) in our tradition of political conduct in order to resolve any 'incoherence' (*ibid.*, p. 147, 149) or 'incoherencies' (*ibid.*, p. 157) in our social arrangements that press 'convincingly for remedy' (*ibid.*, p. 147). Oakeshott's view of what constitutes appropriate political education follows from this understanding of the nature of politics. Political education consists in imparting to young people a knowledge and understanding, as profound, as searching and as comprehensive as it is possible to make it, of the spirit and the pattern of the political arrangements of their society. The ecological style of political education involves initiation into the tradition of political activity as it has come to be, and as it is currently, practised in that society. Though generally there will 'remain something of a mystery' (Fuller, 1989, p. 151), about how civic learning takes place, Oakeshott suggests that we come to acquire it in the manner in which we learn our native language by 'the observation and imitation of the behaviour of our elders' (*ibid.*, p. 152). He maintains that the 'greater part ... perhaps the most important part – of our political education we acquire haphazardly in finding our way about the natural-artificial world into which we are born' (*ibid.*) Oakeshott does deal in some detail with the kind of education appropriate to those who as politicians, political party managers, or as government officials, are professionally involved in politics – this involves a specialised vocational education along with some form of apprenticeship. But he says little enough about political education in schools and makes no mention of pedagogical theories on the subject. This failure to investigate the mechanics of moral and political education is somewhat surprising in the light of the analysis that he has made of the activities of teaching and learning that was examined in the previous chapter and, indeed, to the high profile enjoyed by his seminal essay, 'Political Education' (Fuller, 1989).

This account of civic life does not show why Oakeshott is so unenthusiastic regarding the place of argument in moral and political matters. How is this lack of enthusiasm to be explained?

Rules in Moral and Civic Learning

The most important reason for Oakeshott's reservations about debate and argument in these areas derives from his hostility to intellectualised forms of moral and civic learning that give primacy to formulated ideals, rules, and principles. In his mind, these tend to be associated with the exaggerated emphasis given to them by the 'morality of the Rationalist' (Oakeshott, 1981, p. 35). According to the Rationalist's understanding of the moral life, people first determine their moral ideals in the abstract and then learn to formulate them in words. Next they learn to defend these ideals from the criticism of others and to regulate their conduct in accordance with them. What Oakeshott fears is that people will come to place excessive reliance on the invocation of ideals, rules, and principles and thereby give primacy to thought over actual good conduct. Quite correctly, he believes that what people practise is more important than what they preach. How we actually behave represents what we really believe and expresses our real, as opposed to professed, convictions. For example, a teacher cannot be said to be genuinely opposed to the use of corporal punishment in schools if she routinely inflicts it on the pupils in her charge. Oakeshott compares our actual moral behaviour to a religion that remains primarily a way of life, rather than merely a compendium of theological propositions (see Oakeshott, 1981, pp. 71–2). In any event, moral rules and principles will usually 'require interpretation in terms of persons and circumstances' (Fuller, 1989, p. 55). They cannot specify substantive performances because there exists no principle that tells us which moral ideals to choose or how to implement them in specific actions (see Oakeshott, 1975a, pp. 69, 90–1). As with the exercise of skills considered in the preceding chapter, there is always a gap between propositional knowledge of rules and the ability to apply them or, as Oakeshott more accurately puts it, 'to *illustrate*' (*ibid.*, p. 90) or to use (see *ibid.*, p. 68) them in action. Of necessity, therefore, moral rules, ideals and principles must rest 'upon a foreshortened understanding of the character of a moral practice' (*ibid.*, p. 70). To adapt a famous metaphor of Oakeshott's with regard to role of ideology in politics, a moral principle is less the 'quasi-divine parent' of moral conduct than its 'earthly stepchild' (Fuller, 1989, p. 142).

Another reason for Oakeshott's negative attitude towards formulated rules and principles is his fear that these formulations will make conduct too self-conscious and will come to supervene upon the unselfconscious spontaneity of 'morally educated conduct' (Oakeshott, 1975a, p. 70). By invoking rules and principles a person becomes thereby engaged upon a 'casuistical enterprise' (*ibid.*), and casuistry he calls 'the grave of moral sensibility' (Oakeshott, 1978, p. 301) or of 'moral judgement' (Fuller, 1989, p. 55). Too rigid an emphasis on rules could restrict full participation in moral life to the kind of person who is 'something of a philosopher and something of a self-analyst' (Oakeshott, 1981, p. 68). Moreover, as the application of rules to conduct is not easy to do, reflection and analysis could come to paralyse action. Where thought and reflection are given priority at the expense of behavior, intellectual coherence can come to be valued more than a form of moral life. The intellectualised form of moral life, as just noted, is like a religion where the construction of a theology has become more important than the practice of way of life (*ibid.*, p. 72). Or, in another apposite and typically illuminating analogy from Oakeshott, in this form of moral life, the preaching of moral ideals such as '"social justice"' is considered a greater achievement than exhibiting 'ordinary decent behaviour" (*ibid.*, p. 75).

Oakeshott also maintains that an individual who does not have a broad intellectual grasp of different moral ideals can become obsessional in the pursuit of one particular ideal. A broad intellectual grasp is not easy to acquire with the result that 'a passion for righteousness' can make people 'hard and merciless' (*ibid.*, p. 69), a memorable insight that sadly has lost none of its force in the twentieth-first century. Oakeshott's insight reflects that of George Eliot who remarks that in 'transactions between fellow-men it is well to consider a little, in the first place, what is fair and kind towards the person immediately concerned, before we spit and roast him on behalf of the next century but one' (Eliot, 1995, p. 64). Like 'archangels with awful brow and flaming sword ... (w)ide-reaching motives, blessed and glorious as they are, and of the highest sacramental virtue, have their dangers, like all else that touches the mixed life of the earth' (*ibid.*).

What Oakeshott advocates is a form of moral life in which rules are observed implicitly and unselfconsciously, '*tacitement, naturellement et sans art*' (Oakeshott, 1981, p. 20) or 'as nearly as possible without reflection' (*ibid.*, p. 61) His preferred form of moral education is by following the example of adults who 'habitually behave in a certain manner' (*ibid.*, p. 62) in the way we learn to speak our mother tongue. Just as people learn to speak their mother tongue without being overtly and concurrently aware of the rules of grammar and syntax that they are following so too people may learn to behave morally without acquiring an intellectualised knowledge of the principles and ideals in terms of which they are acting. An example of the kind of moral behaviour that Oakeshott would find congenial is provided in Elizabeth Gaskell's description of one of her characters, Captain Brown. Gaskell refers to Captain Brown's 'infinite kindness of heart, and the various modes which, unconsciously to himself, he manifested it' (Gaskell, 1963, p. 15). To say that Captain Brown manifests his good nature 'unconsciously to himself' means that he habitually acts in a kindly manner, without conscious deliberation about ideals and rules. This, of course, is not to deny to Captain Brown the possibility justifying his actions. What Oakeshott would wish to deny is that the Captain, or any morally educated individual, must explicitly advert to this business of reflection before, or in the course of, performing actions that have become part a 'settled disposition' (Oakeshott, 1981, p. 248). Oakeshott would almost be sympathetic to the view human conduct articulated by the Nazi officer in Alan Judd's novel *The Kaiser's Last Kiss* who believes that we are what we do and that 'the rest' is 'froth' (Judd, 2004, p. 56).

Yet this does not represent Oakeshott's view because the quite proper priority that he attributes to actual conduct over professed convictions does not lead him to deny the importance of critical reflection on moral principles. In 'The Tower of Babel' he argues that 'education in moral ideology' (Oakeshott, 1981, p. 71) is necessary in order that our tradition of moral conduct retain 'the power to criticize, to reform and to explain itself, and the power to propagate itself beyond the range of the custom of a society' (*ibid.*, p. 70). An important part of moral education consists in being given an opportunity to reflect upon moral ideals, rules, and principles (see *ibid.*, p. 108 and Oakeshott, 1975a, p. 68). This is because moral ideals, which are the outcome of reflection, have 'power as critics of human habits' (Oakeshott 1981, p. 73), just as in politics reflection on principles has a role as 'critic of political habit' (*ibid.*, p. 22). Without knowledge of formulated rules, we can never know for certain whether or not our behaviour is in accordance with tradition. An education in such rules is also necessary to be aware of there being genuine alternatives before us in action and to equip us with the ability to defend and explain our conduct. Otherwise our moral virtues will be cloistered and our patterns of behaviour may collapse under threat, or they may degenerate into a form of superstitious allegiance to our past. Both responses are common to people brought up in uncritical and closed religious environments who are exposed to the world outside their community.

Ideally for Oakeshott, as for Shakespeare's (1997b) Coriolanus, 'action is eloquence' (Act III, Sc. ii, line 76) and articulated knowledge would usually therefore be superfluous. Nonetheless, he does provide a careful account of the different forms that justification may take (Oakeshott, 1975a, pp. 68–70), so Peters's criticism that for Oakehsott principles are 'somehow spurious in relation to justification' (Peters, 1974, p. 451 and Benn and Peters, 1959, pp. 317–8) is certainly untrue of the later work. Regrettably though, as already noted, Oakeshott does not get to grips with the pedagogy involved in the transmission of moral values. In his writings there is a parsimony of elucidation on how facility in the 'language of moral converse' (Oakeshott, 1975a, pp. 59, 64) is actually acquired. In his theory of learning, as Peters points out, '(t)heories about roles, imitation, or identification are never mentioned' (Peters, 1974, p. 449) and there is no reference to empirical studies on the transmission of values. Oakeshott cannot really be taken to task for failing to elaborate an account of the pedagogy of moral and political education since this was never his intention.

So, in summary it could be said that Oakeshott recognises, in principle, the place of crtical debate but that, personally, he is less than sympathetic towards it. His endorsement of 'critical self-understanding' (Fuller, 1989, p. 26) is not extended to social critique. Reasonably enough, he might say that conversations about moral and political values are not conversations that he himself would wish to join in. Now I can understand why someone would wish to avoid encounters with the assertions of 'critical theorists' and of their conservative counterparts. As noted in chapter 5, these assertions generally represent what Oakeshott would condemn as points of view rather than '*thoughts*' (Fuller, 1989, p. 102). Much of this discourse is well described by novelist, Ian McEwan, as 'that old business of theorising, taking up a position, planting the flag of identity and self-esteem, then fighting all comers to the end' (McEwan, 1988, p. 80). But this agenda-driven theorising represents one rationalistic extreme and Oakeshott's attitude could be said to represent another. If his educational conversation is to be an honest engagement then young people must be allowed to be critical without incurring the polite, civilised indifference of those adults whose values they are invited to criticise. Unless such questioning of moral and political values is not only permitted, but also encouraged and promoted, then Oakeshott's conversation of mankind is not a genuine dialogue at all.

Concluding Critique

Here we should note another important reason for his scepticism regarding moral and political argument and this is his own deep conservative instincts. Most memorably, in 'On Being Conservative' he expresses this allegiance to conservatism in personal and political life. This essay serves to convey the nature and temper of the conservative attitude itself, which Oakeshott describes as a 'disposition' (1981, p. 168) as opposed to a creed, doctrine, ideology or specific set of beliefs. The conservative disposition is distinguished by a propensity to use, to enjoy, and to delight in the present, in what is currently available, in what is familiar. The conservative makes use of the opportunities for satisfaction offered by the present and neither lives for future pleasures nor dwells on those which the past may have offered.

Unsurprisingly his conservatism is deeply hostile to socialism in all its forms, whether social democratic or Marxist. This view pervades Oakeshott's work and is very explicitly enunciated in, for example, *On Human Conduct* (1975a), 'The Political Economy of Freedom' (1981), 'Contemporary British Politics' (1947–8) and 'Political Laws and Captive Audiences' (1964). In his writings there seems little awareness, as Bhiku Parekh notes, that the socialist ideal emerged from moral outrage at what Parekh describes as 'unrestrained and exploitative nineteenth-century capitalism' (1979, p. 502). Oakeshott sees the extension of the functions of government as a response to the craven pusillanimity of the masses rather than as a response to human suffering and to 'a desire to create conditions in which individuality may be brought within the reach of all' (*ibid.*). Oakeshott is not unaware that for someone to prefer 'present laughter to utopian bliss' (Oakeshott, 1981, p. 169), her or his present situation must offer significant opportunity for enjoyment. Yet he fails to elaborate on the fact that conservatism is hardly an appropriate attitude for the poor and the disadvantaged. Oakeshott does not acknowledge the crucial role played by ownership of, and access to, financial resources making possible and sustaining the values of personal autonomy. '(W)ealth' he concedes, affords 'some superficial protection' (Oakeshott, 1975a, p. 275) to those who wish to express their individuality and autonomy. But economic security is less a form of 'superficial protection' than a condition necessary to enable many to exploit 'the adventure and risk of self-enactment' (*ibid.*, p. 276).

And it is not only a question of wealth, it is also a question of power. And, unfortunately, there exist societies where power is exercised by men, for example, in a manner as to frustrate the aspiration of women even to the enjoyment of privacy let alone to the expression of individuality. Here, for example, is Äsne Seierstad's description of the life of the unmarried adult daughter, Leila, of a well-to-do family in Kabul.

> Alone is an unknown idea for Leila. She has never, ever, any-where, at any time, been alone. She has never been alone in the apartment, never gone anywhere alone, and never remained any-where alone, never slept alone. Every night she sleeps on the mat beside her mother. She quite simply does not know what it is to be alone, nor does she miss it. (Seierstad, 2003, p. 169)

This is not to deny the value of Oakeshott's ideal of autonomy but merely to show how far lies its realisation from the lives of many.

There are two further reservations to be raised regarding Oakeshott's ideal of the morally autonomous individual. In the notions of the individual who learns to 'make the most of or the best of himself' (Fuller, 1989, p. 47), and of selves as 'his-toric personalities' (*ibid.*, p. 48), there is, arguably, an exagger-ated assumption regarding the unitary quality of the moral personality. As noted in Chapter 1, Oakeshott's conception of autonomy can be understood in broad and nuanced terms but he does not raise the possibility that our beliefs and attitudes may not form a singular whole. In a wonderful essay on Emily Brontë and *Wuthering Heights*, Somerset Maugham captures something of what I feel is missing from Oakeshott's account of moral identity. 'We are', writes Maugham, 'none of us all of a piece; more than one person dwells within us, often in uncanny companionship with his fellows' (Maugham, 1971, p. 226). In Chapter 2 it was noted that our motivation to learn can be multi-faceted—likewise the beliefs and conduct that inform our moral lives can exhibit contrary impulses. George Eliot in fact disparages the application of 'that fallacious standard of what is called consistency to a man's moral nature' (Eliot, 1995, p. 63) because people can give evidence of 'fine impulses or habits of feeling in relation to . . . actions generally' (Eliot, 1995, p. 63), which may be absent from some episodes of their behaviour. The 'dews of fellowship and pity' can be found in a person whose actions can on other occasions be 'unfair, equivocal, and even cruel' (*ibid.*, pp. 64–5). The narrator in Maugham's story 'A Friend in Need' makes the same point very well. '(S)elf-contradictory is what most of us are. We are a haphazard bundle of inconsistent qualities' (Maugham, 2006, p. 86). I am not claiming that Oakeshott would disagree with this, but I do think that the complex, multi-faceted character of the moral life is overlooked in his writing.

The other reservation concerns Oakeshott's dismissive attitude towards the 'morality of communal ties' and of the 'common good' (1981, p. 249). The self is socially situated and this social situation is very salient when it comes to moral duties. To affirm this dimension of the moral life is not to deny the significance of individuality. Nor is it to embrace current inflated rhetoric about solidarity and global citizenship. One lesson that Oakeshott well teaches is the need to treat with caution ideals of universal benevolence and generosity that may have little purchase in daily living. It is easy to be generous with the money of other people. Yet our response to the suffering of other people can spring from a sense of sharing 'communal ties' with people both within and beyond national boundaries and from a sense that '"every other person is basically you"'.[2] The affirmation of individual morality in opposition to a 'morality of communal ties' risks obscuring the social context of moral and civic conduct and reflects once more Oakeshott's tendency to work with over-simplified categories conceived in an oppositional or either/or way.

Despite these reservations, there remains much that is commendable in Oakeshott's conception of individuality and autonomy. But the questions that arises once more is whether the kind of education that fosters and supports these values is exclusivist and elitist and I turn to this question in the penultimate chapter.

---

[2]   This is the explanation of one man for his efforts to rescue Jewish victims of the Nazis (quoted in Callan, 1992, p. 440).

Chapter Eleven

Equality and Civil Association

Oakeshott's view of society and of education had been charged with elitism (see Lawn, 1996, p. 276). The elitist spirit in some of his educational writing has been described as 'chilling' by John Searle (1990, p. 41) and his educational vision has been described by John B. Bennett, a very sympathetic commentator, as 'cloaked in elitist garments' (Bennett, 2001, p. 37). In this chapter I propose to consider this charge before addressing the relationship between educational opportunity and his philosophy of civil life. I hope to show that the charge of elitism is not justified but that but there are tensions in Oakeshott's theory of politics when it comes to accommodating the kind of political action necessary to secure significant equalising of educational opportunity (see McCabe, 2000).

Oakeshott's Invitation to the Educational Conversation

Though Oakeshott's is a fairly uncompromising statement of the traditional view of education, his is not an exclusivist or elitist epistemology. And, as was shown in Chapter 3 of this volume, Oakeshott is well aware that historically the poor have not enjoyed equality of educational opportunity and he deplores their exclusion from the curriculum of high culture by what he calls 'socialisation'. 'Socialisation', it will be recalled, is the term he uses to describe instruction in vocationally oriented skills and, according to Oakeshott, was originally designed to accommodate the masses who on account of their poverty were excluded from any education whatsoever. 'Socialisation' is indicted as a misguided 'alternative apprenticeship to adult life' (Fuller, 1989, p. 80) that can, in no sense, be said to provide initiation into the educational conversation. Instead of offering this culturally, intellectually and emotionally impoverishing apprenticeship to what were assumed to be the needs of their future adult life, Oakeshott believes that governments should have endeavoured to extend the opportunity of genuine education to those who had hitherto been deprived of it. And it is for their efforts to do precisely this that he commends those religious orders such as the Brothers of the Common Life (Oakeshott, 1975a, p. 306).

As explained in Chapter 5, with regard to university education, Oakeshott stresses that the opportunity to develop a participant's fluency in one of the universes of discourse offered by the traditional university was not something which only one social class could appreciate or something suited only to a '"leisured class"' (Fuller, 1989 p. 128). Nevertheless, as even such a sympathetic critic as R.S.Peters points out, Oakeshott remains remarkably unaware of the extent to which opportunity to avail of education, particularly at senior cycle in second level and at third level, is related to socio-economic background (Peters, 1974, p. 436, see also Falk, 1963, p. 69 and Kneller, 1984, pp. 225, 250, Moberley, 1950, pp. 207–8). To appreciate his lack of awareness on the issue it is necessary to say something further on the distribution of educational opportunity.

Equality of Opportunity in Education

Before considering empirical data on the issue, there is a general point regarding access to education to be first noted. Access to educational institutions is subject to necessary restriction since that provision for education, as for health and social welfare services, represents a charge on 'the scarce resources of the world (Oakeshott, 1975a, p. 45, note 3). To explore the human cultural inheritance is to make demands on the world's resources: on schools, universities, libraries and on the time and energy of teachers and administrators. Obviously enough the opportunity to engage full-time in the pursuit of learning is open only to those of independent means or to those with positions in research institutes or who otherwise enjoy funding. Such opportunity is therefore determined by the availability of individual or community resources. And I should not wish to quarrel with Oakeshott's view that it is necessary to devise some method or methods, however fallible, which will allow us to determine the relationship between the 'abilities and . . . ambitions' (Oakeshott, 1967, p. 140) of those who wish to pursue further study or to find careers in academic life. But what he fails to take into account sufficiently is the relationship between access to education and at least some element of 'pre-existing privilege' (Fuller, 1989, p. 128). And the case that access by the poor to the educational conversation is significantly restricted is abundantly borne out by the vast research on the issue.

Before commenting on this research, it is worth noting the salience of the profile of the relationship between education and privilege in fiction that deals with education. In four recent popular novels (Cooper, 2006, Harris, 2006, Sittenfeld, 2006, Benameur, 2006) and in the memoir, *Teacher Man* (McCourt, 2005), the relationship between class and schooling is the main theme. The school system is portrayed as a very vivid expression of the social division between the rich and the poor. In no sense serving as partisan special pleading, these works communicate imaginatively the continuing, pervasive and powerful role that wealth plays in securing the kind of education that will ensure that this wealth will remain within the charmed circle of the privileged. The rich and the poor do indeed inhabit contrasting universes and different levels of affluence provide different lifestyles. Part of these lifestyles is access to the form of education that will serve to perpetuate the privilege bestowed by wealth.

Turning next to the research on the subject, it is as unnecessary, as it would be tedious, to review this research in detail but its main findings are worth rehearsing briefly. This is because empirical questions regarding the accessibility of particular educational pursuits must be raised when adjudicating on the justifiability of assigning them a central role in the school curriculum. Even if Oakeshott's characterisation of education as initiation into the cultural patrimony composed of the languages of human understanding and of art is found to be compelling, the question must be asked as to whether in practice, rather than merely in principle, it is open to everyone to avail of the invitation to participate in this educational conversation. In Chapter 6, attention was drawn to the significance of access to education in determining life chances. This is why the disturbingly high correlation between participation in education and social class origins gives cause for concern. For many years research findings reported by Halsey, Heath and Ridge (1980), Whelan and Whelan (1984) and Wolf (2002) show that internationally, in spite of increased rates of participation in education by pupils from lower socio-economic backgrounds, disparities in participation relative to class origin persist. The higher the educational level, the greater are the disparities in rates of educational participation relative to class origins (see Wolf, 2002, pp. 187–99). And, of course, this leads to a vicious circle in reinforcement of class barriers, given that employment status greatly depends on the level of educational attainment and that level of educational attainment correlates closely with the occupational status of one's parents. Though children today do not usually directly inherit their parents' occupational positions, the consequence of the differential in access to the qualifications conferred by education is that socio-economic advantage tends to pass indirectly from one generation to the next. Admittedly, there has been a huge increase in the numbers attending university but, as Alison Wolf explains with close analysis of statistics over a period of more than 40 years, the middle- and upper-middle classes have benefited the most, and continue to do so, from the increase in participation at third level. These are the classes made up of the AB groups of the advertising agencies and the classes I and II as defined by social scientists. The international evidence is overwhelmingly the same — the middle classes 'swamp' (*ibid.*, p. 190) the universities, while children from working-class and poor backgrounds 'only trickle in' (*ibid.*, p. 188).

And this leads us to the second aspect of the issue of access to education, namely, those research findings that show that pupils from lower socio-economic classes are at a disadvantage in relation to the language in which Oakeshott's educational conversation is conducted. Since the 1970s research internationally shows that deeply-rooted cultural and family factors play a crucial role in determining the accessibility of this language and the written word in which it is inscribed (see, for example, Bullock, 1975, Bernstein, 1975, 1971, Bowles, 1976, Martell, 1976). Middle-class children tend to have a greater capacity to generate the context-free, universalistic meanings of educational discourse than do young people from working-class backgrounds whose meanings tend to be context-bound and particularistic (Bernstein, 1971, pp. 63–4, see also Donaldson, 1987, pp. 86–95). In addition, the written form in which this language is characteristically presented reinforces this disadvantage simply because, as George Martell puts it, 'as you move down the socio-economic class scale, the kids read and write less and less well' (Martell, 1975, p. 107). Hardly surprising therefore is Bernstein's famous conclusion that 'the working-class child may be placed at a considerable disadvantage in relation to the *total* culture of the school. It is not made for him; he may not answer to it' (Bernstein, 1971, p. 64). And it is lack of facility in using the language of this culture that leads to what sociologists describe as 'systematic under-achievement' by the working class (Whelan and Whelan, 1984, p. 189). I believe that access by young people from backgrounds of socio-economic disadvantage to the language of educational discourse can be facilitated by the provision of curricula that are imaginatively designed, epistemologically coherent and taught in a pedagogic style appropriate to the experience of the pupils. But it will involve more than this – for the simple reason that many young people from such backgrounds do not remain within the educational arena for long enough to acquire significant familiarity with the languages of the conversation of mankind.

As already noted, research shows that in practice socio-economic factors are a powerful influence both on making accessible the language of education and in facilitating access to educational institutions. Consequently, the educational pursuits to which Oakeshott assigns a central role are not equally accessible to every member of the community. In practice the invitation to the educational conversation is extended predominantly to the relatively advantaged because many young people from lower socio-economic classes are not in a position to accept it. Why then is Oakeshott so reticent on the issue of access to education and on the socio-economic factors that so significantly govern educational opportunity? I suggest that the main reason for this failure to take due measure of the practical problems involved in promoting equality of educational opportunity derives from the form of political life or 'civil association' (Oakeshott, 1975a, p. 119) that he advocates. This form of civil life, and in particular the role that he attributes to government, makes problematic the achievement of such equality of opportunity in education as he would in fact wish to see. The tension between Oakeshott's attitude to the issue of equality of opportunity in education and his political philosophy points to an ambivalence at the heart of his theory of civil life. This is the tension between the conceptual limits that define the ideal of civil association and the '"inner morality"' (Oakeshott, p. 153, note 1) of this form of civil life. The nature of this tension can be shown if we understand the basis of Oakeshott's political philosophy. This now requires some attention.

Oakeshott's Political Philosophy: The Conceptual Framework

Behind Oakeshott's political philosophy is the commendable impulse of providing an account of civil life which accommodates the maximum exercise of human freedom. This philosophy is based on a theory of the state that is in turn based on a theory about forms of human association. He argues that human beings can be joined together in two forms of association, one of which he calls enterprise or purposive association, and the other civil association.

Enterprise Association

An enterprise association is made up of individuals joined together in 'terms of the pursuit of some common purpose, some substantive condition of things to be jointly procured, or some common interest to be continuously satisfied' (*ibid.*, p. 114). The concept comes from the Latin term *universitas* which is exemplifed in the medieval university, in which, together with craft guilds, monasteries and military orders, individuals are joined in a 'corporate mode of association' (*ibid.*, p. 203) as a 'corporate body' (Fuller, 1989, p. 97) in what Oakeshott calls a 'co-operative enterprise' (*ibid.*), thus constituting 'a many joined in the pursuit of a common substantive satisfaction' (Oakeshott, 1975a, p. 217). As well as the 'joint pursuit of a common purpose' (*ibid.*, p. 115) that the individuals associated acknowledge as such, membership of an 'enterprise association' also involves 'joint recognition of "managerial" choices of response to contingent situations contingently connected with the pursuit of a joint purpose or interest' (*ibid.*, p. 117). Members are further associated 'in making or acknowledging "managerial" decisions' (*ibid.*, p. 121) in the pursuit of these joint purposes or interests. Consequently 'joint enterprisers' are bound to one another in two respects, both in their 'agreed choice of wants to be satisfied and [also] of "managerial" decisions about how to satisfy them' (*ibid.*, p. 158).

The right to exercise authority within an enterprise association derives from the consent of the members to comply with the demands of those duly authorised to manage the pursuit of the purpose. Obligation to comply with authoritative demands subsists as long as individuals remain members of the association. But they can extricate themselves from the association and thereby release themselves from the obligation whenever they so desire (see *ibid.*, pp. 115–9, 157–8). This is the situation of a member of a tennis club who undertakes to abide by the rules of the club and who thereby becomes obligated to do so in order to remain a member, although in choosing to join the club the individual does not, of course, choose the rules. The rules or laws of such a club are designed to promote the interests of the club and its members; rules within an enterprise association are therefore necessarily instrumental to its purpose or purposes. Normally, an enterprise association will offer authorised procedures for changing its rules or for reconciling disagreement regarding these rules, and in this way enterprise association accommodates a form of politics. An individual who wishes to change a rule has therefore recourse to these recognised procedures but in the event of his failing to secure this change or in reaching some compromise regarding it she must either conform or dissociate herself from the organisation.

As shown in Chapter 3, Oakeshott believes that a state can be conceived as an enterprise association. In a state so conceived the interests of the inhabitants are seen as being vested in and expressed through the agencies of government. This corporate interest consists in the promotion of the well-being of the inhabitants and this well-being is understood as the 'satisfaction of their endlessly proliferating wants (*ibid.*, p. 290). Within such a state the activity of politics will be concerned with identifying and clarifying the nature of the putative general interest or common good, and in establishing the most appropriate policy to achieve this corporate purpose, in particular by deciding how benefits might be most appropriately redistributed to this end. If the interests of individuals and of organisations diverge from the general interest, it is the task of the government to ensure the conciliation and integration of such private interests with the common purpose either by means of persuasion, threat, or ultimately by the use of force. It is Oakeshott's opinion that in most contemporary states government and citizens alike tend to think of the state as an enterprise association. What he calls the 'teleocratic drift' (*ibid.*, p. 311), which mobilisation for two world wars has imparted to all governments, has made increasingly pervasive and acceptable this concept of the state. An essential feature of the state's involvement in the management of its citizens' lives has been its concern to provide 'compulsory generalized education and technological training' (*ibid.*, p. 301).

Oakeshott's repudiates most passionately any 'deed' or 'attempt' to make of the state an enterprise association (Oakeshott, 1976, p. 367). This is because the compulsory quality of membership of a state is incompatible with the choice that characterises membership of an enterprise association. In respect of a normal enterprise association such as a sports club, a business, or a university, individuals' freedom is expressed in their right to choose whether or not to join in the enterprise and to make the joint undertaking their own, and in their right to terminate their membership when they so desire. But if a state is conceived as an enterprise with a common purpose shared by its members, then not only are citizens precluded from opting out of the enterprise, but they are also obliged to have their individual private purposes subsumed within, and made subordinate to, the shared purpose. Oakeshott would want not only to question the possibility of identifying a 'common good or general interest' (Oakeshott, 1975a, p. 152) within a state, but he would also claim that even if it were possible to identify a common social purpose, the prosecution by the state of such a purpose would involve an undesirable concentration of power and resources in the hands of a few. A state organised in such a way would deny the freedom inherent in the concept of personhood by severing 'the link between belief and conduct which constitutes moral agency' (*ibid.*, p. 158). In affronting the moral autonomy of its citizens such a state would, represent in Oakeshott's words, a 'moral enormity' (Oakeshott, 1976, p. 367, see also p. 356). Here we should note that compulsion and membership of an enterprise association are not contradictory. A compulsory enterprise association may be described as a 'moral enormity' but not, as Oakeshott states elsewhere a 'self-contradiction' (Oakeshott, 1975a, p. 119). [1]

Civil Association

The second kind of association identified by Oakeshott is relationship in terms of a practice rather than in terms of the pursuit of a purpose. By choosing to participate in a practice we choose to observe the conditions which it entails and to be thus obligated by these conditions and the restrictions that they impose upon our freedom. But our freedom cannot thereby be said to be compromised because the choice to engage in a practice does not include the choice of the conditions of association. The nature of this form of association becomes clear if we think of association in terms of the rules of a game. By agreeing to play a game of tennis, for example, we undertake to accept the rules of the game as binding and, whether or not we like some of the rules, we must conform to them in order to play the game. In agreeing to play the game of tennis we choose to be obligated by the conditions or demands that its rules impose upon our freedom. But as Oakeshott puts it in 'being obligatory conduct does not become non-optional, it becomes conditional' (Oakeshott, 1975a, p. 155, see also p. 154, note 1).

In civil association Oakeshott sees people joined together, not in the pursuit of a joint purpose or purposes, but rather in terms of the recognition of the authority of rules of a practice which in this case is the rule of law. This is what he calls the practice of civility or of civil life or the 'practice of "just" conduct' (*ibid.*, p. 182). The form of relationship between citizens and the rules of civil life is analogous to that between speakers of a common language and the rules of grammar and syntax. The rules of grammar and syntax do not determine whether or when individuals should speak, but they do provide the rules to be followed if they wish to make intelligible utterances.

---

[1] On this issue see the criticism of, for example, Pitkin (1976, pp. 308-10) and Parekh (1979, pp. 494 and 502-3) and Liddington, 1984, pp. 296-7). Originally I also considered this to be a contradiction within Oakeshott's philosophy of society (the school being a pre-eminent example of a compulsory enterprise association), but now I am inclined to see it as an oversight on his part. A writer attempting to construct a complex and lengthy explanation of civil life needs such indulgence from readers who do better, at least on occasions, to attend to the spirit of the writing rather than to the fine detail.

Likewise the rules of civil society prescribe not substantive actions but rather the conditions to be observed in the performance of all our actions. The essence of civil rules is their non-instrumental character, so that unlike the rules of enterprise associations, they have no function in the realisation of substantive purposes of designated individuals. Their sole function is to allow citizens of a state who are joined together in the acknowledgement of the rule of law to pursue their purposes without interference from others and subject only to the rule of these laws. And it is the burden of Oakeshott's political philosophy that only relationship in terms of the rules of civil association is compatible with the moral autonomy of the citizens of a state, membership of which is compulsory.

Within the state conceived as a civil association the term 'politics' refers not to the whole network of relationships between persons in society, but rather to a 'specific and limited activity' (Oakeshott, 1981, p. 189) within civil life. Oakeshott argues that the existence of a 'political system is primarily for the protection and occasional modification of a recognised legal and social order' (Oakeshott, 1939–1940, p. 148). Political activity is concerned with considering the desirability of the laws or rules with a view to their conservation or alteration (see Oakeshott, 1975a, pp. 163, 184 and Oakeshott, 1976, pp. 361–2). Engaging in politics demands acknowledgment of the authority of the law in force and, consequently, acceptance of the procedures whereby laws are enacted, amended, and repealed. According to Oakeshott the rules of civil life derive their authority by virtue of their being acknowledged as authoritative and categorically binding by those who fall within their jurisdiction. Refusal to acknowledge the authoritative nature of these rules is, claims Oakeshott, a repudiation of the conditions of civil association and in such repudiation lie the seeds of civil war (see Oakeshott, 1975a, pp 164, note 1). Thus to question the desirability of any law is a political act, whereas to impugn the authority of the law is an act of civil dissociation.

Oakeshott's definition of government has a stipulative force similar to that of his definition of politics. The concern of government is solely with the custody and promulgation of law and therefore government has no function in the appropriation, control, or distribution of material goods. Because it has nothing to own, a government cannot be an agency of ownership. As 'civil rulers have nothing to distribute', a government cannot be 'a distributor in possession of what is to be distributed' (*ibid.*, p. 153, note 1; see also Oakeshott, 1983, p. 141). Conferring upon a political/legal system a distributive function would be inconsistent with the non-instrumental character that Oakeshott attributes to law within the practice of civility. If a government were to become an agency of ownership concerned to devise laws which would distribute benefits to designated individuals or groups then the state would become an enterprise association and civil association would have come to an end. Oakeshott's preferred version of civil life is therefore based on the conceptual conditions that must be respected if civil association is not to become enterprise association. Accordingly he argues that the only power that a government requires is that which will enable it to provide 'that small amount of compulsory civilization' (Oakeshott, 1975a, p. 152) necessary to ensure the survival of the civil order. This means that a government needs an apparatus of power sufficient only 'to maintain the authority of an arbiter of this kind' (Oakeshott, 1981, p. 189). The role of government, as Oakeshott sees it, is similar to that of an umpire or referee in ensuring that those subject to its jurisdiction are enabled to prosecute their private endeavours unhindered and unobstructed, and limited only by the rule of law.

And it is this view of the nature of civil life which provides the parameters of the form of governance advocated by Oakeshott, and in particular his attitude to the right to private property. Consistent with his non-interventionist form of government is his commitment to the right to private ownership and control of wealth and resources. The institution of private property, argues Oakeshott, serves to protect citizens from an over-concentration of power in the hand of the government. Consequently the right to ownership and control of wealth is the social arrangement most conducive to the freedom of the individual (see *ibid.*, pp. 43–8).[2] Accordingly he defends the individual's right to private ownership of anything 'obtained by the methods of acquisition recognized' in a society (*ibid.*, p. 45). Acquisition of wealth and property, he maintains, is a matter of 'investment, inheritance, and luck' (*ibid.*). Indeed

---

[2] The very explicit references to property rights are made in *Rationalism in Politics* but the existence of the same rights is assumed in *On Human Conduct* and in the later work.

Oakeshott even goes as far as to defend 'those who do not earn their living' from the 'preposterous' charge that they 'unavoidably engage in worthless activity' (Fuller, 1989, pp. 120, 121).

Here it might be helpful to draw together the strands in Oakeshott's theory of civil association by developing his analogy between participating in such association and participating in a game (see Oakeshott, 1975a, p. 154, note 1). Someone who undertakes to play in a game, let's say of soccer, thereby consents to accept the authority of the rules of the game and to be obligated accordingly. These rules are laid down in the rule book issued by FIFA, soccer's international governing body, and, for the game in question, they are interpreted by the referee who is appointed to his task in terms of accepted and established procedures to which players are taken to have consented. By handling the ball a player breaks one of the rules of the game, but his failure to conform to this rule does not constitute a denial of the authoritative status of the rule. Recognition of this status is signalled by his acceptance of the penalty exacted of him and his team by the referee. Irrespective of the consequences in terms of advantage or otherwise to him, he must accept the rules as binding. In handling the ball he hoped to give his team an advantage, but by so doing he has committed an offence, and so he must be prepared to suffer the consequences of his delinquency. Furthermore, though a player may feel that the referee is incompetent and biased, to play in any particular game he must accept the referee's legitimate occupation of the office of authority and abide by his decisions in spite of his alleged personal shortcomings. Refusing to recognise the authority of a duly appointed referee is equivalent to a refusal to recognise the authority of the rules. By such refusal a player ceases any longer to play the game; in other words, he refuses any longer to be obligated by its rules. Although there may be procedures for having an incompetent and biased referee lose his licence to referee soccer matches, until this occurs any referee, appointed in accordance with recognised procedures, is a legitimate occupant of the referee's office of authority. In terms of this analogy, we can see that players are like citizens and the rules of soccer are comparable to the rules of civil life, with FIFA, the international governing body for soccer in the role of the legislature and the referee in the role of both the executive and judiciary.

Some Clarifications

Before offering any criticism of Oakeshott's account of civil association, it is necessary to clarify some issues. I accept that the distinction between enterprise and civil association, which is a distinction between a form of social life that is based on the pursuit of shared purposes and one that is based on the acknowledgement of rules, is plausible. It is possible to meet the objection that the provision of conditions of peace and security to enable individuals to pursue their different goals by ensuring that the rules of law be upheld is itself a shared social purpose.[3] Oakeshott indicates the direction which an answer to this objection might take by claiming that peace and security are not 'substantive purposes' and hence do not change the status of civil association to that of enterprise association (Oakeshott, 1975a, pp. 119, 118, note 1). The point he wishes to make is the reasonable one that the maintenance of peace and security is not a purpose of a managerial type such as that of increasing gross national product. The presence of peace and security, and a concern that the rules that accommodate them be acknowledged, are conditions necessary to the exercise of individual freedom. Civil law provides for the peace and security of those subject to it, not as an end in itself, but rather as the condition in which freedom can flourish. Peace and security are then conditions of civil association rather than determinate ends to which the rule of law is the means. And to the possible objection that freedom is consequently the end to which the rule of law is the means, the answer must be that the freedom to pursue the activities of one's choice is a feature rather than an end of civil association. Freedom is no more the end to which civil association is the means than the acquisition of intellectual qualities and virtues is the end to which education is the means or that the feelings of exhilaration and closeness to nature are the ends to which mountaineering is the means. To recall an argument made in different contexts in Chapter 2 and 7, freedom, peace and security must not be understood as consequences of civil association, rather they must be understood to characterise it or to be 'inherent in its character' (Oakeshott, 1983a, p. 161).

---

[3] This objection is to be found in Copp (1977, p. 237), Raphael (1975, p. 454) and Barber (1976, pp. 457-460)

Next there is the objection that it is no more likely that the inhabitants of a state would recognise the authority of its laws as share in its purposes (see Copp, 1977, pp. 237–8 and Parekh, 1979, pp. 504–5). In practice, given the complex ethnic and religious configurations of many nation-states, the acceptance by all citizens of the authority of the law may not be common. Yet the notion of such a state is a perfectly coherent one and arguably some western democracies are of such a character. Certainly insistence only on the recognition of the authority of law rather than on the pursuit of shared purposes is more compatible with maximising human freedom and with circumventing tyranny by majority rule.

This point also applies to Oakeshott's account of political activity. His stipulation of what he sees as the legitimate limits of this activity is not designed to describe what people involved in the everyday business of politics actually do. He well realises that in practice political activity is very often concerned with attaining and exercising power and with the distribution of substantive benefits (Oakeshott, 1975b, pp. 409–14). His version of civil association is, he writes, 'ideal, not in the sense of being a wished-for perfect condition of things but in being abstracted from the contingencies and ambiguities of actual goings-on in the world' (Oakeshott, 1975a, p. 109). It is therefore, as he acidly observes in a reply to critics, '". . . nothing like the state of California"' (Oakeshott, 1976, p. 356). This is because, as Josiah Auspitz points out, Oakeshott's definition is philosophical in nature and as such 'neither describes everything that goes on nor proposes slogans for action' (Auspitz, p. 1976, p. 283). In Oakeshott's terms, as Auspitz explains, the sole purpose of a philosophical definition is to elucidate 'organizing categories' (*ibid.*).

Philosophy and Politics

At this point it is appropriate to say something on the nature of Oakeshott's concept of philosophy and how it relates to his concept of politics. As noted in Chapter 1, his categories of knowledge and experience are discrete and autonomous but philosophy is somewhat ambiguously situated within his epistemological universe. On the one hand, in its primary and constructive role, Oakeshott believes that the main task of philosophy is to search for the most comprehensive explanation of experience. What the philosopher aims to do is to raise to a higher level of understanding what in some sense we already know or understand, and thereby to encompass and transcend the understanding achieved in practical experience and in scientific or historical inquiry. Philosophy is, on this account, the ultimate epistemological 'adventure' (Oakeshott, 1975a, p. 11) whereby the philosopher, through the constant critique of assumptions, endeavours to achieve the most comprehensive and complete point of view on whatever subject is under consideration. In his earlier writings philosophy is described as 'experience without presupposition, reservation, arrest, or modification' (Oakeshott, 1978, p. 2 and see also p. 82) and as 'the search for a context which does not require a further setting in order to be understood, a universal, self-complete context' (Oakeshott, 1938, p. 350).

It is the terms of his discrete and autonomous epistemological categories that commit Oakeshott to view philosophy in its constructive role as essentially disjoined from the world of practical experience and from those features (considerations of power and of human interests) of social/political life that are peculiar to practical experience. Accordingly when translated into the idiom of purely philosophical experience, his definition of politics is purged of reference to the influence of human interests. What philosophy can say about politics is therefore not only very circumscribed but is also, in principle, indifferent in respect of conflicting human interests. Accordingly a philosophical definition of politics must be neutral and impotent in the world of political action where the distribution of educational opportunity is decided.

On the other hand, Oakeshott attributes to philosophy a secondary, critical function as what he calls 'pseudo-philosophical experience' (Oakeshott, 1978, p. 332; see also Oakeshott, 1981, pp. 132–3). But in this role philosophy would also appear to be precluded from having any direct bearing on the world of practical political action. In this secondary, critical role, as 'pseudo-philosophical experience', philosophy mediates between the claims of other forms of understanding by correcting inconsistencies and contradictions between them. In particular, philosophy performs this critical function by helping us to clarify our thinking on practical affairs by removing inconsistencies from our thinking on such matters. But, in performing this task of clarification, the philosopher *qua* philosopher cannot tell us what to do in the moral or prudential spheres; she cannot make moral or prudential judgements for us. If the philosopher attempts to tell us how a state should be organised either on the basis of justice/moral appropriateness or of efficiency, then she commits an *ignoratio elenchi*. Decisions of this nature are the province of citizens and administrators rather than of philosophers. Accordingly philosophy in its secondary critical role can have nothing to tell us regarding such matters as the distribution of educational opportunity.

Elements of a Critique

I want to take issue with Oakeshott on two grounds, philosophical and moral. On general philosophical grounds questions must be asked about the relationship between Oakeshott's conception of the philosopher's central task and the world of practical living.[4] I accept that philosophical explanations cannot normally be said to provide direct injunctions as to how to live, and I agree with Oakeshott's argument that we 'should listen to philosophers only when they talk philosophy' (Oakeshott, 1978, p. 355). Nevertheless, and this is my first point of criticism of Oakeshott's view, work in philosophy can have dramatic implications for how we live and for how we conceive of our purposes in life. Work done by philosophers in the areas of philosophy of religion and of philosophy of mind can contribute to human understanding on such issues as the existence of God, the soul and the possibility of an afterlife. Likewise, work done by political philosophers, Marxist, liberal and conservative, can be said to have had a major impact on how the activities of politics and government are understood and conducted in different countries.

A converse criticism concerns Oakeshott's attempt to treat the term 'politics', a term which belongs very much to the world of practical experience, as if it could be detached entirely from this world and placed in a realm of thought beyond the reach of 'all breathing human passion'.[5] What I should want specifically to call into question is the plausibility of his attempt to construct a philosophical definition of politics free of ideological loading. This is not to claim that every essay

---

[4]   For a full consideration of this issue, see Raphael (1964), Oakeshott (1965) Raphael (1965); Greenleaf (1966), Greenleaf (1968); Modood (1980); Hall and Modood (1982); and Liddington (1982).

[5]   This phrase is taken from John Keats's poem, 'Ode on a Grecian Urn'.

in philosophical elucidation derives from the personal ideological predilections of those who offer it. But one cannot produce a definition of politics in the manner that one might offer a conclusion to a theorem in geometry or to a proof in formal logic. No definition of politics can be neutral in the practical world of human affairs, and this is conspicuously the case in respect of the definition offered by Oakeshott. In particular his definition carries a commitment to the law of private property consistent with the values of conventional liberal conservatism to which he subscribes. And this brings me to the main burden of my criticism of Oakeshott's theory of politics, namely, the moral values that inform this theory, especially in so far as these bear on people's opportunity to avail of the invitation to join in the educational conversation.

The ahistorical nature of his definition of politics leads to Oakeshott's failure to consider the possibility that powerful and influential interests may be established in the law of property itself. He shows no awareness that 'the methods of acquisition recognized' (Oakeshott, 1981, p. 45) in western societies have been those which serve the interests of those who already exercised power and influence. What Oakeshott ignores, as Samuel Coleman observes, is 'the existence of unequal clumps of power' that have facilitated 'a relative few who had the power and position' to get laws enacted that had to be accepted by the other members of society (Coleman, 1968, p. 258, note 1). Somewhat ironically, in the light of Oakeshott's hostility towards government intervention in civil life, it could in fact plausibly be argued that, through its laws and policies and by the protection afforded to owners of property by the police and army, the state has played a crucial role in the distribution of property in economically advanced nations. It is as if the rules were established in the course of a game while the stronger team had the advantage. In Oakeshott's writings one certainly finds a complacency regarding the justness of the laws which have provided sanction and support to property rights, rights which have significantly influenced educational opportunity.

At this point it is worth trying to establish how precisely Oakeshott conceives of the relationship between law and justice. Admittedly there is some degree of truth in John Gray's charge that his account of this relationship seems 'obscure' (Gray, 1984, p. 453), and it is understandable that David McCabe find 'maddeningly vague' Oakeshott's account of the 'rules governing civil association' (McCabe, 2000, p. 462). Yet Oakeshott does address the issue directly in his essay 'The Rule of Law'. Here he argues that what he describes as the *jus* of *lex* must not be seen to lie in such instrumental, non-moral considerations as the propensity of the law to promote any particular distribution of material goods or any social purpose such as the 'common good' (Oakeshott, 1983a, p. 141), or identified with its mere 'faithfulness to the formal character of law' (*ibid.*, p. 160; see also Oakeshott, 1975a, 152–3). Rather, argues Oakeshott, the *jus* of *lex* lies in:

> the negative and limited consideration that the prescriptions of the law should not conflict with a prevailing educated moral sensibility capable of distinguishing between the conditions of 'virtue', the conditions of moral association ('good conduct'), and those which are of such a kind that they should be imposed by law ('justice'). (Oakeshott, 1983a, p. 160) [6]

In a later review essay, he observes that the content of laws 'reflects the character of the culture from which they spring' (Oakeshott, 1988, p. 60). But Oakeshott never calls into question the nature of the culture from which laws spring and nor does he raise questions about the relationship between the 'educated moral sensibility' that should find expression in the law and actual laws. In particular he fails to consider the possible relationship between the character of a 'culture' and the interests of the rich and powerful, and specifically the relationship that might be said to exist between this 'educated moral sensibility' and these same interests. The kind of property law to be found in western countries should at least lead Oakeshott to ask questions about the possible entrenchment of the interests of the powerful in the law itself.[7] As Hanna Pitkin points out, he does not ask whether the system that provides for the ownership and control of resources in western countries secures freedom for some 'at the price of social conditions making freedom impossible for others (Pitkin, 1976, p. 311). Unfortunately, as J.A. Bradley comments in his review of *On Human Conduct*, Oakeshott simply refuses 'to allow the cate-

---

[6]   It is somewhat surprising that David McCabe (2000) misses this notion of 'educated moral sensibility' in his criticism of Oakeshott because his essay is otherwise excellent

[7]   In his magisterial essay on Oakeshott, Josiah L. Auspitz raises this as a possible objection to Oakeshott's concept of civil association and, although he does not appear to subscribe to the objection, somewhat surprisingly he does not offer any arguments against it (Auspitz, 1976, p. 282).

gories of radical politics—for example, economic or social-class categories—to enter the vocabulary and concerns of our political philosophy' (Bradley, 1977, p. 204). Accordingly he refuses even to entertain the possibility that the monopoly of society's resources by a few has led to the exclusion of the many, both from political power and from the arena in which the educational conversation takes place.

Some Qualifications

Arguably there is something in Oakeshott's writings to counter this criticism and to qualify somewhat this extreme doctrine regarding the right to private property, as well as the severity of his non-interventionist view of the role of government. In 'The Political Economy of Freedom', for example, he observes that:

> it may happen that a society determines to withdraw from the possibility of private ownership certain things not inherently excluded by the right of private property itself, and there may be good reasons for taking this course. (Oakeshott, 1981, p. 46)

And in 'On Being Conservative', he writes that the tendency to attribute to government a distributive role is 'not at all unintelligible, and there is much in our circumstances to provoke it' (*ibid.*, p. 186). In the same essay, as already noted, he also admits that the conservative disposition that he advocates will not commend itself to those for whom 'the present is arid, offering little or nothing to be used or enjoyed' (*ibid.*, p. 169). And, subsequently, in *On Human Conduct*, Oakeshott appears to support Aristotle's view that the '"good life"or "human excellence"is difficult if not impossible of attainment in the absence of certain substantive conditions (e.g. good health and adequate material means)' (Oakeshott, 1975a, pp. 118–9, note 1). Presumably this also commits Oakeshott to the view that adequate education is also necessary in order to attain 'human excellence' or the 'good life'. Specifically with regard to education, Oakeshott does accept that state intervention may be necessary in providing for the poor (Fuller, 1989, pp. 85, 90). And elsewhere he attributes to Hegel the following views on poverty and wealth of which he apparently approves:

> Modern poverty was a relative not an absolute condition, and it was the counterpart of modern wealth rather than a sign of personal inadequacy .... great disparities of wealth were an impedi-

ment (though not a bar) to the enjoyment of civil association; and
this hindrance could and should be reduced by imposing civil
conditions upon industrial enterprise ... and where necessary by
the exercise of a judicious "lordship" for the relief of the destitute.
(Oakeshott, 1975a, pp. 304–5, note 3)

The extent and degree of the civil conditions to be imposed
is left unspecified but they are compared to 'those designed to
prevent fraud or the pollution of the atmosphere' (*ibid.*). David
McCabe (2000, p. 462) reminds us too that Oakeshott acknowledges fairness as one of the 'general moral ideas' (Oakeshott,
1975a, p. 177) that may be given expression within civil
society.

On the basis of such observations as these we can understand how Ken Minogue, a sympathetic commentator on
Oakeshott's work, can go as far as to claim that 'nothing in
Oakeshott's political writing is logically incompatible with
whatever radical programme of any complexion . . . . Philosophy indeed does leave everything as it is' (Minogue, 1975,
p. 82). And on a similar note, in his review of *On Human Conduct*, Timothy Fuller argues that it would be 'difficult for anyone to imagine that the result of attempting to actualize these
[Oakeshott's] views in the life of any current polity would be
"conservative"' (Fuller, 1976, p. 186). Likewise in his essay,
'The Legend of Oakeshott's Conservatism: sceptical philosophy and limited politics', Jeremy Rayner urges that we distinguish between Oakeshott's 'conservative disposition' and his
putative allegiance to 'conservatism as a political ideology'
(Rayner, 1985, p. 316). Accordingly, the fact that the material
interests of the powerful have historically been associated
with the nature of law does not, in Oakeshott's theory of politics, entail that the law must always serve the interests of this
or of any other group. Moreover, it might well be argued that
the terms of his definition of politics do not in themselves preclude consideration of the desirability of the laws which
govern access to, and control of, wealth and resources.

With specific reference to education there is a tension in
Oakeshott's account of civil association. Josiah Auspitz argues
that the '"inner morality"' (Oakeshott, 1975a, p. 153, note 1) of
any state, in terms of Oakeshott's version of civil life, could be
said to require 'certain levels of education and security to give
citizens the effective ability to exercise their formal civil equality' (Auspitz, 1976, p. 285). From a socialist perspective, Colin

Falck makes the case that the emphasis that Oakeshott puts on human freedom is 'a *prima facie* argument for equalising our opportunities to become knowledgeable and educated' (Falck, 1963, p. 70) in order to be able to exercise this freedom. A sufficient level of education, just like the presence of peace and security, becomes a condition for the exercise of free agency and for the flourishing of civil society. David McCabe argues that in Oakeshott's terms education may be defended on account of its 'constituent role in securing the conditions of free agency' (2000, p. 463) and in developing the capacities whereby citizens can come to choose their own purposes and thus exercise their freedom.

There can be no doubt that the '"inner morality"' of a legal system would have to be very flexible in order to equalise the opportunity for all citizens 'to become knowledgeable and educated' (Falck, 1963, p. 70). To facilitate access to the language of education and to educational institutions by young people from backgrounds of social disadvantage, the law would have to allow extensive curtailment of the right to private property in the interests of the disadvantaged. It would have to accommodate a massive shift in resources to eliminate material inadequacies in the schools themselves and in the conditions of people who live in disadvantaged areas. And this redistribution of resources should be undertaken not as a paternalistic response to what Oakeshott calls '"the problem of the poor"' (Oakeshott, 1975a, pp. 301, 304), but as a necessary precondition in enabling the poor to find their own '*potestas vivendi ut velis*' (*ibid.*, p. 304). Unless the 'inner morality' of Oakeshott's ideal of civil association can be shown to be sufficiently comprehensive to provide for a shift in resources to the advantage of the poor, then many people will continue to be denied the opportunity to join in the conversation of mankind.

A reading of Oakeshott that makes such a shift in resources an acceptable political project discloses the tension in his conception of civil association. This is because, as already noted, conferring upon a political/legal system a distributive function would be inconsistent with the non-instrumental character that Oakeshott attributes to law within the practice of civility. If a government were to become an agency of ownership concerned to devise laws that would distribute benefits to designated individuals or groups then the state would become an enterprise association, and civil association would come to an end. Therefore the conceptual limits inherent in Oakeshott's definition of civil association preclude the state from having a distributive role and they also preclude the creation of any other agency that might realise the project of redistribution. Moreover, Oakeshott has a moral aversion to much state interference in people's lives because he fears that such interference may have a debilitating effect on their capacity and willingness to exploit 'the adventure and risk of self-enactment' (*ibid.*, p. 276). Certainly he implies that a 'single compulsory educational system' (*ibid.*, pp. 321–2, note 1 and Oakeshott, 1981, pp. 57–8) would not only represent an undesirable monopoly, but would also tend to vitiate the individual's capacity for autonomous self-enactment. All of this is consistent with the anti-determinism examined in Chapter 1 that makes Oakeshott opposed to the idea that human beings are simply passive victims of their genetic endowment or of their environment. He believes that the character of each person is the 'outcome of a self-education' rather than 'somehow imposed by such circumstances as poverty or wealth' (Oakeshott, 1975a, p. 325, see also pp. 96–7). Yet, as research shows and as contemporary fiction continues to embody imaginatively, this self-education will be greatly shaped by the individual's economic status. In spite of this, Oakeshott's entire conceptual repertoire seems hostile to the state's intrusion in the lives of its citizens and to interference with the institution of private property. Consequently, within the terms of the form of civil association that Oakeshott advocates, the extent to which measures can be taken to eliminate the conditions of socio-economic disadvantage that restrict the educational opportunity of the poor is a matter for debate. Whether Oakeshott's ideal of civil association has the potency to address these conditions is a question that will be addressed in the next, concluding chapter. As will become clear it is not easy for the political conservative to be a closet egalitarian. Yet a reading of Oakeshott's complete *oeuvre* does not reveal him as an elitist or exclusivist and I hope to defend the view of those commentators who argue that his ideal of civil association can be read with spectacles of a more rather than a less distributivist character. In this way, the essence of the distinction between civil association and enterprise association can be retained as a fruitful way of understanding civil life rather than discarded as a tendentious form of antinomianism

obscuring the possible existence of alternative conceptual-
isations and as another outcome of Oakeshott's excessive zeal
for contrastive categorisations (see Pitkin, 1976, pp. 308–9).

Chapter Twelve

Oakeshott's Educational Legacy

So how should Oakeshott's legacy be appraised? Despite identifying important elements in his writings on education that merit criticism, I hope that this volume has also disclosed much that is unambiguously positive in his work. In this chapter several strands will be drawn together in a concluding assessment. Having reviewed the general plausibility of Oakeshott's conception of liberal education and the extent to which it is appropriate for the conditions of the twenty-first century, the questions of access raised in the preceding chapter will be further considered. Oakeshott's prescience regarding the reprehensible rise of the culture of control in educational policy will be illustrated because unfortunately it still retains an extraordinary currency.

Does the kind of education that Oakeshott advocates still have a place in our times? With some significant reservations the answer is yes. His critique of narrow or thin versions of utility and the pre-eminence he assigns to the enrichment aims of education make practical as well as educational sense. His emphasis on the relational element in education is an affirmation of what lies at the heart of teaching and learning.

Has Liberal Education a Place in the Twenty-First Century?

In spite of this endorsement of central features of Oakeshott's philosophy of education, there is a serious flaw in his thought that needs to be revisited. Diagnosed over 30 years ago by Auspitz, the flaw in question is a tendency to work with a conceptual repertoire that is too rigid and restricted, a tendency raised several times in the course of this volume. This 'over-economy of concepts' (Auspitz, 1976, pp. 266) comes from his having 'insufficiently multiplied essences' (*ibid.*, p. 288). Underlying this tendency is his dichomotomising impulse, that is, the allocation of experience in an oppositional or either/or way to one of two categories. This generates an epistemological separatism that is unsustainable in the form in which he presents it. As Hanna Pitkin explains, Oakeshott's tendency to establish 'a limited number of alternatives' should alert us to the possible existence of 'other alternatives' (Pitkin, 1976, pp. 308–9). Bhikhu Parekh makes a similar argument, pointing out that showing that two categories are 'mutually exclusive' does not entail that they are 'collectively exhaustive' (Parekh, 1979, p. 494). Oakeshott's separatism can at times obscure the presence of alternatives and lead him to make demarcations that are too rigid. For example, the contrast drawn between the morality of the autonomous individual and the 'morality of communal ties' (1981, p. 249) and of the '"common good"' (1975a, p. 277) is far too severe.

But as noted previously in this volume, Oakeshott's thinking is often more subtle than it first appears in the sharp contrasts that he draws. For example, Oakeshott correctly identifyies contemplative delight as a feature of aesthetic experience but then, implausibly and restrictively, he seeks to make delight the sole criterion of the aesthetic. The separatism that seeks to make delight the sole criterion of the aesthetic is inconsistent with a common conception of the relationship between literature and life, and indeed, truth. Yet if he had dwelt on the implications of his remarks about the role of literature in education, this would have allowed Oakeshott to clarify aspects of his theory of art and would probably have led him to temper its separatism. Another example concerns his analysis of teaching and learning where his richest account emerges when his writing is unencumbered by the sharp contrast between the categories instruction and imparting. Nonetheless, his separatism does lead to a wider lack of nuance in accounting for the relationship between the theoretical and the practical worlds. For instance, his analysis of intellectual motivation lacks a satisfactory account of the connection between practical experience and the languages of human understanding. Such an account is necessary in order to make sense of the curiosity that it is the business of schools and universities to promote. Three other important areas where his epistemological separatism also gives rise to difficulties need to be recalled here.

Firstly, despite his criticism of the Greek distinction between arts and crafts, Oakeshott's focus on the theoretical makes him insufficiently alert to the joy and great playfulness of overt interaction between beings and their material environment. Identity creation, *Bildung* or making 'the most or the best' (Fuller, 1989, p. 47) of oneself or can also assume an embodied quality. As argued in Chapter 1 this is a possibility suggested in Oakeshott's writing but, unfortunately, its implications are not explored. Secondly, the rigidity of the distinction that Oakeshott draws between university education and vocational education is unsustainable in the extreme form in which he represents it. There is more to vocational learning than mere mastery of its literature and even of its particular language. The excitement prompted by an intellectual problem, followed by the absorbed attention involved in pursuing it, is as likely to be promoted by research in engineering or medicine as by research in pure science.

Thirdly, Oakeshott's view that the preparation of young people for work is necessarily anti-educational is misguided. As well as providing a context through which identity can be expressed and autonomy exercised, work and work-related learning are capable of yielding an *Arbeitsfreude* (joy in work) that can be experienced as a source of pleasure rather than as a chore, burden or disutility. These activities can offer profound satisfactions that contribute hugely to human flourishing. The contrast that Oakeshott draws between work and play explored Chapter 2 is too stark and requires more nuance. It is a contrast that may not be at all strongly marked in the lives of people for whom work is one of the sources of satisfaction and even of enjoyment in their lives. The irony is that Oakeshott seems not to appreciate that the wider notion of identity creation or of *Bildung* implied in his writing is hospitable to the educational significance of engagement in practical and work-related activities. Oakeshott's conceptual repertoire needs to be more discriminating and sensitive to capture the complexity of important practices. We do not have to choose between the sharply drawn alternatives that Oakeshott often sets before us.

Yet as argued in Chapter 4, in curriculum design, theoretical pursuits must ultimately have priority over practical pursuits.

This is because theoretical pursuits normally have a more intimate connection with human understanding and consequently with human identity. Oakeshott is correct in drawing attention to the enriching potential of literate culture for everyone irrespective of social class background. His philosophy of the curriculum avoids the social divisiveness of, for example, G.H. Bantock, who argues that different social groups can be distinguished on the basis of their capacity for consciousness. Literary and historical studies have been well described as 'identity or person-constitutive' (Carr, 2003, p. 12) because they make a special and vital contribution to the self-understanding of everyone. These aspects of liberal education most certainly have a place in the twenty-first century. But practical pursuits and preparation for work should also have a place. What counts as eligible for inclusion within the educational conversation can assume more encompassing forms than are proposed by Oakeshott.

It is one thing for the curriculum of liberal education to be expansive but it is another for it to be accessible to the whole population. At this point, the question of access raised at the end of the preceding chapter arises once more. Is access to the experience of liberal learning open to all?

The Issue of Access

As already noted, Oakeshott's *oeuvre* does not reveal him as an elitist or exclusivist and his view of civil association is compatible with a distributivist impulse. There are two strands to the argument that to be made here. The first relates to the status of the system of taxation that is the principal mechanism in western democracies for the re-distribution of resources. The taxation code is a system of rules that can be altered through an activity of politics as a result of appropriate argument. This is far from the politics of enterprise association that involves the identification of a corporate purpose, and then deciding how benefits might be most appropriately redistributed to this end. On the contrary, arguments regarding taxation represent the politics of civil association because they involve considering the desirability of laws or rules with a view to their conservation or alteration (see Oakeshott, 1975a, pp. 162–3, 184 and Oakeshott, 1976, pp. 361–2). Engaging in this form of politics demands acknowledgment of the authority of the law embodied in the taxation code and, consequently, an acceptance of the procedure whereby its provisions are enacted, amended, and repealed. Accordingly it does not turn civil association into enterprise association. The second strand concerns the '"inner morality"' (Oakeshott, p. 153, note 1) of Oakeshott's ideal of civil association. This can be understood to permit the substantial shift in resources necessary in order to facilitate a more extensive and extended access by the poor to education. There is no reason in principle why this '"inner morality"' should not accommodate a 'pursuit of intimations' (Fuller, 1989, p. 148) hospitable to a distribution of resources that would put participation in education within the reach of everyone in practice as well as in theory.

The distributivist project may be necessary not only to secure access to education but also to ensure the exercise of full citizenship. A distinction made by T.H. McLaughlin is helpful here. On a thin or 'minimal' interpretation, citizenship is construed merely in 'formal legal, juridical terms', whereas on a thick, wider or 'maximal' interpretation it is construed in 'social, cultural and psychological terms' (McLaughlin, 1992, p. 236). The exercise of 'maximal' citizenship can be undermined by social disadvantage (see *ibid.*). It seems to me that Oakeshott's theory of civil life, as several commentators mentioned in Chapter 11 have suggested, is compatible with the form of social democratic interventionism necessary both to ensure access to education and also to make possible the exercise of 'maximal' citizenship.

Civic education itself can be one dimension of this project. As explained in Chapter 10, Oakeshott says little about the dynamics of civic learning in general and in the school context in particular. His essay 'Political Education' was published long before the notion of active citizenship designed to promote the widest possible participation in political activity became popular. Extensively canvassed today as an aim in curricula of civic education, the notion of active citizenship that is promoted with such a proselytising zeal would probably meet with a sceptical response from Oakeshott. Yet there is nothing in his account of political education that is incompatible with active citizenship. After all, he sees civic learning as imparting to young people a knowledge and understanding as profound, as searching and as comprehensive as it is possible to make it, of the spirit and the pattern of the political arrangements of their society. The spirit of western democracies is essentially participative and the encouragement of universal participation is part of the ecology of civic life. So too is enabling students to become sensitive to those intimations in our political culture of social arrangements that press 'convincingly for remedy' (Fuller, 1989, p. 147). Among these arrangements susceptible to change are the rules governing income acquisition and distribution. These rules are open to challenge on the grounds that they favour the interests of the wealthy. And just as distributive aims do not transform civil association into enterprise association, alerting young people to the possibility of changing these laws does not reduce civic education to the mere advocacy of ideologies. As explained in Chapter 10, Oakeshott's own preferences would probably be hostile to the interventionism such changes would entail but we are concerned not with his personal preference but rather with the implications of his theory. As noted by Josiah Lee Auspitz, any appraisal of Oakeshott's work must be distinguished from merely 'differing with his sympathies (Auspitz, 1976, p. 291).[1]

Yet if access to the form of liberal education defended by Oakeshott were made extensive, it still is appropriate to ask how many people would want such education, even in the expansive form proposed in this volume. Among possible strands of an answer to this question the following two suggest themselves. It is quite clear from all the evidence that is so expertly brought together by Alison Wolf (2002) that young people and their parents are overwhelmingly attracted to liberal education rather than to its vocational alternatives. Secondly, the imaginative and biographical accounts of teaching and learning drawn upon in the course of this volume (see Benameur, 2006, McCourt, 2005, Hynes, 2001, Phinn, 2000) show that even in the most unpromising of circumstances, young people can be engaged in Oakeshott's educational conversation. This may appear idealistic to some readers but what is striking from these accounts of teaching is the educability of young people when taught by committed and resourceful teachers. As one who visits dozens of schools every year, I con-

---

[1]   See also Oakeshott's (1976, p. 361) criticism of this error in the essay of Sheldon Wolin (1976).

stantly admire how such teachers can bring culture to life in the worlds of so many learners.

Inclusiveness and Standards

Oakeshott's negative attitude towards about increasing access to education was noted. Though he does not say so directly, he would probably sympathise with the argument that increased participation leads to a reduction in educational standards. But there is no reason in principle why the participation in education of greater numbers should erode standards. No necessary conflict exists between the democratic values of equality and inclusiveness and traditional respect for high standards. This is not to deny the plausibility of the claim that questionable practices have emerged regarding assessment. Based on research into performance at A-level English in the United Kingdom, Duke Maskell and Ian Robinson (Maskell and Robinson, 2002, 122–50) argue that a misguided conception of 'quality control' has led to the introduction of bland performance 'descriptors' which mean that assessment is less a matter of frank and honest appraisal of scripts by experienced teachers and examiners than the ticking of appropriate 'descriptors'. I also share the concern of these authors and of others that the pressure to award degrees of a high classification at university is reprehensible. Despite these troubling trends, I re-affirm my disagreement with Maskell and Robinson's view that many current students have no place in a university of their mediocre scholarly ability. Students whose intellectual ability is limited can still derive profit and enrichment from university-level studies. Though few will ever become scholars, most will have their lives and analytic abilities enhanced by their studies. To those who will say that this bestows on the university community more of the character of a book club or adult education class, I repeat my conviction that these too are versions of education that can offer models for the university. The 'gift' of higher education can take many forms and it is indeed a gift offered to everyone. I would rather take the risk of being to generous in admitting students to university than to deprive anyone of the opportunity to profit from studying there. But in the light of the commendable impulse towards inclusiveness, there are some features of the notions of standards that are sometimes overlooked.

The standards or criteria of success and norms of achievement in human practices are independent of the desire to be inclusive of individuals in respect of social class origins or indeed of personal qualities. Such qualities as diligence and perseverance are likely to contribute to success at learning but in identifying the criteria of success at such activities as swimming or mathematics, willingness to try hard and other positive psychological dispositions, however admirable, are not relevant. Alas, it can happen that uninterested but able students can do better work than their more enthusiastic but challenged classmates. We must distinguish between the technical merit and the moral, human and psychological merit of performances. We might, for example, wish to applaud a student's interest in the German language and willingness to do his or her best to learn it but if the same student fails to understand or to make the simplest utterance in the language, then we have to say that the individual has been an unsuccessful student of German. But failure to meet the criteria of success in our performances at scholastic, sporting or other activities does not mean that we have failed as human beings. Inability to master the German language, to learn to swim or to play a musical instrument does not diminish our value as persons. All it means is that we lack ability in a certain sphere of human activity.

Likewise norms of achievement are unrelated to inclusiveness. Because it can be important to establish how we are doing in relation to other learners, an element of comparison is a feature of most learning. Assessment is required in order to provide an idea of how our performance compares with that of other learners. This does not mean that we are intrinsically competitive but rather that we require a sense of the norm of achievement within activities in order to get an idea of the relative merit of our own performances. Someone learning to swim all on her own without any idea of what other swimmers can achieve may acquire an exaggerated notion of her ability merely because she is able to swim one width of the pool. There is then nothing inherently objectionable in the notion of norms and they are required in order to appraise abilities relative to the abilities of others. It is possible to be inclusive regarding participation in education while respecting norms of achievement. As was argued in Chapter 2, attributing the relative lack of success of individuals at school to a conspiracy by a socio-economic elite to contrive standards and norms that prevent the poor from achieving success at school subjects is seriously misguided. The economic factors that play an important role in determining the distribution of many of the benefits of education do not define the standards of success or the norms of achievement within academic or other activities.

At this point an important aspect of Oakeshott's legacy needs to be considered. This is his identification of the character, and critique of the corrupting effects, of the culture of control in education policy that he labelled 'rationalism' in the 1950s.

The Culture of Control and Its Consequences

The culture of control in education engendered a strand of profound pessimism in Oakeshott's thought and it continues to prompt concern in the minds of many educators in the twenty-first century. Chapter I drew attention to Oakeshott's dismay at a project aimed at the future 'abolition of man' (Fuller 1989, p. 77) and of his perception of education as an important instrument of manipulative social engineering, supported by the spurious science of behaviourism, designed to realise the purposes of the state. And this was before the rise of forms of state control that have become even more insidiously pervasive in the last two decades. It is surely an irony that the culture of control that Oakeshott so perceptively diagnosed and indicted in the 1950s has come to dominate education in the twenty-first century. The impulse of the positivism that had its genesis at the time of the Enlightenment was designed to control nature. The positivism that developed in the 1950s, and became a pillar of educational policy in the 1980s, had a different purpose, namely, to bring social institutions under the control of government and employers. As mentioned in the Introduction to this volume, it is significant that one of Oakeshott's most celebrated essays, 'Rationalism in Politics', is more about the folly of rationalism or the culture of control in education than in politics, a point perceptively noted by Ephraim Podoksik (2003).

It is not surprising that his work has served as a point of departure in criticising the dominance of this culture in our times. Desmond Ryan invokes Oakeshott's essay 'Political Education' in his account of the 'collateral damage' that was done to 'the delicate eco-system' of university culture (Ryan, 2002, pp. 134–5). Against the managerialism of our times, Michael Smith (1999) bases a persuasive account of the school as an educational community on Oakeshott's work. Paul Standish (2000a, p. 226) salutes Oakeshott's 'remarkable prescience' in his sceptical appraisal of the way the 'talk of the mission statement of the university was spreading' (*ibid.*). Standish endorses Oakeshott's point about the derivative nature of 'missions' as shorthand for how to behave rather than programmes for action. To adapt Oakeshott's memorable metaphor concerning the nature of ideology, a so-called mission statement is less the 'quasi-divine parent' of an educational institution than 'its earthly step child' (Fuller, 1989, p. 142). Elsewhere Standish draws upon Oakeshott's metaphor of education as initiation into a conversation to show how university studies should be conceived (2005, p. 61). This conception is absolutely at odds with the 'closed economy' (*ibid.*, p. 54) of the current ideology of 'proceduralism, coding and performativity' (*ibid.*, p. 63) in higher education.

Regimes of accountability have inflicted grave damage on education for over two decades now. As noted in Chapters 3, 6 and 9 of this volume, a project has been afoot for many years to base teaching at all levels on a 'closed economy' of teaching and learning (*ibid.*, 54). By this Standish means a system requiring a rigid and pre-defined specification of aims, objectives and outcomes. Everything is designed to reflect a belief 'that what teachers and learners are required to do will be fully specified' (*ibid.*). Quality is supposed to be assured and 'transparent to scrutiny' via this comprehensive and exhaustive specification that purports to provide 'clear measures of performance and means of comparison with rival institutions' (*ibid.*). 'Achieving the best ratings' is less a matter of striving for excellence in teaching and learning as 'vigilance against slip-ups, and a judicious containment of risk' (*ibid.*, p. 56). Positivism, as Richard Smith notes, has taken a form whereby institutions are supposed to be 'Highly Reliable Organizations' (Smith, 2005, p. 139) from which risk and uncertainty have been eliminated. In the context of a '"transparent"' or '"audit"' society, the educational climate is one governed by recognition of the '"inevitable and the necessary"' rather than as the outcomes of choices made by administration and management (*ibid.*, p. 140).

Much of which is done under the rubric of quality audits is also a great waste of time and energy. Prickett argues quite rightly that the highly prestigious, private universities in the USA would not spend money on the 'the unproductive monitoring of . . . results that the British now routinely spend' (Prickett, 2002b, p. 198). As Prickett remarks, and as Alison Wolf has demonstrated so ably, students are astute in their appraisal of universities and their courses and student choice is a much more reliable indicator of these than Quality Assurance audits (*ibid.*, p. 182; Wolf, 2002, pp. 200–43). So then we need to ask who benefits from the pervasiveness of auditing measuring and accountability; the answer is not difficult to find. The money being channelled into the endeavour is being used to provide jobs for the people involved in the audit industry (Prickett, 2002b, p. 200). Regrettably this investment is not being used to improve teaching and learning. The new managerial regime 'has created a Frankensteins's Monster in the form of a new class of professional assessors, who, unlike the old inspectorate, are not there to help, but have a vested interest in maintaining their own "management" status—in short, their own power' as well of course as their own jobs. Universities find themselves having to maintain '"management teams"... to co-ordinate Quality Assurance and Research Assessment returns, and to give advice on improving the paperwork generated by those bodies' (*ibid.*).

But not only are current regimes a waste of money and inimical to the conduct of the conversation of mankind but they are also an affront to common sense and it is important to identify why. 'Performance indicators' have to facilitate measurement and so can only focus on the surface of professional activity. Monitoring and measurement can lead to a kind of teaching-to-the-test mentality throughout the educational system. The result is that paperwork takes precedence over the activities of teaching and learning. Teachers and administrators can end up so preoccupied with ensuring that the paperwork is in order that the actual quality of teaching and learning becomes secondary. '(R)egimes of performativity' (Standish, 2005, p. 70) or 'rituals of verification' (Power, 1997) can come at a great price. Over two decades ago Roderick Martin, Professor of Industrial Psychology at Imperial College London, in a letter to the *Times Higher Educational Supplement* noted that the introduction of performance indicators would lead to a regime of '"chase the indicator"' instead of doing the job as well as possible...' (quoted in Ryan, 2000, p. 128). Clyde Chitty (2004, pp. 202–6) also addresses the dangers of over-accountability drawing on the work of Patricia Broadfoot, the philosopher, Onora O'Neill and others. He calls into question the current rationalistic assumption that a regime of 'performativity' applied to public institutions, and to the work of educators as well as to other professionals, is both possible and desirable.

The following are two specific examples of the malign impact of the culture of control in education.

The Work of the Teacher

Much of what occurs in teaching and learning cannot be accommodated in terms of prescribed outcomes because 'so much depends on the teacher's judgement' especially 'in responding to the rhythms of the occasion', all of which relates more to Aristotle's notion of practical reason – 'doing the right thing, at the right time, in the right circumstances' (Standish, 2005, p. 65). Standish gives an account of the teacher in this situation that is very much consistent with the idiom of Michael Oakeshott. The 'good teacher', he writes, 'is in part the orchestrator' of propitious circumstances but she or he is 'also something less centred, more exposed and perhaps more vulnerable, more open to the event' (*ibid.*, pp. 65/66). Though there is, 'no recipe', writes Standish, 'this does not mean that, for the aspiring or practising teacher, nothing can be learned: such abilities are gained by attending to examples of good practice and through readiness to learn from these' (*ibid.*, p. 66).

The same point is made by retired primary school principal, Margaret Sutcliffe (2002). Indicting the over-prescriptive nature of the National Curriculum, she explains that every experienced teacher knows that 'some of the most valuable teaching is done on the spur of the moment' (*ibid.*, p. 156). When an appropriate teaching moment comes up in the classroom a 'good teacher does not waste the opportunity but springs into action to give an instant lesson ... instead of the planned lesson' (*ibid.*). Unfortunately the regime of National Curriculum does not accommodate this kind of spontaneity.

The University

The spirit of Oakeshott's conception of a university is far from the current reductionist view of policy-makers. The current regime of monitoring and measuring exhibits little sense that universities are first and foremost human communities. As Stephen Prickett explains, universities are '*collegial*' rather than 'commercial' or 'bureaucratic' institutions (2002b, p. 185). Staff members in universities and schools are most of all '*colleagues*' and as colleagues 'are collectively responsible for the development of their pupils, and for the advancement of their discipline' (*ibid*.). Richard Smith rightly argues that universities have a responsibility to respond to student concerns. This 'ongoing dialogue, open and sensitive at its best' should not be 'an add-on' to teaching but rather an integral part of it (Smith, 2005, p. 141). The drive for efficiency that 'threatens to eliminate contingency from the university' also threatens to destroy 'forms of human relating, intimacy, intellectual passion, and much else' that have traditionally characterised university life (Smith, 2005, p. 148). In other words, this misguided search for 'efficiency' is corrosive of the very notion of the university as a human community.

To endorse this critique of the culture of control in education is not to deny that there must be accountability on the part of those who are in receipt of public funds, but over-accountability and over-prescriptiveness are inimical to the work of educators. Nor is there anything reprehensible in expecting that educators must sometimes undertake administrative or organisational tasks. Stephen Prickett draws attention to the confusion between organisation and management. It is perfectly reasonable to expect academics to take responsibility for organising aspects of their department's activities but this is different from expecting them to possess management expertise in the sense of 'skills in control and motivation of people, a knowledge of the principles of economics, accountancy and bookkeeping' (Prickett, 2002b, p. 182). Still, the negative aspects of the culture of control recall an important lesson that Oakeshott taught for many decades. When human judgement takes second place to the rigid systems of control, what is good for human beings is overlooked. The lesson is an important part of his legacy.

Oakeshott was particularly uneasy about the role of the state in promoting a culture of control. Chapter one referred to his parody in 'The Tower of Babel' (Oakeshott, 1983) of the notion of a state bent on the pursuit of a futile project and marshalling all its resources to this end. One aspect of his pessimism derives from his fear that the contemporary state is subverting education proper for ulterior purposes. Are there grounds for this fear and for his hostility towards state involvement in education?

The Role of the State

Oakeshott is justified to condemn the kind of state inference in education that has led to the excesses of the culture of control. Though he was indeed prescient in the 1950s to identify the dangers of this trend in government policy, other aspects of his hostility towards state involvement in education are not well–founded. These should be re-visited here. His assumption that this involvement normally leads to an illiberal form of vocationalism is misguided. In many countries state-supported schools strive to provide exactly the kind of educational experiences that Oakeshott espouses. Many of the positive experiences referred to throughout this volume occurred in this context and exemplify the activity of liberal learning.

The previous chapter noted his concession that some intervention by the state may be necessary in providing for the poor (Fuller, 1989 pp. 85, 90). Often, however, access to educational institutions requires significant state involvement and this intervention is an expression of interest of the community in ensuring maximum access to the intrinsic and positional advantages of education. The law of the market and the vagaries of philanthropy are highly unlikely ever to assure the full benefits of education (or of health care) to the population at large. It is one thing to tolerate private schooling but it is naïve to think that private agencies will assume responsibility for the education of the poor and the hard to teach. Without public support Oakeshott's model of liberal learning as articulated throughout this volume will not become the legacy of every citizen in our societies.

And where education is publicly-funded, it is not unreasonable to insist that it give value to the tax-payer. It is possible to ensure appropriate accountability in a manner that respects the nature of education and without recourse to destructive, mechanistic regimes of auditing. The kind of school inspection described in the work of Gervase Phinn (2000) mentioned in Chapter 4 is a model of how this can be undertaken. Publicly-funded universities must give value to the tax-payer and Gordon Graham (2005) shows how this can be one sanely while respecting the nature of the university's true purpose and without using malign forms of monitoring and auditing.

Oakeshott also envisaged the state as promoting a project of social engineering designed to control humankind. This trend led him to fear for a future 'abolition of man' (Fuller 1989, p. 77). This alarmism is understandable but exaggerated. The categories or postulates that form the infrastructure of Oakeshott's thought reveal a rich and persuasive conception of the human person. This version of the human person is not susceptible to the reductionism of policy-makers and social scientists. This conception of the human person is quite properly inimical to impoverished versions of outcomes-driven teaching, learning and assessment. The achievement of committed teachers mentioned in this volume shows that young people are teachable in unpredictable ways that will never be captured in schedules of assessable outcomes. Resistance to current reductionist trends is robust and pervasive and gives grounds for confidence that respect for the human person will prevail over the culture of control.

In concluding this volume, attention should be drawn again to what is of enduring and indestructible value in Oakeshott's vision of liberal education as initiation into the conversation of mankind.

Summing Up

His affirmation of what is positive and life-enhancing about teaching and learning is an important part of his legacy for the twenty-first century. Paul Standish (2000b) is one contemporary philosopher who identifies and eloquently endorses the value of this legacy. We have, he writes, scarcely begun 'to realise the rich significance of the idea of conversation as this runs through Oakeshott's thought' (Standish, 2000b, p. 168). 'The "conversation of mankind" reconvenes the words of the dead, in reading and writing, and in so doing draws a kind of vitality from what cannot be made present' (*ibid*.). As has been noted, Standish is one of many philosophers who develops the legacy of Oakeshott's work.

It is a legacy can be made accessible to all social classes and, appropriately presented, to young people of all levels of ability. Admittedly Oakeshott's conception of what counts as eligible for inclusion within the educational conversation is narrow. Yet the curriculum of a liberal education can be conceived more generously than he appreciates and it can assume more encompassing forms than he proposes. Subject to this reservation and to the other criticisms and qualifications that have been made in the course of this volume, Oakeshott's articulation of the tradition of liberal education can meet the challenge of providing education in mass industrial democracies. What is most important in this legacy is his affirmation of the integrity and sovereignty of liberal education and of its contribution to making our sojourn in this world not only fulfilling and worthwhile but also enjoyable and delightful.

Bibliography

Publications by Oakeshott

The Essays on Education

The following are the details of the essays in Timothy Fuller (ed) (1989) *The Voice of Liberal Learning: Michael Oakeshott on Education* (New Haven and London, Yale University Press).

A place of learning, pp. 17–42. First published 1975.

Learning and teaching, pp. 43–62. First published 1967.

Education: The engagement and its frustration, pp, 63–94. First published 1972.

The idea of a university, pp. 95–104. First published 1950.

The universities, pp. 105–35. First published 1948–9

Political education, 136–58. First published 1951.

Two Essays Not Included in the Collection

The study of 'politics' in a university (1981) in *Rationalism in Politics and Other Essays*. London, Methuen. First published 1962.

The definition of a university (1967). *Journal of Educational Thought*, 1, pp.129–42.

Other Publications by Oakeshott

Work and play (1995). *First Things*, 54, pp. 29–33.

Religion, Politics and the Moral Life (1993). Edited by Timothy Fuller. New Haven, Yale University Press.

Oakeshott on his schooldays (1990). Appendix in Robert Grant, *Thinkers of Our Time: Oakeshott*. London, The Claridge Press.

Scrutinising the conservative disposition (1988). *The Spectator*, 261, p. 60.

On History and Other Essays. (1983a). Oxford, Blackwell.

Photocopy of letter from Oakeshott to Kevin Williams(1983b). library-2.lse.ac.uk/archives/handlists/ Oakeshott/m.html. Accessed 11 March 2007.

Rationalism in Politics and Other Essays (1981). London, Methuen. Originally published in 1962 by the same publisher and now available in an expanded edition edited by Timothy Fuller, Indianapolis: Liberty Press, 1991.

On misunderstanding human conduct: a reply to my critics (1976). *Political Theory*, 4, pp. 353–67.

Experience and Its Modes (1978) (first published 1933). Cambridge, Cambridge University Press.

On Human Conduct (1975a). Oxford, Clarendon Press.

The vocabulary of a modern European state (1975b). *Political Studies*, 23, pp. 319–41, 409–14.

Rationalism in Politics: a reply to Professor Raphael (1965). *Political Studies*, 13, pp. 89–92.

Political laws and captive audiences (1964) in *Talking to Western Europe*. Edited by G.P. Urban. London, Eyre and Spottiswoode, pp. 291–301.

The masses in representative democracy (1961) in *Freedom and Serfdom: An Anthology of Western Thought*. Edited by A. Hunold. Dordrecht, Reidel, pp. 151–70.

The human coefficient, review of *Personal Knowledge* by Michael Polyani (1958). *Encounter* 11, pp. 77–80.

The B.B.C. (1950/51). *Cambridge Journal*, 4 pp. 543–54.

Review of *The State and the Citizen* by J.D. Mabbot (1949). *Mind*, 58, pp. 378–89.

Contemporary British politics (1947–8). *Cambridge Journal*, 1, pp. 474–90.

The concept of a philosophical jurisprudence (1938). *Politica*, 3, pp. 203–22 and 345–60.

Religion and the Moral Life (1927) The "D" Society Pamphlets, No. 2 Cambridge, Bowes and Bowes. Re-printed in *Religion, Politics and the Moral Life*, pp. 39–45.

The claims of politics (1939–40) *Scrutiny*. 8, pp. 146–51. Re-printed in *Religion, Politics and the Moral Life*, pp. 91–6.

Secondary Sources Dealing with or Referring to Oakeshott

Abel, Corey & Fuller, Timothy (2005) (eds) *The Intellectual Legacy of Michael Oakeshott*. Thorverton, Exeter and Charlottesville, VA, Imprint Academic.

Arcilla, René V. (2002) Modernising media or modernist medium? The struggle for liberal learning in our information age. *The Journal of Philosophy of Education*, 36, pp. 457–65.

Arcilla, René Vincente (1995) *For the Love of Perfection: Richard Rorty and Liberal Education*. New York/London, Routledge.

Auspitz, Josiah Lee (1976) Individuality, civility, and theory: the philosophical imagination of Michael Oakeshott. *Political Theory*, 4, pp. 261–94.

Bantock, G.H. (1981) *The Parochialism of the Present*. London, Routledge and Kegan Paul.

Barber, Benjamin (1976) Conserving politics: Michael Oakeshott and political theory. *Government and Opposition*, 11, pp. 446–63.

Benn, S.I. and Peters, R.S. (1959) *Social Principles and the Democratic State*. London, Allen and Unwin.

Bennett, John B. (2001) Liberal learning as conversation. *Liberal Education*, 87, pp. 32–9.

Bradley J.A. (1977) Review of *On Human Conduct* by Michael Oakeshott. *The Heythrop Journal*, 18, p. 202–4.

Coats, Wendell John, Jr. (2000) *Oakeshott and His Contemporaries*. Selinsgrove, PA, Susquehanna University Press.

Coleman, Samuel (1968) Is there reason in tradition? in *Politics and Experience: Essays Presented to Michael Oakeshott on the Occasion of His Retirement*. Edited by Preston King and B. C. Parekh. Cambridge, Cambridge University Press, pp. 239–82.

Corey, Elizabeth Campbell (2006) *Michael Oakeshott on Religion, Aesthetics, and Politics*. Colombia, MO, University of Missouri Press.

Copp, David (1977) Review of *On Human Conduct*, by Michael Oakeshott. *Philosophical Review*, 86, pp. 235–8.

Crawley, Francis, Smeyers, Paul and Standish Paul (eds) (2000) *Universities Remembering Europe: Nations, Culture and Higher Education*. New York/Oxford, Berghahn Books.

Crick, Bernard (1963) The world of Michael Oakeshott: or the lonely nihilist. *Encounter*, 20, pp. 65–74.

Davis, Howard (1975) Poetry and the voice of Michael Oakeshott, *British Journal of Aesthetics*. 15, pp. 59–68.

Duncan, G.C. (1963) Review of *Rationalism in Politics and Other Essays* by Michael Oakeshott. *Australasian Journal of Philosophy*, 41, pp. 112–20.

Falck, Colin (1963) Romanticism in politics. *New Left Review*, 18, pp. 60–72.

Franco, Paul (1990) *The Political Philosophy of Michael Oakeshott*. New Haven, Yale University Press.

Franklin, Julian H. (1963) Review of *Rationalism in Politics and Other Essays* by Michael Oakeshott. *Journal of Philosophy*, 60, pp. 811–20.

Fuller, Timothy (1976) Review of *On Human Conduct*, by Michael Oakeshott. *The Journal of Politics*, 38, p. 184–6.

Gallagher, Shaun (2002) Conversations in postmodern hermeneutics in *Lyotard: Philosophy, Politics and the Sublime*. Edited by Hugh Silverman. London, Routledge, pp. 49–60

Gerencser, Steven Anthony (2000) *The Skeptic's Oakeshott*. Basingstoke, Macmillan.

Gray, John (1984) Review of *On History* by Michael Oakeshott. *Political Theory*, 12, p. 449–53.

Grant, Robert (1990) *Thinkers of Our Time: Oakeshott*. The Claridge Press, London.

Green Maxine (2005) Imagining futures: the public school and possibility in *The RoutledgeFalmer Reader in Philosophy of Education*.

Edited by Wilfred Carr. London and New York, Routledge, pp. 161–73.

Greenleaf, W.H. (1966) *Oakeshott's Philosophical Politics*. London, Longman's, Green.

Greenleaf W. H. (1968) Idealism, modern philosophy and politics in *Politics and Experience: Essays Presented to Michael Oakeshott on the Occasion of His Retirement*. Edited by Preston King and B.C. Parekh. (Cambridge, Cambridge University Press), pp. 93–124.

Gribble James (1983) *Literary Education: A Revaluation*. Cambridge, Cambridge University Press.

Hall, Dale and Modood, Tariq (1982) Oakeshott and the impossibility of philosophical politics. *Political Studies*, 30, pp. 157–77

Hinchliffe, Geoffrey (2001) Education or pedagogy. *Journal of Philosophy of Education* 35, pp. 31–45.

Hogan, Pádraig (1998) Europe and the world of learning: orthodoxy and aspiration in the wake of modernity. *The Journal of Philosophy of Education*, 32, pp. 361–76.

Inglis, Fred (1975) Ideology and the curriculum: the value assumptions of system builders in *Curriculum Design*. Edited by Michael Golby, Jane Greenwald and Ruth West. London, Croom Helm/Open University Press.

Kleining, John (1982) *Philosophical Issues in Education*. London, Croom Helm/St. Martin's Press.

Kneller, George (1984) *Movements of Thought in Modern Education*. New York, John Wiley and Son.

Lawn, Chris (1996) Adventures of self-understanding: Gadamer, Oakeshott and the question of education. *Journal of the British Society for Phenomenology*, 27, pp. 267–77.

Lawson, K.H. (1979) *Philosophical Concepts and Values in Adult Education*. London, Open University Press.

Liddington, John (1984) Oakeshott: freedom in a Modern European State in *Conceptions of Liberty in Political Philosophy*. Edited by Z. Pelczynski and J Gray. London. The Athlone Press, pp. 289–320.

Liddington, John (1982) Hall and Modood on Oakeshott. *Political Studies*, 30, pp. 177–83

Looker, R.J. (1965) Is there a conflict between reason and tradition? *Inquiry*, 8, pp. 301–8.

Løvlie, Lars, Standish, Paul, *Bildung* and the idea of a liberal education, age. *The Journal of Philosophy of Education*, 36. Special Issue: Educating Humanity: Bildung in Postmodernity, pp. 317–40.

Matthews, Michael R. (1980) *The Marxist Theory of Schooling*. Brighton, Harvester.

Moberly (1950) The universities. *Cambridge Journal*, 3, pp. 195–213.

McCabe, David (2000) Michael Oakeshott and the idea of liberal education. *Social Theory and Practice*, 26, pp. 443–64.

McCarney, Joe (1985) Edifying discourses in *Radical Philosophy Reader*. Edited by Roy Edgley. London, Verso, pp. 398–405.

McIntyre, Kenneth B. (2004) *The Limits of Political Theory: Oakeshott's Philosophy of Civil Association*. Thorverton, Exeter and Charolottesville, VA, Imprint Academic.

Mendus, Susan (2000) Thick and thin in culture and higher education in *Universities Remembering Europe: Nations, Culture and Higher Education*. Edited by Francis Crawley, Paul Smeyers and Paul Standish. New York/Oxford. Berghahn Books, pp. 69–80.

Minogue, Ken (1975) Oakeshott and the idea of freedom. *Quadrant*, 19, p. 77–83

Modood, Tariq (1980) Oakeshott's conceptions of philosophy. *History of Political Thought*, 1, pp. 315–22.

Nardin, Terry (2001) *The Philosophy of Michael Oakeshott*. University Park, Pa, The Pennsylvania State University Press.

Novak, Bruce (2003) "National standards" vs the free standards of culture: Matthew Arnold's *Culture and Anarchy* and contemporary educational philistinism. *Philosophy of Education Yearbook*, pp. 376–383.

O'Hear, Anthony (2005) Michael Oakeshott 1901–1992 in *Fifty Modern Thinkers on Education: From Piaget to the Present*. Edited by Joy A. Palmer. London and New York, Routledge, pp. 44–8.

O'Sullivan, Noel (2005) Why read Oakeshott, *Prospero: A Journal of New Thinking in Philosophy for Education*, 11, pp. 10–14.

Palmer, Joy A. (ed) (2001) *Fifty Modern Thinkers on Education: From Piaget to the Present*. London and New York, Routledge.

Parekh, Bhikhu (1979) Review article: The political philosophy of Michael Oakeshott. *British Journal of Political Science*, 9, pp. 481–506.

Peters, R.S. (1974)*Psychology and Ethical Development*. London, Allen and Unwin, Includes chapter entitled Michael Oakeshott's philosophy of education, pp. 433–54.

Phillips Griffiths, A. (1974) A deduction of universities in *Philosophical Analysis and Education*. Edited by Reginald, D. Archambault. London, Routledge and Kegan Paul. pp. 187–297.

Pitkin, Hanna F. (1976) Inhuman conduct and unpolitical theory: Michael Oakeshott's *On Human Conduct*. *Political Theory*, 4, pp. 301–20.

Pitkin, Hanna (1974) The roots of conservatism: Michael Oakeshott and the denial of politics in *The New Conservatives: A Critique from the Left*. Edited by Lewis A. Coser and Irving Howe. New York, Quadrangle/New York Times Book Co, pp. 243–88.

Podoksik, Ephraim (2003a) *In Defence of Modernity: vision and philosophy in Michael Oakeshott*. Thorverton, Exeter and Charlotesville, VA, Imprint Academic.

Podoksik, Ephraim (2003b) Oakeshott's theory of freedom as recognized contingency. *European Journal of Political Theory*, 2, 57–77.

Prospero: A Journal of New Thinking in Philosophy for Education (2005) Special Issue: Oakeshot's Ideas, the Conversation and Related Issues, 11.

Raphael D.D. (1964) Professor Oakeshott's *Rationalism in Politics*. *Political Studies*. 12, pp. 202–15.

Raphael, D.D. (1965) *Rationalism in Politics*: a note on Professor Oakeshott's reply. *Political Studies*, 13, pp. 395–7.

Raphael, D.D. (1975), Review of *On Human Conduct*, by Michael Oakeshott. *Political Quarterly*, 46, pp. 550–454.

Rayner, Jeremy (1985) The legend of Oakeshott's conservatism: sceptical philosophy and limited politics. *Canadian Journal of Political Science*, 18, pp. 313–38.

Ryan, Desmond (2002) Neo-Luddism in *Education! Education! Education: Managerial Ethics and the Law of Unintended Consequences*. Edited by Stephen Prickett, and Patricia Erskine-Hill. Thoverton Exeter and Charlottesville, VA, Imprint Academic/Higher Education Foundation, pp. 103–36,

Rorty, Richard (1998) *Philosophy and the Mirror of Nature*. Oxford, Blackwell.

Searle, John (1990) The storm over the university. *New York Review of Books*, 37, pp. 34–42.

Seller, Anne (1976) Review of *Hobbes on Civil Association* and *On Human Conduct* by Michael Oakeshott. *Philosophical Books*, 17, pp. 54–7.

Smith, Michael (1999) After managerialism: towards a conception of the school as a learning community. *The Journal of Philosophy of Education*, 33, pp. 317–33.

Standish, Paul (2005) Towards an economy of higher education. *Critical Quarterly*, 47, pp. 53–71.

Standish, Paul (2000a) The spirit of the university and the education of the spirit in *Universities Remembering Europe: Nations, Culture and Higher Education*. Edited by Francis Crawley, Paul Smeyers and Paul Standish. New York/Oxford, Berghahn Books, pp. 217–36.

Standish, Paul (2000b) Fetish for effect. *The Journal of Philosophy of Education*, 34, pp. 151–68.

Watkins J.W.N. (1952) Political tradition and political theory: an examination of Professor Oakeshott's political philosophy. *Philosophical Quarterly*, Vol. 2, pp. 323–37.

White, John (2007) Wellbeing and education: issues of culture and authority. *The Journal of Philosophy of Education*, 41, pp. 17–28.

White, P.A. (1975) Socialization and education in *A Critique of Current Educational Aims*, Part 1 of *Education and the Development of Reason*. Edited by R.F. Dearden, P.H. Hirst and R.S. Peters. London and Boston, Routledge and Kegan Paul, pp. 111–29.

Williams, Kevin (2005) The limits of aesthetic separatism; literary education and Michael Oakeshott's philosophy of art in *The RoutledgeFalmer Reader in Philosophy of Education*. Edited by Wilfred Carr. London and New York, Routledge, pp. 174–84.

Williams, Kevin (1989) Reason and rhetoric in curriculum policy: an appraisal of the case for the inclusion of Irish in the school curriculum. *Studies: An Irish Quarterly Review*, 78, pp. 191–203.

Williams, Kevin (1983) A conservative perspective: a critical assessment of Michael Oakeshott's philosophy of education. *Irish Educational Studies*, 3, pp. 33–46.

Wilson, John (1977) *Philosophy and Practical Education*. London, Routledge and Kegan Paul.

Winch, Peter (1980) *The Idea of a Social Science and Its Relation to Philosophy*. London, Routledge and Kegan Paul.

Wolin, Sheldon (1976) The politics of self-disclosure. *Political Theory*, 4, pp. 321–34.

Wood, Neal (1959) A guide to the classics: the skepticism of Professor Oakeshott. *The Journal of Politics*, 21, pp. 647–62.

Other Sources Referred to

Abelson, Raziel (1965) Because I want to. *Mind*, 74, pp. 540–53.

Arnold, Matthew (1966) *Culture and Anarchy*. Edited by J. Dover Wilson. Cambridge, Cambridge University Press.

Austen, J. (1987) *Northanger Abbey, Lady Susan, The Watsons, Sanditon*. Oxford, Oxford University Press.

Benameur, Jeanne (2006) *Présent?* Paris, Denoël.

Berg, Ivar (1970) *Education and Jobs*. New York, Praeger.

Bernstein, Basil (1975) *Class Codes and Control*, 3 vols. London, Routledge and Kegan Paul.

Bernstein, Basil (1971) Education cannot compensate for society in *School and Society: A Sociological Reader*. Edited by B.R. Cosin, I.R. Dale, G.M. Esland and D.F. Swift. London, Routledge and Kegan Paul in association with the Open University Press).

Biddlecombe, Peter (1994) *French Lesson in Africa: Travels with My Brief-case through French West Africa*. London, Abacus.

Blake, Nigel, Smeyers, Paul, Smith, Richard, Standish (eds) (1998) *Thinking Again: Education after Postmodernism*. Westport, Connecticut, Bergin and Garvey.

Bloom, Harold (2001) *How to Read and Why*. London, Fourth Estate.

Bowles, Samuel (1976) Unequal education and the reproduction of the social division of labor in *Schooling and Capitalism: A Sociological Reader*. Edited by Roger Dale, Geoff Esland and Madeleine McDonald. London and Henley, Routledge and Kegan Paul/Open University Press, pp. 32–41.

Bullock, Alan (1975) *A Language for Life*. London, HMSO.

Callan, Eamonn (1997) *Creating Citizens: Political Education and Liberal Democracy*. Oxford, Oxford University Press.

Callan, Eamonn (1992) Finding a common voice. *Educational Theory*, 42, pp. 429–41.

Carr, David (2003) *Making Sense of Education: an introduction to the philosophy and theory of education and teaching*. London and New York, RoutledgeFalmer.

Chitty, Clyde (2004) *Education Policy in Britain*. Basingstoke and New York, Palgrave Macmillan.

Collins, Randall (1979) *The Credential Society*. New York, Academic Press.

Cooley, Mike (1997) *My Education in My Education*. Edited by John Quinn. Dublin: Town House and Country House, pp. 55–63.

Cooper, Jilly (2006) *Wicked: A Tale of Two Schools*. London, Bantam Press.

Confederation of Irish Industry (1990) Human resources — the key issues. *CII Newsletter*, 53, pp. 1–7.

Dale, Roger, Esland, Geoff and McDonald, Madeleine (eds.) (1976) *Schooling and Capitalism: A Sociological Reader*. London and Henley, Routledge and Kegan Paul/Open University Press.

Costa-Lascoux, Jacqueline and Auduc, Jean Louis, *La Laïcité à L'École: Un Principe, une Éthique, une Pédagogie*. Créteil, Scérén.

Dale, Roger, Pires, Eurico (1984) Linking people and jobs: the indeterminate place of educational credentials in *Selection, Certification and Control: Social Issues in Educational Assessment*. Edited by Patricia Broadfoot. London and New York, The Falmer Press, pp. 51–65.

De Botton, Alain (1998) *How Proust Can Change Your Life*. London, Picador.

Debray, Régis (2004) *Ce Que Nous Voile le Voile: La République et le Sacré*. Paris, Gallimard.

Debray, Régis (2002) *L'Enseignement du Fait Religieux dans L'École Laïque*. Paris, Editions Odile Jacob.

Defoe, Daniel (1980) *Moll Flanders*. London, Penguin, 1980.

Denby, David (1997) *Great Books: My Adventures with Homer, Rousseau, Woolf and Other Indestructible Writers of the Western World*. New York, Simon Shuster/Touchstone.

De Selincourt, Ernest (ed) (1974) *Wordsworth: Poetic Works*, original editor, Thomas Hutchinson. London, New York, Toronto, Oxford University Press.

Donaldson, Margaret (1987) *Children's Minds*. London, Fontana.

Doyle, Roddy (1993) Republic is a beautiful word in *My Favourite Year: A Collection of New Football Writing*. Edited by Nick Hornby. London: H., F. and G. Witherby, pp. 7–21.

Doyle, Roddy (1999) *A Star Called Henry*. London, Jonathan Cape.

Duru-Bellat, Marie (2006) *L'Inflation Scolaire: Les Désillusions de la Méritocratie*. Paris, Éditions du Seuil.

Eliot, George (1995) *The Impressions of Theophrastus Such*. Everyman, Dent, London.

Dupuis, Marc (2005) *S'ouvrir à l'immense domaine de l'être humain. Le Monde de Éducation*, 335, pp. 20–2.

Fowler, Karen Jay (2005) *The Jane Austen Book Club*. London, Penguin.

European Commission (1996) *Teaching and Learning: Towards the Learning Society. White Paper on Education and Training.* Brussels, European Commission.

Friel, Brian (2005) *The Home Place.* Oldcastle, Gallery Books.

Floc'h, Benoît (2007) *Deux classes, trois professeurs. Le Monde de L'Éducation,* 356, pp. 64–5.

Galston, William (1991) *Liberal Purposes.* Cambridge, Cambridge University Press.

Garforth, F. W. (1964) Values in society and education. *Education for Teaching,* 64, pp. 22–8.

Gaskell, Elizabeth (1963) *Cranford, The Cage at Cranford, The Moorland Cottage.* London, Oxford University Press.

Gibbon, Monk (1981) *The Pupil.* Dublin, Wolfhound Press.

Graham, Gordon (2005) *The Institution of Intellectual Values: Realism and Idealism in Higher Education.* Thoreverton, Exeter and Charolottesville, VA, Imprint Academic.

Gregory I. M. M and Woods, R.G. (1971) Valuable in itself. *Educational Philosophy and Theory,* 3, pp. 51–64.

Gregory, Ian (1999) Williams on learning for its own sake. *Prospero: A Journal of New Thinking in Philosophy for Education,* 5 (1999), pp. 41–3.

Gribble James (ed) (1967) *Matthew Arnold.* London, New York, Toronto, Collier-Macmillan.

Halsey, A.H., Heath A.F. and Ridge, J.M. (1980) *Origins and Destinations: Family, Class and Education in Modern Britain.* Oxford, Clarendon Press.

Haski, Pierre (ed) (2004) *The Diary of Ma Yan: The Life of a Chinese Schoolgirl Transformed.* London, Virago.

Hammersley, Martin and Woods, Peter (eds) (1976) *The Process of Schooling: A Sociological Reader.* London and Henley, Routledge and Kegan Paul/Open University Press.

Harris, Kevin (1979) *Education and Knowledge: The Structured Misrepresentation of Reality.* London, Routledge and Kegan Paul.

Harris, Joanne (2006) *Gentlemen and Players.* London, Black Swan.

Havighurst, Robert J. (1964) Youth in exploration and man emergent in *Man in a World at Work.* Edited by Henry Burrow. Boston, Houghton, Mifflin.

Hawley, Richard A. (1984) *The Headmaster's Papers.* New York, Bantam Books.

Heaney, Seamus (1988) *The Government of the Tongue.* London, Faber and Faber.

Hegel, G. W. F. (2005) *L'école se situe entre la famille et le monde effectif. Le Monde de L'Éducation,* 338, pp. 8–9.

Hynes, James (2001) *The Lecturer's Tale.* New York, Picador.

Jaurès, Jean (2006) *Contre l'ignorance des désinhérités. Le Monde de Éducation,* 242, pp. 26–7.

Jonathan, Ruth (1986) Cultural elitism explored: G. H. Bantock's educational theory. *The Journal of Philosophy of Education*, 20, No. 2 pp. 265–77.

Johnson, Richard (1976) Notes on the schooling of the English working class in *Schooling and Capitalism: A Sociological Reader*. Edited by Roger Dale, Geoff Esland and Madeleine McDonald. London and Henley. Routledge and Kegan Paul/Open University Press, pp. 44–54.

Judd, Alan (2004) *The Kaiser's Last Kiss*. London, Harper Perennial.

Kipling Rudyard (2000) *The Complete Stalky and Co*. Oxford, Oxford University Press.

Knowles, John (1966) *A Separate Peace*. New York, Bantam Books.

Lawrence, D.H. (1977) *The Rainbow*. London, Heinemann.

Lewis, Theodore (1997) Towards a liberal vocational education. *The Journal of Philosophy of Education* 31, pp. 477–89.

Lewis, Theodore (1991) Difficulties attending the new vocationalism in the USA. *Journal of Philosophy of Education* 25, pp. 95–108.

Louchs, James F. (1979) (ed) *Robert Browning's Poetry*. New York and London, Norton.

Lynch, Kathleen (1992) Education and the paid labour market, *Irish Educational Studies*, 11, pp. 13–33.

Madox Ford, Ford (1987) *The Good Soldier: A Tale of Passion*. London, Penguin.

Martell, George (1976) The politics of reading and writing in *Schooling and Capitalism; A Sociological Reader*. Edited by Roger Dale, Geoff Esland and Madeleine McDonald. London and Henley, Routledge and Kegan Paul/Open University Press, pp. 105–9.

Maskell, Duke and Robinson, Ian (2002) *The New Idea of a University*. Thorverton, Exeter and Charolottesville, VA, Imprint Academic.

Maugham, W. Somerset (2006) *Nouvelles Brèves*/Very Short Stories. Paris, Pochet-Langues pour Tous.

Maugham, W. Somerset (1971) *Ten Novels and Their Authors*. Harmondsworth, Penguin.

McCarthy, Mary (1967) *Memories of a Catholic Girlhood*. Harmondsworth, London, Penguin.

McCourt, Frank (2005) *Teacher Man*. London, Harper Perennial.

McEwan, Ian (1988) *The Child in Time*. London, Picador.

McLaughlin, T.H. (1992) Citizenship, diversity and education: a philosophical perspective. *Journal of Moral Education*, 21, pp. 235–50.

McSweeney, Siobhán (1983) The poets' picture of education. *The Crane Bag*, 7, pp. 134–42

Midgley, Mary (1990) The use and usefulness of learning. *European Journal of Education*, 25, pp. 283–94.

Midgley, Mary (1980) *Beast and Man: The Roots of Human Nature*. London, Methuen.

Miles, Siân (1986) *Simone Weil: An Anthology*. London, Virago.

Murphy, Daniel (1987) *Education and the Arts*. Dublin, School of Education, Trinity College.

Nafisi, Azar (2004) *Reading Lolita in Tehran: A Memoir in Books*. London, Fourth Estate.

Némirovsky, Irène (2006) *Suite Française*. London, Chatto and Windus.

Newman, John Henry (1901) *The Idea of a University: Defined and Illustrated*. London, New York, Bombay, Longman, Green and Co.

Nussbaum, M.C. (1995) *Poetic Justice: The Literary Imagination and Public Life*. Boston, Beacon Press.

O'Connor, Frank (1968) Guests of the nation in *Modern Irish Short Stories*. Edited by Frank O'Connor. London, Oxford University Press, pp. 172–87.

Oxenham, John (1988) What do employers want of education? in *Vocationalizing Education*. Edited by Jon Lauglo and Kevin Lillis. Oxford, Pergamon Press, pp. 69–80.

Parini, Jay (2005) *The Art of Teaching*. New York, Oxford University Press.

Perucca, Brigitte (2006) Marie Duru-Bellat: *On m' a reproché an discours du renoncement*, *Le Monde de Éducation*, 242, pp. 22–4.

Phinn, G. (2001) *Over Hill and Dale*. London, Penguin.

Pirsig, R (1988) *Zen and the Art of Motorcycle Maintenance: An Inquiry into Values*. London, Corgi.

Popper, Karl (1999) *The Open Society and its Enemies*. Vol. 1, *Plato*. London, Routledge and Kegan Paul.

Power, Michael (1997) *The Audit Society: Rituals of Verification*. Oxford, Clarendon Press.

Prickett, Stephen (2002a) Polyphony, the idea of education and social utility in *Education! Education! Education: Managerial Ethics and the Law of Unintended Consequences*. Edited by Stephen Prickett, and Patricia Erskine-Hill. Thoverton and Charlottesville, VA. Imprint Academic/Higher Education Foundation, pp. 85–101.

Prickett, Stephen (2002b) Managerial ethics and the corruption of the future. In Stephen Prickett and Patricia Erskine-Hill (eds), pp. 181–204.

Renaut Alain, Finkielkraut Alain (2005) *Débat: Comment réinventer l'autorité*. *Le Monde de L'Éducation*, 338, pp. 38–41.

Russell, Ben (1999) Students prefer exotic languages. *The Independent*, 24 August, p. 7.

Ruskin, John (1893) *The Political Economy of Art*. London, Collins.

Ryle, Gilbert (1973a) *The Concept of Mind*. Harmondsworth, London, Penguin.

Ryle, Gilbert (1973b)Teaching and training in *The Concept of Education*. Edited by R.S. Peters. London, Routledge and Kegan Paul, pp. 105–19.

Ryle,Gilbert (1969) *Dilemmas*. Cambridge, Cambridge University Press.

Seierstad, Åsne (2003) *The Bookseller of Kabul*. London, Virago.

Shakespeare, William (1997a) *As You Like It* in *The Norton Shakespeare Based on the Oxford Edition*. New York and London, W.W. Norton and Co.

Shakespeare, William (1997b) *The Tragedy of Coriolanus* in *The Norton Shakespeare Based on the Oxford Edition*. New York and London, W.W. Norton and Co.

Shakespeare, William (1997c) *The Tragedy of Macbeth* in *The Norton Shakespeare Based on the Oxford Edition*. New York and London, W.W. Norton and Co.

Shakespeare, William (1997d) *The Tragedy of Hamlet* in *The Norton Shakespeare Based on the Oxford Edition*. New York and London, W.W. Norton and Co.

Schofield Harry (1972) *The Philosophy of Education: An Introduction*. London, George Allen and Unwin.

Siegel, Harvey (1997) *Rationality Redeemed: Further Dialogues on an Educational Ideal*. New York and London, Routledge.

Skinner, B.F. (1982) *Beyond Freedom and Dignity*. Harmondsworth, Penguin.

Sittenfeld, Curtis (2006) *Prep*. London, Picador.

Smith, Richard (2005) Dancing on the feet of chance: the uncertain university. *Educational Theory*, 55, pp. 138–50.

Smith, Richard (2000) Democratic education and the learning society in *Universities Remembering Europe: Nations, Culture and Higher Education*. Edited by Francis Crawley, Paul Smeyers and Paul Standish. New York/Oxford, Berghahn Books, pp. 187–202,

Smith, Richard (1987) Skills: the middle way. *The Journal of Philosophy of Education*, 21, pp.197–201.

Steiner, George (2003) *Lessons of the Masters*. Cambridge, Mass and London, Harvard University Press.

Sutcliffe, Margaret (2002) Bureaucracy and the growth of anxiety in a small independent school in *Education! Education! Education: Managerial Ethics and the Law of Unintended Consequences*. Edited by Stephen Prickett, and Patricia Erskine-Hill. Thoverton, Exeter and Charlottesville VA, Imprint Academic/Higher Education Foundation, pp. 149–58.

Tan, Amy (2004) *The Opposite of Fate*. London, Harper Perennial.

Thubron, Colin (1988) *Behind the Wall: A Journey through China*. London, Penguin.

Truong, Nicolas (2007) *Entretien*: Mona Ozouf. *Le Monde de Éducation*, 355, pp. 68–73.

Truong, Nicolas (2007) *Entretien à deux voix*: Nancy Huston et Tzvetan Todorov. *Le Monde de Éducation*, 354, pp. 68–73.

Vaizey, John (1979) The school in question; an economist's viewpoint. *Oxford Review of Education*, 5, pp. 207–14.

Walsh, Paddy (1993) *Education and Meaning: Philosophy in Practice*. London, Cassell.

Weijers, Ido (2000) *Bildung versus* benefit in *Universities Remembering Europe: Nations, Culture and Higher Education*. Edited by Francis

Crawley, Paul Smeyers and Paul Standish. New York/Oxford, Berghahn Books, pp. 121–33.

Weil, Simone (1973) *Waiting for God*. New York, Harper and Row.

Wharton, Edith. (1995) *Madame de Treymes*, Penguin 60s. London, Penguin.

Whelan, C.T. and Whelan B.J. (1984) *Social Mobility in the Irish Republic: A Comparative Perspective*, Paper No.116. Dublin, The Economic and Social Research Institute.

White, Edmund (2000) *Proust*. London, Phoenix.

White, John (1997) *Education and the End of Work: A New Philosophy of Work and Learning*. London, Cassell.

Whitehead, A.N. (1926) *Religion in the Making*. Cambridge, Cambridge University Press.

Williams, Kevin (2004) Critical pedagogy and foreign language education, *The Journal of Philosophy of Education*, 38, pp. 143–8.

Williams, Kevin (2000) *Why Teach Foreign Languages in School? A Philosophical Response to Curriculum Policy*, Impact No. 5. London, Philosophy of Education Society of Great Britain.

Wilson, P.S. (1974) *Interest and Discipline in Education*. London, Routledge and Kegan Paul.

Winch, Christopher (2002) The economic ends of education. *The Journal of Philosophy of Education*, 36, pp. 101–18.

Wolf, Alison (2002) *Does Education Matter? Myths about Education and Economic Growth*. London, Penguin.

Zola, Émile (1969) *Contes Choisis*. Edited by J.S. Woods. London. University of London Press.

INDEX

85

91

95 MB
96
97

225